21世纪英语专业系列教材　　　　　总主编　胡壮麟

英语泛读教程

（第二版）

第4册

主　编：陈正发　戚　涛　姜亚军

副主编：姜占好　苏锑平

编　者：姚学丽　于元元　朱玲麟

北京大学出版社

PEKING UNIVERSITY PRESS

图书在版编目（ＣＩＰ）数据

英语泛读教程.第4册/陈正发,戚涛,姜亚军主编.—2版.—北京:北京大学出版社,2014.2
（21世纪英语专业系列教材）
ISBN 978-7-301-23938-4

Ⅰ.英…　Ⅱ.①陈…②戚…③姜…　Ⅲ.英语–阅读教学–高等学校–教材　Ⅳ.H319.4

中国版本图书馆CIP数据核字(2014)第022670号

书　　　　名：英语泛读教程(第二版)第4册
著作责任者：陈正发　戚涛　姜亚军　主编
责 任 编 辑：李　娜
标 准 书 号：ISBN 978-7-301-23938-4/H·3484
出 版 发 行：北京大学出版社
地　　　　址：北京市海淀区成府路205号　　100871
网　　　　址：http://www.pup.cn　　新浪官方微博:@北京大学出版社
电 子 信 箱：zbing@pup.pku.edu.cn
电　　　　话：邮购部 62752015　发行部 62750672　编辑部 62759634　出版部 62754962
印 刷 者：北京大学印刷厂
经 销 者：新华书店
　　　　　　787毫米×1092毫米　16开本　17印张　450千字
　　　　　　2008年12月第1版
　　　　　　2014年2月第2版　2017年1月第2次印刷
定　　　　价：42.00元

《21世纪英语专业系列教材》
编写委员会

（以姓氏笔画排序）

王立非	王守仁	王克非
王俊菊	文秋芳	石 坚
申 丹	朱 刚	仲伟合
刘世生	刘意青	殷企平
孙有中	李 力	李正栓
张旭春	张庆宗	张绍杰
杨俊峰	陈法春	金 莉
封一函	胡壮麟	查明建
袁洪庚	桂诗春	黄国文
梅德明	董洪川	蒋洪新
程幼强	程朝翔	虞建华

总　序

北京大学出版社自2005年以来已出版"语言与应用语言学知识系列读本"多种,为了配合第十一个五年计划,现又策划陆续出版"21世纪英语专业系列教材"。这个重大举措势必受到英语专业广大教师和学生的欢迎。

作为英语教师,最让人揪心的莫过于听人说英语不是一个专业,只是一个工具。说这些话的领导和教师的用心是好的,为英语专业的毕业生将来找工作着想,因此要为英语专业的学生多多开设诸如新闻、法律、国际商务、经济、旅游等其他专业的课程。但事与愿违,英语专业的教师们很快发现,学生投入英语学习的时间少了,掌握英语专业课程知识甚微,即使对四个技能的掌握也并不比大学英语学生高明多少,而那个所谓的第二专业在有关专家的眼中只是学到些皮毛而已。

英语专业的路在何方?有没有其他路可走?这是需要我们英语专业教师思索的问题。中央领导关于创新是一个民族的灵魂和要培养创新人才等的指示精神,让我们在层层迷雾中找到了航向。显然,培养学生具有自主学习能力和能进行创造性思维是我们更为重要的战略目标,使英语专业的人才更能适应21世纪的需要,迎接21世纪的挑战。

如今,北京大学出版社外语编辑室的领导和编辑同志们也从教材出版的视角探索英语专业的教材问题,从而为贯彻英语专业教学大纲做些有益的工作,为教师们开设大纲中所规定的必修、选修课程提供各种教材。"21世纪英语专业系列教材"是普通高等教育"十一五"国家级规划教材和国家"十一五"重点出版规划项目"面向新世纪的立体化网络化英语学科建设丛书"的重要组成部分。这套系列教材要体现新世纪英语教学的自主化、协作化、模块化和超文本化,结合外语教材的具体情况,既要解决教学内容、教学方法和教育技术的时代化,也要坚持弘扬以爱国主义为核心的民族精神。因此,今天北京大学出版社在大力提倡专业英语教学改革的基础上,编辑出版各种英语专业技能、英语专业知识和相关专业知识课程的教材,以培养具有创新性思维和具有实际工作能力的学生,充分体现了时代精神。

北京大学出版社的远见卓识,也反映了英语专业广大师生盼望已久的心愿。由北京大学等全国几十所院校具体组织力量,积极编写相关教材。这就是说,这套教材是由一些高等院校有水平有经验的第一线教师们制定编写大纲,反复讨论,特别是考虑到在不同层次、不同背景学校之间取得平衡,避免了先前的教材或偏难或偏易的弊病。与此同时,一批知名专家教授参与策划和教材审定工作,保证了教材质量。

当然,这套系列教材出版只是初步实现了出版社和编者们的预期目标。为了获得更大效果,希望使用本系列教材的教师和同学不吝指教,及时将意见反馈给我们,使教材更加完善。

航道已经开通,我们有决心乘风破浪,奋勇前进!

胡壮麟
北京大学蓝旗营

第二版前言

国家级规划教材《英语泛读教程》自2008年问世以来，受到了全国英语专业老师和学生的一致好评。过去五年的教材使用与教学实践证明，本教材选材方向正确，既兼顾语言表达与人文知识的相得益彰，又注重西方文化传统与现代文化的融会贯通，既注重经典传承，也关注时代变迁。

《英语泛读教程》第二版基本保持了第一版的编写思想。修订内容之一是更换了部分课文，以求选材的时代性、内容的丰富性、文本的趣味性和文体的多样性。在筛选文章的过程中，我们既考虑提升学生的英语水平与人文知识基础，也注重整套教材内容的前后衔接。

第二版对课文后面的练习也做了调整。具体的考量有三：第一，注重从具体课文到所涉及领域之间的递进关系，通过具体的课文使学生对相关领域的知识有所了解。第二，注重学生对篇章结构的理解。第三，注重课内阅读与课外阅读之间的配合。具体修订内容如下：

一、为了提高学生的学习兴趣，本次修订替换了约30%的课文，新的课文内容多启发人文思考，更能体现通过文化思考来带动语言习得，同时注重学生思辨能力的提升。

二、移除各单元练习中的翻译部分，加入了词汇题，有助于学生进一步掌握和复习课文中的重点词汇。

三、新增命题拓展。通过此题的延伸，可以引导学生有意识地进行批评性阅读，从而使其更深刻地领会和理解西方文化的内涵与实质。

四、新设一个引导性的课外拓展题，让学生自己学会如何围绕课本提供的主题进行拓展学习，从大学基础学习阶段就培养良好的自主深入学习的习惯，更有利于学生知识面的扩展。

五、每个单元后面新增二十分钟的阅读材料，材料选自历年英语专业四级阅读真题，以提高学生的限时阅读水平，提升学生阅读的有效性。

我们相信，通过此次修订，这套泛读教材将更好地服务于英语人才的培养。借此机会，感谢为本套教材改版而默默奉献的老师们，也感谢北京大学出版社的领导、各位编辑和工作人员为本套教材的成长所提供的关爱与支持。

英语专业教学任重道远,教材建设永无止境。本套教材旨在适应新形势下的英语专业教学,探索教学新路,缺点与不足之处在所难免,衷心希望得到专家学者的批评指正,听到广大师生的改进意见。

编者

2013 年 1 月

第一版前言

本教程根据《高等学校英语专业英语教学大纲》编写,为英语基础课教材,供高等学校英语专业二年级第二学期使用。教材致力于通过阅读训练扩大学生的词汇量,增强英语语感,丰富文化知识,提高人文素质,并重点培养学生以下诸方面的能力:(1)英语阅读及快速阅读能力;(2)假设判断、分析归纳、推理检验等逻辑思维能力;(3)略读、寻读、细读、评读等阅读技巧。

本教材共分12个单元,每单元由Text A和Text B两篇课文、辅学资料及相关练习构成。所录24篇课文从近百年来众多英语美文中精选出来,遴选的原则包括以下几点:

(1)覆盖尽可能广阔,涉及文化、环保、科技、教育、职业、性别、大学生活等社会生活的诸多方面,以满足扩充词汇量、拓展知识面的需要;

(2)在文字优美的前提下,侧重选择思辨性较强的文章,以培养学生的逻辑思维能力;

(3)优先选择趣味性强、贴近学生生活、容易产生共鸣的文章,以提高学生的学习兴趣;

(4)注重选择时代感强、观点成熟且兼容并蓄的文章,以启发学生对人生、世界的认识与思索,提高人文素质;

(5)考虑到英语文化的多元性,选文来源尽可能广泛,来自主要英语国家——美、英、加、澳等国作者的文章均有收录;

(6)在全球化背景下,让外部世界了解中国文化是我国对外交往的重要课题之一,本册教材特意安排了一个介绍中国文化的单元,方便学生掌握相关的词汇与知识,以促进日后可能进行的文化交流。

本册教材在单元的编排顺序上,主要依照由浅入深的原则。每一单元中,通常Text A的难度较大,适合学生在教师的指导下细读;Text B相对难度较小,适合学生自主、快速阅读。与之相对应,A、B两篇课文辅学资料及相关练习的设计,也有所不同。Text A通常由 Cultural Notes, Comprehension Questions, Paraphrase, Translation, After-reading Discussions, Inference 六部分组成;Text B 由 Cultural Notes, Comprehension Questions, After-reading Discussions, Inference 四部分组成。各部分的设计基于以下考虑。

第一，Cultural Notes 就文章涉及的人物、文化背景和专有名词进行必要的解释和说明，拓展学生的知识面，帮助其更好地理解课文。

第二，Comprehension Questions 用以检验学生对课文中表达的观点、逻辑关系及个别难句的理解程度。设计问题时尽量做到触及文章的深层涵义，借以培养学生的逻辑思辨和理解能力，从中掌握更多的知识。

第三，After-reading Discussions 引导学生深入思考课文的内容并展开讨论。

第四，Paraphrase 旨在检验学生在快速阅读中，对部分关键句及难句的理解程度。

第五，Translation 旨在检验学生在快速阅读中，对部分关键句及难句的精确掌握程度，以求"泛"中有"精"。

第六，Inference 考查学生能否在理解字面意思的基础上，掌握文章内部的逻辑关系，以培养学生的寻读、假设判断、分析归纳、推理检验等逻辑思维能力。

鉴于泛读教程的特殊性，练习没有涉及应由其他课程培训的技能，如词汇的使用、修辞技巧等。

本册教材由安徽大学外语学院编写，陈正发教授、戚涛副教授担任主编，参加编写的还有于元元、姚学丽、朱玲麟等。教材编写期间得到教程总主编——胡壮麟教授的大力指导，胡先生提出了许多宝贵的建议；北大出版社也为编写工作的顺利进行，付出了很多心血。编者在此一并表示衷心感谢！

本册教材若有疏漏之处，敬请广大读者及业界人士批评指正！

编　者
2008 年 12 月

Contents

Unit One
Book Review and Chinese Culture

Unveiling and Consuming Art
in the Multifarious Spaces of Early Modern China
By Zaixin Hong

Working simultaneously on a similar frontier of scholarship, two eminent scholars mark a breakthrough in their new books on the study of Chinese visual arts and material culture. Jonathan Hay's *Sensuous Surfaces*, focusing on portable interior decorative objects of the Ming and Qing periods, circa 1570—1840, examines the fascinating yet little-explored sensuous surfaces of what the Qing taste-maker Li Yu called *wanhao zhi wu* or "pleasurable things". James Cahill's *Pictures for Use and Pleasure*, with a focus on scroll paintings, which have survived from between 1661 and 1794, reconstructs what had been an excluded area in mainstream Chinese art history, namely the pleasure and use of "vernacular paintings".

As a genre, the "vernacular painting" of Cahill's book exists in neither Chinese art historiography nor traditional literati-biased collecting practices. The standard narrative of High Qing paintings is dominated by named painters from either "orthodox" or "individualistic schools" working in both court and non-court settings. A great number of surveys and case studies on paintings of this period have been written in recent decades, yet few have paid attention as Cahill has done to those urban studio artists who created quality pictures for use and pleasure in and beyond the

frontier /ˈfrʌntɪə/ *n.* the limits of what is known about something

eminent /ˈemɪnənt/ *adj.* famous, important, and respected

portable /ˈpɔːtəb(ə)l/ *adj.* able to be carried or moved easily

circa /ˈsɜːkə/ *prep.* used before a date to show that something happened close to but not exactly on that date

sensuous /ˈsenʃʊəs/ *adj.* pleasing to your senses or attractive in a sexual way

reconstruct /riːkənˈstrʌkt/ *v.* to produce a complete description or copy of an event by collecting together pieces of information

genre /ˈʒɒnrə/ *n.* a particular type of art, writing, music, etc., which has certain features that all examples of this type share

literati /ˌlɪtəˈrɑːtɪ/ *n.* a small group of people in a society who know a lot about literature

orthodox /ˈɔːθədɒks/ *adj.* ideas, methods, or behaviour are accepted by most people to be correct and right

Imperial court. Primarily defined by its function, "vernacular painting" refers to those which "were intended not so much for pure aesthetic appreciation as for hanging on particular occasions such as New Year's celebrations and birthdays, or for serving particular functions, such as setting the tone in certain rooms of the house or illustrating a story" (Cahill, p. 3). Their content, style, and format, according to Cahill, "were executed in the polished 'academic' manner of fine-line drawing and colors, usually on silk, and were valued for their elegant imagery and their lively and often moving depictions of subjects that answered the needs and desires of those who acquired and hung

aesthetic /iːsˈθetɪk/ *adj.* connected with beauty and the study of beauty

tone /təʊn/ *n.* the general character and attitude of sth such as a piece of writing, or the atmosphere of an event

execute /ˈeksɪkjuːt/ *v.* to do something that has been carefully planned

akin /əˈkɪn/ *adj.* very similar to something

ephemeral /ɪˈfem(ə)r(ə)l/ *adj.* existing or popular for only a short time

anonymous /əˈnɒnɪməs/ *adj.* done, sent, or given by someone who does not want their name to be known

unprecedentedly /ʌnˈpresɪdentɪdli/ *adv.* never having happened before, or never having happened so much

obscurity /əbˈskjʊərɪti/ *n.* the state of not being known or remembered

controversial /kɒntrəˈvɜːʃ(ə)l/ *adj.* causing a lot of disagreement, because many people have strong opinions about the subject being discussed

secular /ˈsekjʊlə/ *adj.* not connected with or controlled by a church or other religious authority

antiquarian /ˌæntɪˈkweərɪən/ *adj.* concerned with old and rare objects

them, or enjoyed them in album and hand-scroll (horizontal scroll) form" (p. 3). As a term, "vernacular painting" is akin to "secular painting" since Cahill has excluded all religious subjects. We may, to a certain degree, compare it to "genre painting" within Western traditions, such as in seventeenth-century Dutch painting. However, "vernacular painting" does not include "still life" as it would in the West. Often ephemeral objects of urban culture and ceremony, the authorship of these works is oftentimes anonymous, less known, or misattributed. Unprecedentedly, Cahill has in his book taken issue with mainstream approaches and, in doing so, rescued an amazing body of "vernacular paintings" from obscurity. His five chapters present important, oftentimes controversial ideas, by which Cahill unveils some marvelous social spaces visualized in this formerly understudied genre.

Hay has also pursued an original inquiry, with his study of a choice group of interior decorative objects for domestic consumption from the late Ming to mid-Qing periods. In order to explore their "sensuous surfaces", he makes a critical selection of "the secular display objects associated with the residential interior", distinguishing them from the mass of ritual, religious, and antiquarian decorative works (p. 9). Made in a pre-mechanised historical context at the dawn of modern design, these portable decorative objects may have received greater publicity than the High Qing "vernacular painting" in the collectors' circles inside and outside of

China since the sixteenth century, but the <u>sheer</u> task of assessing such a great number of items and related scholarship must have been <u>daunting</u>. Like Cahill, Hay has had to push at the boundaries of <u>prevailing</u> opinions. In twentieth-century China, the taste for possessing these highly collectable luxuries, was condemned as an indication of an aesthetic decline from the high level of the Qin-Han (221 BC—220 CE) and Tang-Song (618 CE—1279 CE). As such, in focusing on the early modern examples, Hay's objects make a valuable contribution to current discourses about the visuality of Ming material culture. In tackling both the objects themselves and of the visuality they construct, Hay starts his discussion of "Decoration as Luxury" by using a three-part structure: "The Decorative Object"; "The Surfacescape's Resources"; and "From Surfacescapes to Objectscapes'. Having chosen a rich and varied body of material and media—such as clay, hardwood, bamboo, lacquer, silk, hardstones (including jade), and copper <u>alloys</u>, in the forms of vases, bowls and cups, teapots and wine pots, brush holders, and incense burners—he observes that these decorative objects may have been socially coded, but appealed nevertheless to three different groups of collectors (wealthy urban residents, <u>lavish</u> court attendees, and elegant literati). While these collectors sought to own examples of earlier achievements, they also looked for *qi* (originality) in newer works. Exploring this shared vision fascinated by the duality of repetition and originality, Hay invites us in two subsequent parts of his book to pay special attention to the complexity of visual spaces through his in-depth discussion of "surfacescapes" and "objectscapes". Making a distinct contribution to remapping the possibilities of our understanding of luxury items, Hay has presented a "conceptual landscape" for "sensuous surfaces"— i.e. a consideration of the <u>multifarious</u> spaces of "pleasurable things" hitherto never examined.

In the formulation of their original "visual arguments", both authors adopt a similar methodology but take on different positions. Based primarily on visual evidence, their narratives cross-examine the written evidence that Ming-Qing writers have left us about everyday life in early modern Chinese centres. Cahill observes that "vernacular painting" <u>elicited</u> in its urban audience in High Qing China "[s]imilar moments of shared aesthetic pleasures are recounted in the late Ming literatus Mao

sheer /ʃɪə/ *adj.* used to emphasize that something is very heavy, large, etc.
daunting /ˈdɔntɪŋ/ *adj.* frightening in a way that makes you feel less confident
prevailing /prɪˈveɪlɪŋ/ *adj.* existing or accepted in a particular place or at a particular time
alloy /ˈælɔɪ/ a metal that consists of two or more metals mixed together
lavish /ˈlævɪʃ/ *adj.* large, impressive, or expensive or very generous
multifarious /ˌmʌltɪˈfeərɪəs/ *adj.* of many different kinds
elicit /ɪˈlɪsɪt/ *v.* to succeed in getting information or a reaction from someone, especially when this is difficult

Xiang's memoir of his life with his beloved concubine Dong Xiaowan" (p. 125). But as far as the art-historical focus on literati-biased collectors and connoisseurs towards "vernacular painting" is concerned, Cahill provides us with a rich collection of counter examples. He has assembled an astonishing collection of more than 120 fine reproductions, mostly in colour, of the excluded genre, convincingly countering the strong bias from the literati circles. For his part, Hay gathers 229 illustrations (mostly in colour as well accompanied by descriptive captions) that support his arguments for those subtle and sensitive appreciations of luxury objects evinced by Ming-Qing writers, particularly by Li Yu—the aforementioned Qing taste-maker. For the domestic consumption of luxury objects with such "shared aesthetic pleasures", Hay points out, "[a] rich and diverse body of textual sources confirms and specifies the metaphoric and affective possibilities of decoration that were made possible by the immediate physicality of surface, allusions to other surfaces, the complication of surface by representations, or the self-consciously rhetorical use of any given surface treatment" (p. 99). Involved in this are the sensory and/or embodied pleasures enabled by these objects, as well as a desire for conspicuous consumption.

memoir /ˈmemwɑː/ *n.* a short piece of writing about a person or place that you knew well, or an event that you experienced

connoisseur /ˌkɒnəˈsɜː/ *n.* someone who knows a lot about something such as art, food, or music

caption /ˈkæpʃ(ə)n/ *n.* words printed above or below a picture in a book or newspaper or on a television screen to explain what the picture is showing

subtle /ˈsʌt(ə)l/ *adj.* not easy to notice or understand unless you pay careful attention

sensitive /ˈsensɪtɪv/ *adj.* able to understand or express yourself through art, music, literature, etc.

evince /ɪˈvɪns/ *v.* to show a feeling or have a quality in a way that people can easily notice

allusion /əˈluːʒ(ə)n/ *n.* something said or written that mentions a subject, person, etc. indirectly

conspicuous /kənˈspɪkjʊəs/ *adj.* very easy to notice

artisan /ˈɑːtɪzæn/ *n.* someone who does skilled work, making things with their hands

With different approaches but complementary results in their observations, these authors of two different generations push us to rethink complex discourses "within the network of binaries—subject-object, centre-periphery, genuine-fake, among others—that continue to define the modern discipline" (Hay, p. 15). They remind us of Niklas Luhmann's theory of social systems, in which a system such as art can react to other social systems only in terms of its "binary codes". Hay's study provides us with an insightful way of associating pleasure with consumption and of underlining the human presence in handling luxury objects. In doing so, the social network of binaries—the south-north, Chinese-Manchu, local-global, literatus-artisan, among others—find new ways to broaden extant debates on the aesthetic characteristics of the Ming-Qing decorative art.

Considering the erotic economy of decoration, we should be aware that discussing "pleasurable things" has been taboo in modern Chinese aesthetics and art history, deriving from a Neo-Confucian condemnation of *wanwu sangzhi* or "excessive attention to trivia which saps the will". Qing scholars were concerned with the anxiety caused by pleasurable commodities, an anxiety which came from a fear of "low tastes" or "bad tastes" infecting art collecting. Such inhibitions have left crucial blind spots that both Hay and Cahill have sought to eliminate, causing us to reflect on what has been missing or excluded in

trivia /ˈtrɪvɪə/ *n.* unimportant or useless details

sap /sæp/ *v.* to make something weaker or destroy it, especially someone's strength or their determination to do something

infect /ɪnˈfekt/ *v.* if a feeling or interest that you have infects other people, it makes them begin to feel the same way or have the same interest

tongue–in–cheek /ˈtʌŋɪnˈtʃiːk/ *adj.* done or said as a joke, not seriously

corrective /kəˈrektɪv/ *n.* something that is intended to correct a fault or mistake

strand /strænd/ *n.* one of the parts of a story, idea, plan, etc.

unveil /ʌnˈveɪl/ *v.* to remove a cover or curtain from a painting, statue, etc. so that it can be seen in public for the first time

episodic /ˌepɪˈsɒdɪk/ *adj.* containing or consisting of many separate and different events

loose /luːs/ *adj.* not exact or thoroughly done or not strictly controlled or organized

substantiate /səbˈstænʃɪeɪt/ *v.* to prove the truth of something that someone has said, claimed, etc.

both traditional and modern art history. To this extent, Cahill's tongue-in-cheek remark that "a full history of the collecting of Chinese painting [. . .] should include a section titled 'In Praise of Bad Taste'" (p. 154) may well apply to the art-historical discipline at large, and not just to new histories of Chinese art. In part, the focus on affect and sensory pleasure is a good corrective to a humanistic strand in art history that over-privileges intellectual, iconographical, and theoretical interpretations.

With their different yet interrelated methodologies, both Hay and Cahill have together unveiled astonishing multifarious spaces for the pleasurable two-and three-dimensional objects consumed by the domestic market. *Pictures for Use and Pleasure* reconstructs an excluded genre of High Qing painting, about which more innovative research can be expected. Cahill's book structure is intentionally episodic with loose ends left for future scholars to pick up. One might ask, for instance, whether such an excluded genre exist before or after the High Qing era of Cahill's focus? In comparison, the structure of *Sensuous Surfaces* seeks to substantiate "a basic understanding of the unwritten rules that made secular luxury decoration a loose, always evolving, but coherent system" (Hay, p. 14), and through analyses of rich layers of objectscapes occupied by the human presence, Hay presents a firm conceptual landscape for his tightly focused case study of material and visual culture in the late Ming and mid-Qing China. However, a broader art-historical issue remains still to be explored: whether such amazing surfaces of

connote /kəˈnəʊt/ v. (of a word) to suggest a feeling, an idea, etc.

decorative objects functioned in similar ways prior to the mid-Ming? In other words, we are inspired to ask if 'sensuous surfaces' of decorative objects were only meaningful to the Ming-Qing taste-makers, or did they also connote certain universal values in people's consumption of luxury objects everywhere and at all times? The two volumes by Cahill and Hay lead the way for further explorations.

Cultural Notes

1. **Li Yu** (1610—1680 AD) (Chinese: 李渔) was a Chinese playwright, novelist and publisher. Born in Rugao, in present day Jiangsu province, he lived in the late-Ming and early-Qing dynasties. Although he passed the first stage of the imperial exams, he did not succeed in passing the higher levels before the political turmoil of the new dynasty, but instead turned to writing for the market. Li was an actor, producer, and director as well as a playwright, who traveled with his own troupe. His play *Errors Caused by the Kite* remains a favorite of the Chinese Kun opera stage. His biographers call him a "writer-entrepreneur" and the "most versatile and enterprising writer of his time". He is the presumed author of *The Carnal Prayer Mat,* a well-crafted comedy and a classic of Chinese erotic literature. He also wrote a book of short stories called *Twelve Towers.* In his time he was widely read, and appreciated for his daringly innovative subject matter. He addresses the topic of same-sex love in the tale *House of Gathered Refinements.* This is a theme which he revisits in the collection *Silent Operas* and his play *Lian Xiangban.* The painting manual *Jieziyuan Huazhuan* was prefaced and published by Li in Jinling. Li was also known for his informal essays and for his gastronomy and gastronomical writings. Lin Yutang championed Li and translated a number of these essays. Li's whimsical, ironic *On Having a Stomach* proposes that the mouth and the stomach "cause all the worry and trouble of mankind throughout the ages." He continues that the "plants can live without a mouth and a stomach, and the rocks and the soil have their being without any nourishment. Why, then, must we be given a mouth and a stomach and endowed with these two extra organs?" Lin also translated Li's *How to Be Happy Though Rich* and *How to Be Happy Though Poor,* and *The Arts of Sleeping, Walking, Sitting and Standing,* which illustrate his satirical approach to serious topics.

2. **scroll paintings:** also known as handing scrolls (c.f. hand-scrolls). A hanging scroll is one of the many traditional ways to display and exhibit Chinese painting and calligraphy. Displaying the art in such way was befitting for public appreciation and appraisal of the aesthetics of the scrolls in its entirety by the audience. The traditional craft involved in creating such a work is considered an art in itself. Mountings can be divided into a few sections, such as hand-scrolls, hanging scrolls, album leaves, and screens amongst others. Hanging scrolls are generally intended to be displayed for short periods of time and are then rolled up to be tied and secured for storage. The hanging scrolls get rotated according to season or occasion, as such works are never intended to be on permanent display. The painting surface of the paper or silk can be mounted with decorative brocade silk borders. In the composition of a hanging scroll, the foreground is usually at the bottom of the scroll while the middle and far distances are at the middle and top respectively.

3. **High Qing:** a period during which the Qing Dynasty reached the zenith of its social, economic and military power, also known as Kang-Qian Golden Age.

4. **genre painting:** also called genre scene or petit genre, depicts aspects of everyday life by portraying ordinary people engaged in common activities. One common definition of a genre scene is that it shows figures to whom no identity can be attached either individually or collectively—thus distinguishing petit genre from history paintings (also called grand genre) and portraits. A work would often be considered as a genre work even if it could be shown that the artist had used a known person—a member of his family, say—as a model. In this case it would depend on whether the work was likely to have been intended by the artist to be perceived as a portrait—sometimes a subjective question. The depictions can be realistic, imagined, or romanticized by the artist. Because of their familiar and frequently sentimental subject matter, genre paintings have often proven popular with the bourgeoisie, or middle class. Genre themes appear in nearly all art traditions. Painted decorations in ancient Egyptian tombs often depict banquets, recreation, and agrarian scenes, and Peiraikos is mentioned by Pliny the Elder as a Hellenistic panel painter of "low" subjects, such as survive in mosaic versions and provincial wall-paintings at Pompeii: "barbers' shops, cobblers' stalls, asses, eatables and similar subjects". Medieval illuminated manuscripts often illustrated scenes of everyday peasant life, especially in the *Labours of the Months* in the calendar section of books of hours, most famously *Les Tres Riches Heures du Duc de Berry*.

5. **Niklas Luhmann** (December 8, 1927—November 6, 1998) was a German sociologist, and a prominent thinker in sociological systems theory. He was born in Lüneburg, Lower Saxony, where his father's family had been running a brewery for several generations. After graduating from the Johanneum school in 1943, he was conscripted as a Luftwaffenhelfer in World War II and served for two years until, at the age of 17, he was taken prisoner of war by American troops in 1945. After the war Luhmann studied law at the University of Freiburg from 1946 to 1949, when he obtained a law degree, and then began a career in Lüneburg's public administration. During a sabbatical in 1961, he went to Harvard, where he met and studied under Talcott Parsons, then the world's most influential social systems theorist. In later years, Luhmann dismissed Parsons' theory, developing a rival approach of his own. Leaving the civil service in 1962, he lectured at University for Administrative Sciences in Speyer, Germany, until 1965, when he was offered a position in Social Research Centre of the University of Münster, led by Helmut Schelsky. In 1965/66 he studied one semester of sociology at the University of Münster. Two earlier books were retroactively accepted as a PhD thesis and habilitation at the University of Münster in 1966, qualifying him for a university professorship. In 1968/1969, he briefly served as a lecturer at Theodor Adorno's former chair at the University of Frankfurt and then was appointed full professor of sociology at the newly founded University of Bielefeld, Germany (until 1993). He continued to publish after his retirement, when he finally found the time to complete his *magnum opus* (the greatest or most important work produced by a writer, artist, musician, or academic), *Society as a Social System*, which was published in 1997.

Comprehension Exercises

I. Answer the following questions based on the text.

1. What is vernacular painting?
2. What are the similarities and the differences between "vernacular painting" in China and "genre painting" in the Western tradition?
3. What are James Cahill's and Jonathan Hay's methodology and positions they have in their books?
4. When it comes to the art-historical focus on literati-biased collectors and connoisseurs towards "vernacular painting", what examples does James

Cahill offer us?

5. What are the author's opinions of both James Cahill's and Jonathan Hay's writings on the study of Chinese visual arts and material culture?

II. Decide whether each of the following statements is true or false according to the text.

1. James Cahill focuses on and examines the amazing surfaces of pleasurable things, a field in paintings that has been dwelled on overwhelmingly in Chinese painting history.

2. James Cahill pays more attention in his writing to paintings of High Qing period than those who have recently made surveys and case studies on the paintings of the same period.

3. Jonathan Hay, in his book, made a critical selection of the secular displayed objects related to the mass of ritual, religious, and antiquarian decorative works.

4. In spite of different methodologies and contradictory results in their observations, James Cahill and his contemporary Jonathan Hay have provided us with insightful food for our rethinking of complex discourses within the network of binaries.

5. According to the author of this article, being indulged in "pleasurable things" has been ruled out in the history of modern Chinese aesthetics and art.

III. Select the most appropriate word or phrase and use its proper form to complete each of the following sentences.

eminent	sensuous	reconstruct	orthodox	aesthetic
execute	sensitive	akin	ephemeral	anonymous
unprecedented	sentimental	controversial	daunting	prevailing
multifarious	sensational	elicit	conspicuous	substantiate

1. Companies that sell foods with added ingredients that are intended to boost health or prevent illness are under increasing pressure to _____ the claims about their products.

2. True, as all my Chinese colleagues tell me, no one takes this stuff seriously, but it shows how writers have to acknowledge the _____ ideology, whether or not they choose to confront it directly.

3. She may not be your _____ telephone caller, but in any case, ask the operator about your options: have your calls intercepted first and callers identified before you speak to them; or go ex-directory.

4. Just as the collapse of intellectual and _____ standards in the universities

and the art world exacerbated the decline of moral standards in the general public, so declining public morality weakened the cohesion of American society, by creating and enlarging a poor black underclass that stood apart from, and threatened, middle-class society.

5. Here students may either study an option offered in another department, for example, Theatre Studies, Philosophy, History of Art, History of Music, Film Studies, Italian, or take a specialised course in an _____ area of English Literature such as the Brontes, Dickens, Shakespeare's History Plays, T.S. Eliot.

6. Small in size, fragile in substance, and pale in color, they are the fickle, _____ , and heart-rending essence of spring.

7. So while redeveloping the character of the American people, or of any substantial portion of the American people, might seem a _____ project, conservatives were reassured when Wilson reminded them that the task had been done before: by the temperance movement of the nineteenth century and by the public school and other municipal reforms of the Progressive Era.

8. There are pubs, emptier than before, and large working-men's clubs, with a little of the atmosphere of empty Victorian churches, and empty Victorian churches, but there is no hotel in Jarrow, nor could I find a bed and breakfast, no disco, no nightclub, nothing that provokes any sort of _____ consumption whatsoever.

9. The company's founder and boss, Michael Dell, agrees that the Internet gives customers _____ power to seek out the lowest prices, but argues that it can also be used to deepen relationships and ultimately build far greater customer loyalty than before.

10. Bits and pieces of black, gold and copperplated beads, chains and rings are encrusted in sparkling black-pigmented, lightweight cement—the results are _____ .

11. The poll did not _____ opinions on non-animal research and testing methods, but other surveys have demonstrated enormous support.

12. With a poet such as Petrarch, who plays with puns, classical references and inter-textual echoes, to capture the _____ and eliding meanings is all but impossible.

13. One might argue differently, and we have in court sometimes argued differently, but one lives with the interpretations that the court renders on law and continues to administer and _____ law consistent with the deeply-felt principles that this President and this administration has on questions of racial injustice.

14. The landlady was making her morning sweep, brandishing a broom so vigorously that the ritual seemed more _____ to exercise than to practical considerations of cleanliness.

15. For example, he found an answer to a question first raised in the 1960s: can you hear the shape of a drum—that is, can you _____ the shape of an object from the pattern of its vibrations?

IV. Try to paraphrase the following sentences, paying special attention to the underlined parts.

1. ...but the <u>sheer</u> task of assessing such a great number of items and related scholarship must have been <u>daunting</u>. Like Cahill, Hay has had to push at the boundaries of <u>prevailing</u> opinions.

_____

_____

2. ...he observes that these decorative objects may have been <u>socially coded</u>, but <u>appealed</u> nevertheless <u>to</u> three different groups of collectors (wealthy urban residents, <u>lavish</u> court attendees, and <u>elegant literati</u>).

_____

_____

3. <u>Exploring</u> this shared vision <u>fascinated by the duality of repetition and originality</u>, Hay <u>invites us</u> in two subsequent parts of his book to pay special attention to the complexity of visual spaces through his in-depth discussion of "surfacescapes" and "objectscapes".

_____

_____

4. For his part, Hay gathers 229 illustrations (mostly in colour as well accompanied by descriptive <u>captions</u>) that support his arguments for those <u>subtle and sensitive appreciations of luxury objects evinced</u> by Ming-Qing writers, particularly by Li Yu—the <u>aforementioned</u> Qing taste-maker.

_____

_____

5. Cahill's book structure is intentionally <u>episodic</u> with <u>loose</u> ends left for future scholars to <u>pick up</u>.

_____

_____

V. Discuss with your partner about each of the three statements and write an essay in no less than 260 words about your understanding of one of them.

1. Excessive attention to trivia saps the will.

_____

_____

2. In doing so, the social network of binaries—the south-north, Chinese-Manchu, local-global, literatus-artisan, among others—find new ways to broaden extant debates on the aesthetic characteristics of the Ming-Qing decorative art.

_____

_____

3. To be part is to be whole; to be bent is to be straight; to be hollow is to be filled; to be worn out is to be renewed; to have little is to have more; to have much is to be confused.

_____

_____

VI. List four websites where we can learn more about how to write book review or Chinese traditional culture and provide a brief introduction to each of them.

1. _____

_____

_____ .

2. _____

_____

_____ .

3. _____

_____

_____ .

4. _____

_____

_____ .

Text B

Book Review of *Mi Fu and the Classical Tradition of Chinese Calligraphy*
By Michael Loewe
(excerpt)

Mi Fu and the Classical Tradition of Chinese Calligraphy. By Ledde-Rose Lothar. Princeton University Press: Princeton, 1979. Pp. xiv, 132; 50 plates.

Calligraphy may be regarded as one of the most esoteric and yet one of the most characteristic forms of Chinese art. The artist works within a prescribed medium of symbols whose meaning is open to comprehension by all literate Chinese; but his subtleties can be appreciated to the full only by a minority of initiates. While the set forms of the medium preclude extravagant innovation, the art comprises scope for infinite variations that respond to a calligrapher's mood and evoke emotional response from his admirers.

The three millennia in which the history of the art may be traced have been punctuated by a few crucial changes which have depended on the introduction of new materials (e.g. silk, and then paper, in place of wood; and the brush in place of the engraver's tool) and the evolution of new types of script in response to intellectual, social and political needs. Simultaneously the progress of the art has been marked both by the stimulus of imperial patronage and by the reaction of a man of letters who seeks refuge from political strife in the beauties of pure form.

One of the first crucial changes that may be defined took place in the fourth century AD, which gave rise to the achievements of Wang Hsi-chih (307—365)

esoteric /ˌesəˈterɪk/ *adj.* known and understood by only a few people who have special knowledge about something
literate /ˈlɪt(ə)rət/ *adj.* able to read and write; well educated
initiate /ɪˈnɪʃɪeɪt/ *n.* someone who has been allowed to join a particular organization, club, or group and has been taught its secrets
preclude /prɪˈkluːd/ *v.* to prevent something or make something impossible
extravagant /ɪkˈstrævəg(ə)nt/ *adj.* doing or using something too much or more than is necessary
evoke /ɪˈvəʊk/ *v.* to produce a strong feeling or memory in someone
millennia /mɪˈlenɪə/ *n.* a period of 1000 years
punctuate /ˈpʌŋ(k)tʃʊeɪt/ *v.* to be interrupted by something, especially when this is repeated
simultaneously /ˌsɪm(ə)lˈteɪnɪəslɪ/ *adv.* happening or done at the same time as sth else
patronage /ˈpætr(ə)nɪdʒ/ *n.* the support, especially financial support, that is given to an organization or activity by a patron
strife /straɪf/ *n.* angry or violent disagreement between two or more people or groups

and his son Wang Hsien-chih (344—388). These two masters may be taken as the pace-setters who led the fashion; and despite the many vicissitudes that beset the preservation of their work, they played a leading role in forming China's calligraphic tradition. This derived considerable strength from the strong imperial patronage of the newly unified court of T'ang, particularly under the encouragement of the second emperor (T'ai-tsung: reigned 626 to 649).

Five hundred years later a further crucial stage was reached in the history of the art. This occurred during the intellectual and artistic flowering of the Sung age, whose institutions provided long leisure hours in which the numerous officials could devote their attention to the cultivation of the arts, the sharpening of their critical ability and the examination of far greater literary and artistic riches than had been available to their predecessors; for the woodblock printers—themselves working from calligraphic models—were now turning out copies of texts or rubbings of inscriptions or other types of literary embellishment. Yet another significant stage in the history of calligraphy may be seen in the Ch'ing period, when emperors such as Ch'ien-lung (reigned 1736 to 1795) set about collecting masterpieces of all forms of Chinese art on an unprecedented scale, and new standards were being reached in most aspects of China's artistic development and aesthetic appreciation.

In the present volume Professor Ledderose concentrates attention on the growth of the tradition from the fourth century, and the critical appreciation of that tradition by Mi Fu in the eleventh century. It should be said at once that the book has been beautifully produced with excellent half-tone plates and the inclusion of Chinese characters in the text; the publishers deserve full praise for maintaining so high a standard of production. The theme of the book is expounded with great lucidity and an agreeable absence of jargon. While the book expects a basic familiarity with Chinese cultural development, it is yet written in such a way that it could form one of the first textbooks that a serious student of calligraphy should read; it is a major contribution to a subject that all

pace-setter *n.* a person or company that is considered to be a leader in a particular area of activity

vicissitude /vɪˈsɪsɪtjuːd/ *n.* the continuous changes and problems that affect a situation or someone's life

beset /bɪˈset/ *v.* to make someone experience serious problems or dangers

considerable /kənˈsɪd(ə)rəb(ə)l/ *adj.* fairly large, especially large enough to have an effect or be important

reign /reɪn/ *v.* to rule a nation or group of nations as their king, queen, or emperor

institution /ɪnstɪˈtjuːʃ(ə)n/ *n.* an important system of organization in society that has existed for a long time

predecessor /ˈpriːdɪsesə/ *n.* someone who had your job before you started doing it

embellishment /ɪmˈbelɪʃmənt/ *n.* a. to make something more beautiful by adding decorations to it

plate /pleɪt/ *n.* a plate in a book is a picture or photograph that takes up a whole page and is usually printed on better quality paper than the rest of the book

expound /ɪkˈspaʊnd/ *v.* to explain or talk about something in detail

lucid /ˈluːsɪd/ *adj.* expressed in a way that is clear and easy to understand elusive /ɪˈl(j)uːsɪv/ *adj.* difficult to describe or understand

discriminate /dɪˈskrɪmɪneɪt/ *v.* to recognize a difference between things

analogy /əˈnælədʒɪ/ *n.* something that seems similar between two situations, processes, etc.

versatile /ˈvɜːsətaɪl/ *adj.* someone has many different skills; having many different uses

chronological /krɒnəˈlɒdʒɪk(ə)l/ *adj.* arranged according to when things happened or were made

contemporary /kənˈtemp(ə)r(ər)ɪ/ *adj.* happening or done in the same period of time

intact /ɪnˈtækt/ *adj.* not broken, damaged, or spoiled

reveal /rɪˈviːl/ *v.* to make known something that was previously secret or unknown; to show something that was previously hidden

yardstick /ˈjɑːdstɪk/ *n.* something that you compare another thing with, in order to judge how good or successful it is

nicety /ˈnaɪsɪtɪ/ *n.* a small detail or point of difference, especially one that is usually considered to be part of the correct way of doing something

epitaph /ˈepɪtɑːf/ *n.* a short piece of writing on the stone over someone's grave

evolve /ɪˈvɒlv/ *v.* to develop and change gradually over a long period of time

unitary /ˈjuːnɪt(ə)rɪ/ *adj.* relating to or existing as a single unit

too often proves to be more than somewhat elusive.

In the first chapter the author charts the growth of the calligraphic tradition, and readers will be grateful for his clear guidance. In the first place it is necessary to discriminate between different types of script (if analogy may be permitted, it would, as it were, be between uncial, Italianate and Black Letter, or Gothic, types), and their sequence of evolution. The second distinction is between the different characteristics of individual artists within those types. However, from Sung times at least, calligraphers were accustomed and even expected to practise their art in several of the basic types; their very versatility increases the difficulty of isolating changes in chronological terms or defining the stages of a particular calligrapher's personal development.

In addition, the early history of the subject is gravely affected by the absence of original material before the T'ang period. A scholar can only proceed by examining the evidence of copies, or copies several times removed from the original, be they made by tracing, rubbing or by engravings on durable substances such as stone. Such evidence, e.g. of the writing of Wang Hsi-chih (307—365) or Yil Shih-nan (558—638) may then be compared with such contemporary evidence of their age that has survived intact and that has been revealed by archaeologists. Here, however, the accidental nature of such evidence constitutes a further difficulty, and it cannot be regarded as forming typical or universal yardsticks for the appreciation of calligraphic niceties. While it is possible to draw certain general inferences (e.g., regarding the choice of styles that were in fashion for engraving funerary epitaphs at particular times), archaeology cannot be asked to provide a corpus of material for the formation of aesthetic standards or judgments.

Professor Ledderose does well to remind his readers that styles were not evolved as part of a unitary process; his warning is of particular application to the

centuries that elapsed between the Han and the Sui dynasties (i.e., from AD 220 to 589). For these were centuries that were especially rich in artistic growth and cultural diversity. China was divided among several ruling houses, each with its own court and officials, and with its need to patronize scholarship and the arts. In intellectual and religious terms, both Taoist and Buddhist establishments were springing up with a new degree of enthusiasm, and requiring copies of holy writings. The successive rise and fall of dynasties resulted in the collection, dispersal or destruction of masterpieces, or in the need to order copies for the delectation of a new set of rulers.

By the T'ang dynasty a further consideration was affecting the growth of the calligraphic tradition and an artist's reputation; this was the need for art critics to follow a lead given by an emperor. Possibly for this reason the reputation of Wang Hsien-chih (344—388) was at times eclipsed in favor of that of his father, Wang Hsi-chih, for whom the second T'ang emperor T'ai-tsung had expressed a marked predilection. But the potential hazards of an imperial choice or whim must be offset, in this case, against T'ai-tsung's great achievement in encouraging calligraphy, scholarship and the arts, at a moment that was singularly ripe for the purpose. In the seventh century the influence of the newly unified imperial institutions was at one of its most effective points in promoting cultural activities; it was largely thanks to T'ai-tsung that famous artists such as Ou-yeng Hsiin (557—641), Yti Shih-nan (558—638) and Ch'u Sui-liang (596—658) have held a prominent place in calligraphy and its criticism for over a millennium.

In addition, it was as a result of the T'ang achievement that the calligraphic tradition came to centre round the southern styles that derived from the two Wangs, rather than the more austere forms that had been finding favour in the north. T'ai-tsung's part in the tragi-comic story of Wang Hsi-chih's most famous production, The Preface for the *Pavilion of Orchids* (*Lan-t'ing hsü*) is perhaps not so inspiring; it provides adequate comment on the lack of scruple prevailing in high places, when imperial ambitions involved the

elapse /ɪˈlæps/ v. if a particular period of time elapses, it passes
successive /səkˈsesɪv/ adj. coming or following one after the other
dispersal /dɪˈspɜːsl/ n. the process of spreading things over a wide area or in different directions
delectation /ˌdiːlekˈteɪʃ(ə)n/ n. enjoyment or amusement
eclipse /ɪˈklɪps/ v. to make sb/sth seem dull or unimportant by comparison
predilection /ˌpriːdɪˈlekʃən/ n. if you have a predilection for something, especially something unusual, you like it very much
whim /wɪm/ n. a sudden feeling that you would like to do or have something, especially when there is no important or good reason
offset /ˈɒfset/ v. to use one cost, payment or situation in order to cancel or reduce the effect of another
singularly /ˈsɪŋɡjələli/ adv. in a way that is very noticeable or unusual
austere /ɒˈstɪə/ adj. plain and simple and without any decoration
scruple /ˈskruːp(ə)l/ n. moral principles or beliefs that make you unwilling to do something that seems wrong

16

posterity /pɒˈsterɪtɪ/ *n.* everyone who will be alive in the future

sporadically /spəˈrædɪkli/ *adv.* happening only occasionally or at intervals that are not regular

palpably /ˈpælpəbli/ *adv.* that is easily noticed by the mind or the senses

staunch /stɔːn(t)ʃ/ *adj.* strong and loyal in your opinions and attitude

deception /dɪˈsepʃ(ə)n/ *n.* the act of deliberately making someone believe something that is not true

perpetrate /ˈpɜːpɪtreɪt/ *v.* to do something that is morally wrong or illegal

appendix /əˈpendɪks/ *n.* a part at the end of a book containing additional information

acquisition of artistic masterpieces.

Mi Fu (1052—1107) is the hero of Professor Ledderose's study. He lived as a member of one of China's most brilliant generations, being a contemporary of literary figures such as Ou-yang Hsiu (1007—1072) and Su Shih (1037—1101), the historian Ssu-ma Kuang(1019—1086), Shen Kua (1031—1095) the master of technology and Wang An-shih (1021—1086) the political reformer. He was also partly contemporary with Hui-tsung, last but one of the northern Sung emperors (reigned 1100—1125), who was best known to history not for his part in dynastic destinies but for his own highly characteristic calligraphy, and the collections that he assembled. With some connections at court, Mi Fu passed through a number of offices, without attaining the highest professional reaches of the civil service. He is known as an outstanding artist, collector, connoisseur and critic of calligraphy, who had access to most of the famous pieces of the day.

Mi Fu's opinions are known to posterity thanks to the survival of his descriptive accounts of several pieces of writing. These notes were produced sporadically and independently, as occasion demanded, and it is hardly surprising that they include some inconsistencies. Nevertheless his achievement stands out as that of a pioneer critic. He paid strict attention to the problems of authorship or ownership of each piece of writing upon which he was called to comment. His descriptions are precise, his arguments logical; and he thereby established a model of art criticism in China. In rejecting the evidence of copies where these were palpably unreliable, Mi Fu sought to isolate the characteristics and essential qualities of the fourth century style of calligraphy that he loved, as against the austere tastes of the staunch Confucians of the eighth century such as Han Yü (768—824). As part of his self-training in connoisseurship, Mi Fu made a practice of copying some of the works of earlier masters such as Yü Shih-nan; in doing so he succeeded in surprising both his friends and himself by the ease with which unintentional deceptions could be perpetrated.

In his third chapter Professor Ledderose gives a critical and scholastic account of the evidence that Mi Fu had before him of the work of the fourth century calligraphers. The chapter, and its supporting appendixes, include a treasure-house of bibliographical information and guidance which will be invaluable to any student of calligraphy. The author deserves the highest praise for treating the whole subject in a professional manner, in the full light of critical canons and scholastic demands. In doing so he reflects the attitude of the Chinese themselves towards the calligrapher's art; so far from being a set of diletantish exercises, it demanded a technical ability

invaluable /ɪnˈvæljʊ(ə)b(ə)l/ *adj.* extremely useful

canon /ˈkænən/ *n.* a standard, rule, or principle, or set of these, that are believed by a group of people to be right and good

dilettantish /ˌdɪləˈtæntɪʃ/ *n. a.* a person who takes up an art, activity, or subject merely for amusement, especially in a desultory or superficial way; dabbler. **b.** a lover of an art or science, especially of a fine art. *adj.* of or pertaining to dilettantes

rigorous /ˈrɪg(ə)rəs/ *adj.* very severe or strict; careful, thorough, and exact

acumen /ˈækjʊmən/ *n.* the ability to think quickly and make good judgments

that derived from a rigorous training, a professional judgment based on scholastic acumen and the inspiration of an artist.

This review will conclude with a few remarks on the growth of the calligraphic tradition in its early stages, before it had received the impact of men such as Wang Hsi-chih and Wang Hsien-chih.

Cultural Notes

1. **Michael Loewe** (born 1922): also known as M. A. N. Loewe, is a British academic and renowned sinologist who has authored dozens of books, articles, and other publications in the fields of classical Chinese and ancient Chinese history. Loewe attended The Perse School in Cambridge and Magdalen College, Oxford. In 1942, he left Oxford to serve as a specialist officer in the British Government Communications' Headquarters working with Japanese issues, while studying classical Chinese in his spare time. The School of Oriental and African Studies at the University of London awarded him a first class honours degree in 1951, and in 1956 he left the government to serve as a lecturer in the History of the Far East at the University of London. Oxford awarded him a PhD in 1963, and he subsequently joined the faculty of the University of Cambridge, where he taught until retiring in 1990 to focus solely on research and scholarship. He is a fellow of Clare Hall, Cambridge.

2. **Mi Fu** (1051—1107) was a Chinese painter, poet, and calligrapher born in Taiyuan during the Song Dynasty. In painting he gained renown for his style of painting misty landscapes. This style would be deemed the "Mi Fu" style

and involved the use of large wet dots of ink applied with a flat brush. His poetry followed the style of Li Bai and his calligraphy that of Wang Xizhi. His uninhibited style made him disliked at the Song court. He is best known for his calligraphy, and he was regarded as one of the four greatest calligraphers in Song Dynasty. His style arises from that of calligraphers in earlier dynasties, but with a unique mark of his own. As a personality Mi Fu was noted as an eccentric. At times they even deemed him "Madman Mi" because he was obsessed with collecting stones and even declared one stone to be his brother. Hence he would bow to his "brother" rock in a display of the filial devotion given to older brothers. He also was known as a heavy drinker.

3. **T'ai-tsung** (28 January 598—10 July 649), or Taizong, his personal name Li Shimin , was the second emperor of the Tang Dynasty of China, ruling from 626 to 649. As he encouraged his father, Li Yuan (later Emperor Gaozu) to rise against Sui Dynasty rule at Taiyuan in 617 and subsequently defeated several of his most important rivals, he was ceremonially regarded as a co-founder of the dynasty along with Emperor Gaozu. He is typically considered as one of the (if not the) greatest emperors in Chinese history. Throughout the rest of Chinese history, Emperor Taizong's reign was regarded as the exemplary model against which all other emperors were measured, and his "Reign of Zhenguan" was considered a golden age of Chinese history and required study for future crown princes. During his reign, Tang China flourished economically and militarily. For more than a century after his death, Tang China enjoyed peace and prosperity. During Taizong's reign, Tang was the largest and the strongest nation in the world. It covered most of the territory of present-day China, Vietnam and much of Central Asia as far as eastern Kazakhstan. It laid the foundation for Xuanzong's reign, which is considered Tang China's greatest era. Unlike many of the nobility of the time, Emperor Taizong was a frank rationalist, openly scorning superstitions and claims of signs from the heavens. He also modified important rites in order to ease the burden of agricultural labour. The modern Chinese historian Bo Yang opined that Emperor Taizong achieved greatness by enduring criticism which others would find difficult to accept whilst trying hard not to abuse his absolute power (using Emperor Yang of Sui as a negative example), as well as through his employment of capable chancellors such as Fang Xuanling, Du Ruhui and Wei Zheng. Emperor Taizong's wife Empress Zhangsun also proved to be a capable assistant.

4. **Chien-lung** (Emperor) (25 September 1711—7 February 1799) was the sixth emperor of the Manchu-led Qing Dynasty, and the fourth Qing emperor to rule over China proper. The fourth son of the Yongzheng Emperor, he reigned officially from 11 October 1735 to 8 February 1796. On 8 February, he abdicated in favor of his son, the Jiaqing Emperor—a filial act in order not to reign longer than his grandfather, the illustrious Kangxi Emperor. Despite his retirement, however, he retained ultimate power until his death in 1799. Although his early years saw the continuation of an era of prosperity in China, his final years saw troubles at home and abroad converge on the Qing Empire. He was a major patron of the arts, seeing himself as an important "preserver and restorer" of Chinese culture. He had an insatiable appetite for collecting, and acquired much of China's great private collections by any means necessary, and reintegrated their treasures into the imperial collection. His massive art collection became an intimate part of his life; he took landscape paintings with him on his travels in order to compare them with the actual landscapes, or to hang them in special rooms in palaces where he lodged, to inscribe them on every visit there. He also regularly added poetic inscriptions to the paintings of the imperial collection, following the example of the emperors of the Song Dynasty and the literati painters of the Ming. They were a mark of distinction for the work, and a visible sign of his rightful role as Emperor. Most particular to the Qianlong Emperor is another type of inscription, revealing a unique practice of dealing with works of art that he seems to have developed for himself. On certain fixed occasions over a long period he contemplated a number of paintings or works of calligraphy which possessed special meaning for him, inscribing each regularly with mostly private notes on the circumstances of enjoying them, using them almost as a diary. One of Qianlong's grandest projects was to assemble a team of China's finest scholars for the purpose of assembling, editing, and printing the largest collection ever made of Chinese philosophy, history, and literature. Known as The Four Treasuries project, or Siku Quanshu, it was published in 36,000 volumes, containing about 3450 complete works and employing as many as 15,000 copyists. It preserved numerous books, but was also intended as a way to ferret out and suppress political opponents, requiring the careful examination of private libraries to assemble a list of around eleven thousand works from the past, of which about a third were chosen for publication. The works not included were either summarized or—in a good many cases—scheduled for destruction.

Comprehension Exercises

I. Answer the following questions based on the text.

1. Who played the leading role in forming China's calligraphic tradition according to Michael Loewe?

2. Why did a further crucial stage in the calligraphic field reach in Sung Dynasty?

3. How many emperors have contributed to the development of the art history of calligraphy in China according to this book review?

4. Why does Michael Loewe think highly of the book *Mi Fu and the Classical Tradition of Chinese Calligraphy* by Ledde-Rose Lothar?

5. What does Michael Loewe warn his readers when it comes the appreciation of calligraphic styles in China?

II. Decide whether each of the following statements is true or false according to the text.

1. Calligraphy, as a typical form of Chinese art, can spark off given emotional reaction from beholders for its multifarious forms of medium may allow for a great legion of creative initiatives in terms of strokes.

2. The history of the calligraphy art has been influenced a lot by a variety of factors such as the introduction of new materials on which Chinese characters are either written or engraved, the imperial support and the men of letters.

3. Michael Loewe makes a very sound and convincing analogy between Chinese scripts in the field of calligraphy and different font types such as uncial, Italianate.

4. Wang Hsien-chih was more popular than Wang His-chich in Tang Dynasty because T'ang T'ai-tsung enjoyed more of the latter's calligraphic art than of the former's one.

5. Mi Fu, as a member of one of China's most brilliant generations, also the hero of Ledde-Rose Lothar's book, is renowned for his versatility as an artist, collector, connoisseur, and critic of calligraphy.

III. Select the most appropriate word or phrase and use its proper form to complete each of the following sentences.

embellish	esoteric	austere	meticulous	eccentric
austere	institution	extravagant	evoke	exemplify
sporadic	tentative	palpable	elusive	staunch
eclipse	elapse	canon	reveal	versatile

1. Every religious holiday features food and its _____ preparation as the central secular theme, and even if you don't like to cook, shop for a particularly delectable holiday assortment of food as a gift for your family.

2. Pinter's superbly crafted, typically pithy script cuts a swathe through the more _____ portions of Kafka's novel without losing any of its depth, resonance of message and draws you deeper into Josef's plight.

3. While it has nothing to do specifically with Pirates, this quote from the New York Herald of November 6 might be of interest: The appearance and manner of the two famous Englishmen greatly believe the published accounts which have found their way across the ocean, and which represented more especially Mr. Gilbert as a man of _____ and haughty temperament.

4. A recent article published by the _____ of Electrical Engineers stated that by the turn of the century approximately 70% of all electrical power will pass through a semiconductor device before it is consumed.

5. He died in 1847 in Van Diemen's Land, as Tasmania was then called, having been transported ten years earlier for what was then a capital crime: he had forged the deeds on a trust fund left to him by his grandfather in order to access the capital, which he then squandered on his _____ lifestyle.

6. Adopting the Proustian method of allowing sensual experience to dictate narrative shape and suddenly re-experienced tastes to _____ long-forgotten childhood memories, John Lanchester's novel idles along on a sentimental and gastronomic journey through France, mixing story-telling, recipes, reminiscence and hints of mysterious crimes to tickle the reader's palate and nudge even the most unwilling audience into admiration of its cleverness.

7. Her vision is that political organizations that do lobbying, consciousness raising, etc., becomes involved in hands-on social services in order to better _____ the plight of those who cause they rally behind, and, more simply, to meet the need of those who find themselves on the outside.

8. As she looked out over the vista, illuminated only by the _____ flickering lights of the tiny settlements in the valley below, she found herself thinking back to what Rick had said about the gorge having once been a dumping

ground for the bodies of those who'd dared to oppose the repressive rule of the gun.

9. After that I was allowed to make a few _____ steps around the grounds of the hospital, which were like wading through treacle, then, three-and-a-half weeks later I was finally allowed home.

10. As people sort out the competing stories, the urgent desire for "the truth" and for stability grows _____.

11. Britton gives us many of the sub-layers, the hints and allusions which are the very nature of the language, but which remain so _____ to most translators.

12. Claritas then linked the addresses of the respondents to each of the state's 6,000 clustered block groups (typically a four-square-block area) and analyzed the poll data to identify the initiative's firm supporters, opponents and persuadable voters.

13. This is an entirely welcome addition to Shostakovich's recorded symphonic canon, because while it fails to _____ Rozhedestvensky's rendition with the old USSR Ministry of Culture Symphony Orchestra, it is a worthy attempt at this often overlooked work.

14. At least 80 minutes _____ before Welles delivered his first speech, a supremely sinister homily on how 500 turbulent years in corrupt while in Switzerland it produced the cuckoo clock.

15. First, he is aware that conventional critical articles in the ongoing debate about the _____ generally appeal to a limited audience, an audience consisting of writers and critics whose careers are directly affected by the vicissitudes of the canon.

IV. Try to paraphrase the following sentences, paying special attention to the underlined parts.

1. One of the first crucial changes that may be <u>defined</u> took place in the fourth century AD, which <u>gave rise to</u> the achievements of Wang Hsi-chih (307—365) and his son Wang Hsien-chih (344—388).

2. Yet another significant stage in the history of calligraphy may be seen in the Ch'ing period, when emperors such as Ch'ien-lung (reigned 1736 to 1795) <u>set about</u> collecting masterpieces of all forms of Chinese art <u>on an unprecedented scale</u>, and new standards were being reached in most aspects of China's <u>artistic development and aesthetic appreciation</u>.

3. The <u>successive</u> rise and fall of dynasties resulted in the collection, <u>dispersal</u> or destruction of masterpieces, or in the need to order copies for the <u>delectation</u> of a new set of rulers.

_____

_____

4. But the potential hazards of an imperial choice or <u>whim</u> must be <u>offset</u>, in this case, against T'ai-tsung's great achievement in encouraging calligraphy, scholarship and the arts, at a moment that was <u>singularly</u> ripe for the purpose.

_____

_____

5. In doing so he reflects the attitude of the Chinese themselves towards the calligrapher's art; so <u>far from being</u> a set of <u>diletantish</u> exercises, it demanded a technical ability that <u>derived from</u> a <u>rigorous</u> training, a professional judgment based on scholastic <u>acumen</u> and the inspiration of an artist.

_____

_____

V. Discuss with your partner about each of the three statements and write an essay in no less than 260 words about your understanding of one of them.

1. Calligraphy may be regarded as one of the most esoteric and yet one of the most characteristic forms of Chinese art.

_____

_____

2. There are things that we don't want to happen but have to accept, things we don't want to know but have to learn, and people we can't live without but have to let go.

_____

_____

3. While the set forms of the medium preclude extravagant innovation, the art comprises scope for infinite variations that respond to a calligrapher's mood and evoke emotional response from his admirers.

_____

_____

VI. List four websites where we can learn more about the history of calligraphic art or famous calligraphers in China and provide a brief introduction to each of them.

1. _____

_____

_____.

2. _____

_____

_____.

3. _____

_____

_____.

4. _____

_____

_____.

Twenty Minutes' Reading

You are required to read the following two sections within 20 minutes.

Section A

Automation refers to the introduction of electronic control and automatic operation of productive machinery. It reduces the human factors, mental and physical, in production, and is designed to make possible the manufacture of more goods with fewer workers. The development of automation in American industry has been called the "Second Industrial Revolution".

Labour's concern over automation arises from uncertainty about the effects on employment, and fears of major changes in jobs. In the main, labour has taken the view that resistance to technical change is unfruitful. Eventually, the result of automation may well be an increase in employment, since it is expected that vast industries will grow up around manufacturing, maintaining, and repairing automation equipment. The interest of labour lies in bringing about the transition with a minimum of inconvenience and distress to the workers involved. Also, union spokesmen emphasize that the benefit of the increased production and lower costs made possible by automation should be shared by workers in the form of higher wages, more leisure, and improved living standards.

To protect the interests of their members in the era of automation, unions have adopted a number of new policies. One of these is the promotion of supplementary unemployment benefit plans. It is emphasized that since the employer involved in such a plan has a direct financial interest in preventing unemployment, he will have a strong drive for planning new installations so as to cause the least possible problems in jobs and job assignment. Some unions are working for dismissal pay agreements, requiring that permanently dismissed workers be paid a sum of money based on length of service. Another approach is the idea of the "improvement factor", which calls for wage increases based on increases in productivity. It is possible, however, that labour will rely mainly on reduction in working time.

1. Though labour worries about the effect of automation, it does not doubt that
   _____.
   A. automation will eventually prevent unemployment
   B. automation will help workers acquire new skills
   C. automation will eventually benefit the workers no less than the employers
   D. automation is a trend which cannot be stopped
2. The idea of the "improvement factor" (Para. 3) probably implies that _____.
   A. wages should be paid on the basis of length of service
   B. the benefit of increased production and lower costs should be shared by workers
   C. supplementary unemployment benefit plans should be promoted
   D. the transition to automation should be brought about with the minimum of inconvenience and distress to workers
3. In order to get the full benefits of automation, labour will depend mostly on
   _____.
   A. additional payment to the permanently dismissed workers
   B. the increase of wages in proportion to the increase in productivity
   C. shorter working hours and more leisure time
   D. a strong drive for planning new installations
4. Which of the following can best sum up the passage?
   A. Advantages and disadvantages of automation.
   B. Labour and the effects of automation.
   C. Unemployment benefit plans and automation.
   D. Social benefits of automation.

Section B

The case for college has been accepted without question for more than a generation. All high school graduates ought to go, says conventional wisdom and statistical evidence, because college will help them earn more money, become "better" people, and learn to be more responsible citizens than those who don't go.

But college has never been able to work its magic for everyone. And now that close to half our high school graduates are attending, those who don't fit the pattern are becoming more numerous, and more obvious. College graduates are selling shoes and driving taxis; college students interfere with each other's experiments and write false letters of recommendation in the intense competition for admission to graduate school. Others find no stimulation in their studies, and drop out—often encouraged by college administrators.

Some observers say the fault is with the young people themselves—they are spoiled and they are expecting too much. But that's a condemnation of the students as a whole, and doesn't explain all campus unhappiness. Others blame the state of the world, and they are partly right. We've been told that young people have to go to college because our economy can't absorb an army of untrained eighteen-year-olds. But disappointed graduates are learning that it can no longer absorb an army of trained twenty-two-year-olds, either.

Some adventuresome educators and campus watchers have openly begun to suggest that college may not be the best, the proper, the only place for every young person after the completion of high school. We may have been looking at all those surveys and statistics upside down, it seems, and through the rosy glow of our own remembered college experiences. Perhaps college doesn't make people intelligent, ambitious, happy, liberal, quick to learn things—maybe it's just the other way around, and intelligent, ambitious, happy, liberal, quick-learning people are merely the ones who have been attracted to college in the first place. And perhaps all those successful college graduates would have been successful whether they had gone to college or not. This is heresy (异端邪说) to those of us who have been brought up to believe that if a little schooling is good, more has to be much better. But contrary evidence is beginning to mount up.

5. According to the passage, the author believes that _____.
   A. people used to question the value of college education
   B. people used to have full confidence in higher education
   C. all high school graduates went to college
   D. very few high school graduates chose to go to college

6. In the 2nd paragraph, "those who don't fit the pattern" refers to _____.

    A. high school graduates who aren't suitable for college education

    B. college graduates who are selling shoes and driving taxis

    C. college students who aren't any better for their higher education

    D. high school graduates who failed to be admitted to college

7. The drop-out rate of college students seems to go up because _____.

    A. young people are disappointed with the conventional way of teaching at college

    B. many young people are required to join the army

    C. young people have little motivation in pursuing a higher education

    D. young people don't like the intense competition for admission to graduate school

8. According to the passage the problems of college education partly arise from the fact that _____.

    A. society cannot provide enough jobs for properly trained college graduates

    B. high school graduates do not fit the pattern of college education

    C. too many students have to earn their own living

    D. college administrators encourage students to drop out

9. In this passage the author argues that _____.

    A. more and more evidence shows college education may not be the best thing for high school graduates

    B. college education is not enough if one wants to be successful

    C. college education benefits only the intelligent, ambitious, and quick-learning people

    D. intelligent people may learn quicker if they don't go to college

10. The "surveys and statistics" mentioned in the last paragraph might have shown that _____.

    A. college-educated people are more successful than non-college-educated people

    B. college education was not the first choice of intelligent people

    C. the less schooling a person has the better it is for him

    D. most people have sweet memories of college life

Unit Two
Campus Life

Take This Fish and Look at It
By Samuel H. Scudder

It was more than fifteen years ago that I entered the laboratory of Professor Agassiz, and told him I had enrolled my name in the Scientific School as a student of Natural History. He asked me a few questions about my object in coming, my previous experience, the way in which I afterwards proposed to use the knowledge I might acquire, and finally, whether I wished to study any special branch. To the latter I replied that, while I wished to be well grounded in all departments of zoology, I planned to devote myself specially to insects.

"When do you wish to begin?" he asked.

"Now," I replied.

This seemed to please him, and with an energetic "Very well." he reached from a shelf a huge jar of specimens in yellow alcohol. "Take this fish," he said, "and look at it; by and by I will ask what you have seen."

With that he left me, but in a moment returned with explicit instructions as to the care of the object entrusted to me. "No man is fit to be a naturalist," said he, "who does not know how to take care of specimens."

I was to keep the fish before me in a tin tray, and occasionally moisten the surface with alcohol from the jar, always taking care to replace the stopper tightly. I was conscious of a passing feeling of disappointment, for gazing at a fish did not seem to be a pleasant beginning

specimen /ˈspesɪmɪn/ *n.* an individual or part regarded as typical of its group or class
entrust /ɪnˈtrʌst/ *v.* to give over (something) to another for care, protection, or performance
naturalist /ˈnætʃərəlɪst/ *n.* a person who specializes in natural history, especially in the study of plants and animals in their natural surroundings

to me, and the smell was horrible. But I said noting and set to work immediately.

In ten minutes I had seen all that could be seen in that fish, and started in search of the Professor—who had, however, left the Museum; and when I returned, after lingering over some of the odd animals stored in the upper apartment, my specimen was dry all over. I <u>dashed</u> the fluid over the fish and looked with anxiety for a return of the normal appearance. This little excitement over, nothing was to be done but to return to a steadfast gaze at my mute companion. Half an hour passed—an hour—another hour; the fish began to look <u>loathsome</u> . I turned it over and around; looked it in the face—<u>ghastly</u>; form behind, beneath, above, sideways — just as ghastly. I was in despair; at an early hour I concluded that lunch was necessary; so, with infinite relief, the fish was carefully replaced in the jar, and for an hour I was free.

> dash /dæʃ/ v. to splash
> loathsome /ˈləʊðsəm/ adj. causing or able to cause loathing; abhorrent
> ghastly /ˈɡɑːstli/ adv. very unpleasantly
> hideous /ˈhɪdɪəs/ adj. extremely ugly or unpleasant
> scale /skeɪl/ n. thin, flat, hard plates that cover a fish
> cork /kɔːk/ v. to close a bottle with a plug
> pore /pɔː/ n. a small opening in the skin or surface of an animal or plant

On my return, I learned that Professor Agassiz had been at the Museum, but had gone, and would not return for several hours. My fellow-students were too busy to be disturbed by continued conversation. Slowly I drew forth that <u>hideous</u> fish, and with a feeling of desperation again looked at it. I might not use a magnifying-glass, nor instruments of any kind. Just my two hands, my two eyes, and the fish: it seemed a limited field. I pushed my finger down its throat to feel how sharp the teeth were. I began to count the <u>scales</u> in different rows, until I was convinced that was nonsense. At last a happy thought struck me—I would draw the fish; and now with surprise I began to discover new features in the creature. Just then the Professor returned.

"That is right," said he; "a pencil is one of the best of eyes. I am glad to notice, too, that you keep your specimen wet, and your bottle <u>corked</u> ."

With these encouraging words, he added:

"Well, what is it like?"

He listened attentively to my brief rehearsal of the structure of parts whose names were still unknown to me: the <u>pores</u> of the head, fleshy lips and forked tail; When I finished, he waited as if expecting more, and then, with an air of disappointment:

conspicuous /kənˈspɪkjuəs/ *adj.* easy to notice; obvious
disconcerting /dɪskənˈsɜ:tɪŋ/ *adj.* causing an emotional dis-turbance
perplexity /pəˈpleksɪti/ *n.* the state of being perplexed or puzzled
cordial /ˈkɔ:dɪəl/ *adj.* warm and sincere; friendly
symmetrical /sɪˈmetrɪkəl/ *adj.* having similarity in size, shape, and relative position of corresponding parts
venture /ˈventʃə/ *v.* to express at the risk of denial, criticism, or censure

"You have not looked very carefully; why," he continued more earnestly. "You haven't even seen one of the most conspicuous features of the animal, which is plainly before your eyes as the fish itself; look again, look again!" and he left me to my misery.

I was hurt. Still more of that wretched fish! But now I set myself to my task with a will, and discovered one new thing after another, until I saw how just the Professor's criticism had been. The afternoon passed quickly; and when, towards its close, the Professor inquired:

"Do you see it yet?"

"No," I replied, "I am certain I do not, but I see how little I saw before."

"That is next best," said he, earnestly, "but I won't hear you now; put away you fish and go home; perhaps you will be ready with a better answer in the morning. I will examine you before you look at the fish."

This was disconcerting. Not only must I think of my fish all night, studying, without the object before me, what this unknown but most visible feature might be; but also, without reviewing my discoveries, I must give an exact account of them the next day. I had a bad memory; so I walked home in a distracted state, with my two perplexities.

The cordial greeting from the Professor the next morning was reassuring; here was a man who seemed to be quite as anxious as I that I should see for myself what he saw.

"Do you perhaps mean," I asked, "that the fish has symmetrical sides with paired organs?"

His thoroughly pleased "Of course!" repaid the wakeful hours of the previous night. After he had talked most happily and enthusiastically—as he always did—upon the importance of this point, I ventured to ask what I should do next.

"Oh, look at your fish!" he said, and left me again to my own devices. In a

entomological /ˌentəməˈlɒdʒɪkəl/ *adj.* of or relating to the scientific study of insects

subsequent /ˈsʌbsɪkwənt/ *adj.* following in time or order; succeeding

worm-eaten *adj.* bored through or gnawed by worms

cork /kɔːk/ *n.* a plug made of outer bark of a Mediterranean oak

little more than an hour he returned, and heard my new catalogue.

"That is good, that is good!" he repeated; "but that is not all; go on", and so for three long days he placed that fish before my eyes, forbidding me to look at anything else, or to use any artificial aid. "Look, look, look," was his repeated instruction.

This was the best entomological lesson I ever had—a lesson whose influence has extended to the details of every subsequent study; a legacy the Professor had left me, of inestimable value, which we could not buy, with which we cannot part.

The fourth day, a second fish of the same group was placed beside the first, and I was told to point out the resemblances and differences between the two; another and another followed, until the entire family lay before me, the odor had become a pleasant perfume; and even now, the sight of an old, six-inch, worm-eaten cork brings fragrant memories.

At the end of eight months, it was almost with reluctance that I left these friends and turned to insects; but what I had gained by this outside experience has been of greater value than years of later investigation in my favorite groups.

(approximately 1200 words)

Reading Time: _____   Reading Rate: _____

Cultural Notes

About the author and the text: Entomologist Samuel H. Scudder (1837—1911) wrote this account of his first learning encounter with the renowned ichthyologist Dr. Louis Agassiz (1807—1873), founder of Harvard University's Lawrence School of Science. The story took place around 1859, was first published (anonymously) in 1873, and has since become a classic lesson in the value of close observation for analysis.

Comprehension Exercises

I. Answer the following questions based on the text.

1. How does the author convey in words the student's initial disappointment at being asked to look at a fish in his biological lesson?

2. What did the professor mean when he said, "a pencil is one of the best eyes"? What did the student mean when he said, "I see how little I saw before"?

3. How to understand "look at the fish" in a larger sense, not just in a literal sense?

4. What is the lesson that Professor Agassiz is trying to get Scudder to learn? Why would this lesson be important for students of history as well as students of science?

5. Have you ever had a similar experience in your life in which you thought something was one way at the beginning, only to find it was another and more significant than you initially thought? Explain.

II. Decide whether each of the following statements is true or false according to the text.

1. Samuel was enrolled at the Scientific School as a student of Natural History and was asked many questions by Professor Agassiz so as to be well-grounded in all departments of zoology.

2. Samuel set about observing the fish specimen the moment Professor Agassiz asked him to do so for none can be qualified to be a naturalist who has no idea of how to strike the iron while it is hot.

3. Samuel examined meticulously the fish specimen from all the perspectives for several hours in the beginning, only to find it was totally impalpable and disgusting.

4. Samuel kept on finding something new about the specimen and realized he saw how little he saw before with the afternoon passing by after he set himself to his task again with a will.

5. Samuel has gained insightful lesson from Professor Agassiz's instruction whose influence was pervasive in his subsequent study and research, which in Samuel's eye, was of great value and significance.

III. Select the most appropriate word or phrase and use its proper form to complete each of the following sentences.

enroll	reluctance	resemblance	subsequent	legacy
venture	symmetrical	cordial	perplexity	disconcerting
wretched	rehearsal	hideous	ground	linger
entrust	naturalist	dash	steadfast	loathsome

1. The news that the governor favors a program that might enable black students from Detroit to _____ in high schools in Birmingham or Grosse Pointe has unaccountably failed to enthrall voters in those towns.

2. Certainly, compared with Russia's lethargic approach to tax and banking reform, and the central bank's continuing _____ to explain properly its holding of some of its reserves in a shell company in Jersey, this burst of financial spin-doctoring is more irksome than horrifying.

3. Initially opened as a retirement area in the 1960s, before the renovation fervor took hold, this flat, checkerboard subdivision of single-story duplex and fourplex homes bears a striking _____ to the ranch-house neighborhoods of Sun City.

4. Microcomputers are available for use here, both for data processing and for the simulation of experiments and they form part of more sophisticated experiments in _____ years.

5. The widespread hostility to the idea that women might "have it all" is partly the _____ of a puritanical culture where "greed" or self-interest are regarded as sinful.

6. We rely on bees and other pollinating insects to transfer pollen from bloom to bloom, but if it's cold at flowering time, insects are reluctant to _____ far and flowers may be inefficiently pollinated.

7. Thomas points out that fossils of Caudipteryx, a primitive feathered cousin of Archaeopteryx, have _____ feathers, which could provide enough drag to stabilise a short fall.

8. Since then, she's established _____ relations with her white neighbors, though their conversations "usually stick to crime in the neighborhood or what's going into someone's garden," she says.

9. The student turned to the professor, saying, "let us play the man a trick: we will hide his shoes, and conceal ourselves behind those bushes, and wait to see his _____ when he cannot find them."

10. As a rarely-staged work by an important gay writer this is well worth a look, but perhaps the abiding and _____ image is of man as beautiful but aloof,

marrying out of put but disdainful of his adoring women.

11. Moldova looks stuck in a _____ economic and geographical plight, a country not so much forgotten as never remembered.

12. First class facilities for performance and _____ are provided in the Music Centre, which comprises practice rooms and an ensemble room which is equipped with a grand piano and a two manual Goble harpsichord.

13. George is wearing a _____ purple jacket, someone's old moustache and the world's worst haircut.

14. He or she has a well- _____ basic understanding of all types of mental illness, which may or may not be of practical use to you.

15. At all times our pace will be unhurried, so that we can go ashore to beachcomb and explore forest trails, or take time to _____ with a group of feeding humpback whales.

IV. Try to paraphrase the following sentences, paying special attention to the underlined parts.

1. With that he left me, but in a moment returned with explicit instructions as to the care of the object entrusted to me.

   _____

   _____

2. I dashed the fluid over the fish and looked with anxiety for a return of the normal appearance.

   _____

   _____

3. But now I set myself to my task with a will, and discovered one new thing after another, until I saw how just the Professor's criticism had been.

   _____

   _____

4. His thoroughly pleased "Of course!" repaid the wakeful hours of the previous night.

   _____

   _____

5. At the end of eight months, it was almost with reluctance that I left these friends and turned to insects; but what I had gained by this outside experience has been of greater value than years of later investigation in my favorite groups.

   _____

   _____

V. Discuss with your partner about each of the three paragraphs and write an essay in no less than 260 words about your understanding of one of them.

1. "That is right," said he; "a pencil is one of the best of eyes."

_____

_____

2. This was the best entomological lesson I ever had—a lesson whose influence has extended to the details of every subsequent study; a legacy the Professor had left me, of inestimable value, which we could not buy, with which we cannot part.

_____

_____

3. I don't think that when people grow up, they will become more broad-minded and can accept everything. Conversely, I think it's a selecting process, knowing what's the most important and what's the least and then be a simple man.

_____

_____

VI. List four websites where we can learn more about how to be a keen observer or a discerning researcher and provide a brief introduction to each of them.

1. _____

_____

_____ .

2. _____

_____

_____ .

3. _____

_____

_____ .

4. _____

_____

_____ .

Text B

Another School Year—What For?
By John Ciardi

Let me tell you one of the earliest disasters in my career as a teacher. It was January of 1940 and I was fresh out of graduate school starting my first semester at the University of Kansas City. Part of the student body was a beanpole with hair on top who came into my class, sat down, folded his arms, and looked at me as if to say "All right, teach me something." Two weeks later we started *Hamlet*. Three weeks later he came into my office with his hands on his hips. "Look," he said, "I came here to be a pharmacist. Why do I have to read this stuff?" and not having a book of his own to point to, he pointed to mine which was lying on the desk.

New as I was to the faculty, I could have told this specimen a number of things. I could have pointed out that he had enrolled, not in a drug-mechanics school, but in a college and that at the end of his course he meant to reach for a scroll that read Bachelor of Science. It would not read: Qualified Pill-Grinding Technician. It would certify that he had specialized in pharmacy, but it would further certify that he had been exposed to some of the ideas mankind has generated within its history. That is to say, he had not entered a technical training school but a university, and in universities students enroll for both training and education.

I could have told him all this, but it was fairly obvious he wasn't going to be around long enough for it to matter.

Nevertheless, I was young and I had a high sense of duty and I tried to put it this way: "For the rest of my life," I said, "your days are going to average out to about twenty-four hours. They will be a little shorter when you are in love, and a little longer when you are out of love, but the average will tend to hold. For eight of these hours, more or less, you will be asleep."

"Then for about eight hours of each working day you will, I hope, be usefully employed.

beanpole /ˈbiːnpəʊl/ *n. (informal)* a very tall, thin person

certify /ˈsɜːtɪfaɪ/ *v.* to confirm formally as true, accurate, or genuine

Assume you have gone through pharmacy school—or engineering, or law school, or whatever—during those eight hours you will be using your professional skills. You will see to it that the cyanide stays out of the aspirin, that the bull doesn't jump the fence, or that your client doesn't go to the electric chair as a result of your incompetence. These are all useful pursuits. They involve skills every man must respect, and they can all bring you basic satisfactions. Along with everything else, they will probably be what puts food on your table, supports your wife, and rears your children. They will be your income, and may it always suffice."

"But having finished the day's work, what do you do with those other eight hours? Let's say you go home to your family. What sort of family are you raising? Will the children ever be exposed to a reasonably penetrating idea at home? Will you be presiding over a family that maintains some contact with the great democratic intellect? Will there be a book in the house? Will there be a painting a reasonably sensitive man can look at without shuddering? Will the kids ever get to hear Bach?"

That is about what I said, but this particular pest was not interested. "Look," he said, "you professors raise your kids your way; I'll take care of my own. Me, I'm out to make money."

"I hope you make a lot of it," I told him, " because you're going to be badly stuck for something to do when you're not signing checks."

Fourteen years later I am still teaching, and I am here to tell you that the business of the college is not only to train you, but to put you in touch with what the best human minds have thought. If you have no time for Shakespeare, for a basic book at philosophy, for the continuity of the fine arts, for that lesson of man's development we call history—then you have no business being in college. You are on your way to being that new species of mechanized savage, the push-button Neanderthal. Our colleges inevitably graduate a number of such life forms, but it cannot be said that they went to college; rather the college went through them—without making contact.

No one gets to be a human being unaided. There is not time enough in a single lifetime to invent for oneself everything one needs to know in order to be a civilized human.

Assume, for example, that you want to be

cyanide /saɪənaɪd/ n. a highly poisonous chemical
suffice /səfaɪs/ v. to be enough or satisfactory for a purpose
Neanderthal /niændətɑːl/ n. a type of primitive man that lived in Europe before 12,000 BC

a physicist. You pass the great stone halls of, say, <u>M.I.T.</u>, and there cut into the stone are the names of the scientists. The chances are that few, if any, of you will leave your names to be cut into those stones. Yet any of you

fragment /ˈfrægmənt/ *n.* an incomplete or isolated portion; a bit
implicitly /ɪmˈplɪsɪtli/ *adv.* without ever expressing so clearly
expertise /ˌekspɜːˈtiːz/ *n.* special skill, knowledge, or judgment

who managed to stay awake through part of a high school course in physics, knows more about physics than did many of those great scholars of the past. You know more because they left you what they knew, because you can start from what the past learned for you.

And as this is true of the techniques of mankind, so it is true of mankind's spiritual resources. Most of these resources, both technical and spiritual, are stored in books. Books are man's peculiar accomplishment. When you have read a book, you have added to your human experience. Read <u>Homer</u> and your mind includes a piece of Homer's mind. Through books you can acquire at least <u>fragments</u> of the mind and experience of <u>Virgil</u>, <u>Dante</u>, Shakespeare—the list is endless. For a great book is necessarily a gift; it offers you a life you have not the time to live yourself, and it takes you into a world you have not the time to travel in literal time. A civilized mind is, in essence, one that contains many such lives and many such worlds. If you are too much in a hurry, or too arrogantly proud of your own limitations, to accept as a gift to your humanity some pieces of the minds of Aristotle, or <u>Chaucer</u>, or <u>Einstein</u>, you are neither a developed human nor a useful citizen of a democracy.

I think it was <u>La Rochefoucauld</u> who said that most people would never fall in love if they hadn't read about it. He might have said that no one would ever manage to become human if they hadn't read about it.

I speak, I'm sure, for the faculty of the liberal arts college and for the faculties of the specialized schools as well, when I say that a university has no real existence and no real purpose except as it succeeds in putting you in touch, both as specialists and as humans, with those human minds your human mind needs to include. The faculty, by its very existence, says <u>implicitly</u>: "We have been aided by many people, and by many books, in our attempt to make ourselves some sort of storehouse of human experience. We are here to make available to you, as best we can, that <u>expertise</u>."

(*approximately 1400 words*)

Reading Time: _____   Reading Rate: _____

Cultural Notes

1. **John Anthony Ciardi** (1916—1986) was an American poet, translator, and etymologist.

2. *Hamlet*: a tragedy by William Shakespeare, believed to have been written between 1599 and 1601. The play, set in Denmark, recounts how Prince Hamlet exacts revenge on his uncle Claudius, who has murdered Hamlet's father, the King, and then taken the throne and married Hamlet's mother. The play vividly charts the course of real and feigned madness—from overwhelming grief to seething rage—and explores themes of treachery, revenge, incest, and moral corruption.

3. **Bach:** a prolific German composer and organist whose sacred and secular works for choir, orchestra, and solo instruments drew together the strands of the Baroque period and brought it to its ultimate maturity.

4. **Neanderthal:** an extinct variety of human that lived throughout Europe and in parts of western Asia and northern Africa during the late Pleistocene Epoch, until about 30,000 years ago. Neanderthals had a stocky build and large skulls with thick eyebrow ridges and big teeth. They usually lived in caves, made flaked stone tools, and were the earliest humans known to bury their dead. Neanderthals were either a subspecies of modern humans or a separate, closely related species. They coexisted with early modern humans (Cro-Magnons) for several thousand years before becoming extinct, but are not generally believed to have interbred with them.

5. **M.I.T.:** the short name for Massachusetts Institute of Technology. Founded in 1861, this private university is located in Cambridge, Mass., USA.

6. **Homer:** a Greek poet probably of the 8th century BC who was believed to be the author of *Iliad* and *Odyssey*, the two earliest epic poems in Greek literature about the Trojan War.

7. **Virgil:** a great Roman poet, best known for his epic poems describing the fall of Troy and the founding of Rome.

8. **Dante:** an Italian poet. His masterpiece, *The Divine Comedy*, describes the journey of a religious pilgrim through Hell, Purgatory and Heaven.

9. **Chaucer:** an English poet, established English as a literary language. His most representative work *Canterbury Tales* provides an excellent source on the life and customs of late medieval England.

10. **Einstein:** a German-born Swiss-American theoretical physicist, the formulator of the theory of relativity.

11. **La Rochefoucauld:** a noted French author of maxims and memoirs, as well as an example of the accomplished 17th-century nobleman.

Comprehension Exercises

I. Answer the following questions based on the text.

1. Why did the student consider reading Shakespeare a waste of time?
2. What is the difference between professional training and university education?
3. What will be a person like if he has no touch with mankind's spiritual resources according to the author?
4. What is the value of a great book?
5. How do you find the tone of the article?

II. Decide whether each of the following statements is true or false according to the text.

1. John Ciardi felt distressful in his early career as a teacher at the University of Kansas City for one of his students was always being particular about his teaching methodology and classroom activities.
2. John Ciardi held that universities should guarantee that students are not only exposed to some of the ideas mankind has generated in its history so as to be humanism-oriented but also be trained professionally to be capable of making a living upon their graduation.
3. John Ciardi didn't tell the beanpole the ultimate purpose of university education directly for in his view, it would definitely take the student much time to have a whole picture of the quintessence of college life.
4. John Ciardi and the beanpole had little in common when it comes to the essence of and the influence of university education, for example, its influence on such issues on the sort of family one may raise, the profound ideas at home children may be exposed to, or the great democratic intellect with whom a family may maintain contact.
5. John Ciardi mentioned the great stone halls of M.I.T and such great literati as Virgil, Dante and Shakespeare in order to demonstrate the impact of both university education and reading books on humanity on the cultivation of a college student, be s/he from a agricultural college or from a university of science and technology.

III. Select the most appropriate word or phrase and use its proper form to complete each of the following sentences.

expertise	peculiar	accomplishment	implicit	humanity
fragment	pest	democratic	arrogant	stuck
suffice	expose	pursuit	penetrating	certify
matter	beanpole	preside	specialize	rear

1. These courses will not only give students the chance to study their subject at university level but will also help them develop particular _____ in teaching it in school as well as preparing them to advise teachers who have specialised in other subjects.

2. There is also a(n) _____ subtext: She who follows the crowd has a weak sense of direction.

3. "Industry and Christianity have pushed aside the sensitive and poetic in _____ and have abused nature," Anelog complains with rising anger: people have let fashion make them mechanical to the point where they no longer know what they feel.

4. Although each county has its own particular and _____ charm (and in no way would I want to see that disrupted) we really have got to come to terms with the fact that if England are going to be successful as a Test side over a sustained period of time the moment has come for revolution and not evolution.

5. You can cope with these situations by inviting a friend along; finding out in advance as much as you can about what you'll find when you arrive; arranging to go alone but be escorted home (as to a dinner party); throwing your shoulders back, lifting your head, and toughing it out by yourself (the pride of _____ is often better than the experience itself!).

6. I shall spare you a lecture on why some of the language worked better on stage than in the movie, where close-ups and cutting further _____ the pieces that need to be combined into a whole to make their proper effect.

7. The contemporary artist is largely illiterate, ignorant of his cultural background, incompetent in his craft, greedy, and _____ in his determination to express and empty and silly self.

8. Once witnessed embarrassing scene when, during opening ceremony of African Nations Cup in March 1988 a parachutist got _____ for 20 minutes in a flood-light pylon, watched by FIFA top brass.

9. Some of them, let me just read you a list: vending services, refuse pickup services, dumpster rental, elevator maintenance services, _____ control,

towing services, international mailing services, bookbinding services, banking, carpet installation, hazardous waste disposal, elevator maintenance, food service, furniture upholstery, travel services, laundry services, microfiche services, child care services, and of course, we have privatized the Lenoir Hall food service and the Carolina Inn.

10. He'd campaigned tirelessly in the run-up to the first _____ elections in the country, to be held after the official ceasefire; and when the party was swept into power, he was rewarded with a position in the cabinet.

11. Organizing holidays away from the ghettos did not _____: as soon as the children came back, peer pressure to be involved in violence was as strong as ever. Most community work and all the government initiatives, in Stewart's view, serve merely to contain the Troubles.

12. It all sounds rather boring, which it would most certainly be were it not for Ferris's _____ eye, and her obvious harmony with not only the foxes and the badgers, but all the wildlife in her corner of Kent.

13. Each year they audit our accounts and _____ them as being true and fair.

14. But I think it's all the more important to do that, because the evidence of prejudice and racism is sometimes subtle and sometimes doesn't ____ itself through the thrown brick or the hurled epithet; it's sometimes a quieter kind of prejudice and bigotry and all the more important to confront it and speak to it in times that are not filled with crisis.

15. For many years the _____ of sexual pleasure, reading about sexual pleasure and studying how to give and receive sexual pleasure were the province of the male of the species; women were supposed to be passive receptacles.

IV. Try to paraphrase the following sentences, paying special attention to the underlined parts.

1. "I hope you make a lot of it," I told him, "because you're going <u>to be badly stuck for something to do</u> when you're not signing checks."

_____

_____

2. You are <u>on your way</u> to being that new species of <u>mechanized savage</u>, the push-button Neanderthal. Our colleges inevitably graduate a number of such life forms, but it cannot be said that they went to college; rather the college <u>went through</u> them—<u>without making contact</u>.

_____

_____

3. For a great book is necessarily a gift; it offers you a life you have not the time to live yourself, and it takes you into a world you have not the time to travel in literal time. A civilized mind is, in essence, one that contains many such lives and many such worlds.

_____

_____

4. ...a university has no real existence and no real purpose except as it succeeds in putting you in touch, both as specialists and as humans, with those human minds your human mind needs to include.

_____

_____

5. The faculty, by its very existence, says implicitly: "We have been aided by many people, and by many books, in our attempt to make ourselves some sort of storehouse of human experience. We are here to make available to you, as best we can, that expertise."

_____

_____

V. Discuss with your partner about each of the three paragraphs and write an essay in no less than 260 words about your understanding of one of them.

1. I could have pointed out that he had enrolled, not in a drug-mechanics school, but in a college and that at the end of his course he meant to reach for a scroll that read Bachelor of Science.

_____

_____

2. ...I am here to tell you that the business of the college is not only to train you, but to put you in touch with what the best human minds have thought. If you have no time for Shakespeare, for a basic book at philosophy, for the continuity of the fine arts, for that lesson of man's development we call history—then you have no business being in college.

_____

_____

3. No one gets to be a human being unaided. There is not time enough in a single lifetime to invent for oneself everything one needs to know in order to be a civilized human.

_____

_____

VI. List four websites where we can learn more about broadening one's vision by reading books or by traveling around and provide a brief introduction to each of them.

1. _____

_____

_____ .

2. _____

_____

_____ .

3. _____

_____

_____ .

4. _____

_____

_____ .

Twenty Minutes' Reading

You are required to read the following two sections within 20 minutes.

Section A

Ours has become a society of employees. A hundred years or so ago only one out of every five Americans at work was employed, i.e., worked for somebody else. Today only one out of five is not employed but working for himself. And when fifty years ago "being employed" meant working as a factory laborer or as a farmhand, the employee of today is increasingly a middle-class person with a substantial formal education, holding a professional or management job requiring intellectual and technical skills. Indeed, two things have characterized American society during these fifty years: middle-class and upper-class employees have been the fastest-growing groups in our working population—growing so fast that the industrial worker, that oldest child of the Industrial Revolution, has been losing in numerical importance despite the expansion of industrial production.

Yet you will find little if anything written on what it is to be an employee. You can find a great deal of very dubious advice on how to get a job or how to get a promotion. You can also find a good deal of work in a chosen field, whether it be the mechanist's trade or bookkeeping. Every one of these trades requires different skills, sets different standards, and requires a different preparation. Yet they all have employeeship in common. And increasingly, especially in the large business or in government, employeeship is more important to success than the special professional knowledge or skill. Certainly more people fail because they do not know the requirements of being an employee than because they do not adequately possess the skills of their trade; the higher you climb the ladder, the more you get into administrative or executive work, the greater the emphasis on ability to work within the organization rather than on technical abilities or professional knowledge.

1. It is implied that fifty years ago _____.
   A. eighty per cent of American working people were employed in factories
   B. twenty per cent of American intellectuals were employees
   C. the percentage of intellectuals in the total work force was almost the same as that of industrial workers
   D. the percentage of intellectuals working as employees was not so large as that of industrial workers

2. According to the passage, with the development of modern industry, _____.
   A. factory laborers will overtake intellectual employees in number
   B. there are as many middle-class employees as factory laborers
   C. employers have attached great importance to factory laborers
   D. the proportion of factory laborers in the total employee population has decreased

3. The word "dubious" (Para. 2) most probably means _____.
   A. valuable
   B. useful
   C. doubtful
   D. helpful

4. According to the writer, professional knowledge or skill is _____.
   A. less important than awareness of being a good employee
   B. as important as the ability to deal with public relations
   C. more important than employer-employee relations
   D. more important as the ability to co-operate with others in the organization

5. From the passage it can be seen that employeeship helps one _____.
   A. to be more successful in his career
   B. to be more specialized in his field
   C. to solve technical problems
   D. to develop his professional skill

Section B

We all know that the normal human daily cycle of activity is of some 7-8 hours' sleep alternation with some 16-17 hours' wakefulness and that, broadly speaking, the sleep normally coincides with the hours of darkness. Our present concern is with how easily and to what extent this cycle can be modified.

The question is no mere academic one. The ease, for example, with which people can change from working in the day to working at night is a question of growing importance in industry where automation calls for round-the-clock working of machines. It normally takes from five days to one week for a person to adapt to reversed routine of sleep and wakefulness, sleeping during the day and working at night. Unfortunately, it is often the case in industry that shifts are changed every week; a person may work from 12 midnight to 8 a.m. one week, 8 a.m. to 4 p.m. the next, and 4 p.m. to 12 midnight the third and so on. This means that no sooner has he got used to one routine than he has to change to another, so that much of his time is spent neither working nor sleeping very efficiently.

The only real solution appears to be to hand over the night shift to a number of permanent night workers. An interesting study of the domestic life and health of night-shift workers was carried out by Brown in 1957. She found a high incidence of disturbed sleep and other disorders among those on alternating day and night shifts, but no abnormal occurrence of these phenomena among those on permanent night work.

This latter system then appears to be the best long-term policy, but meanwhile something may be done to relieve the strains of alternate day and night work by selecting those people who can adapt most quickly to the changes of routine. One way of knowing when a person has adapted is by measuring his body temperature. People engaged in normal daytime work will have a high temperature during the hours of wakefulness and a low one at night; when they change to night work the pattern will only gradually go back to match the new routine and the speed with which it does so parallels, broadly speaking, the adaptation of the body as a whole, particularly in terms of performance. Therefore, by taking body temperature at intervals of two hours throughout the period of wakefulness it can be seen how quickly a person can adapt to a reversed routine, and this could be used as a basis for selection. So far, however, such a form of selection does not seem to have been applied in practice.

6. Why is the question of "how easily people can get used to working at night" not a mere academic question?

    A. Because few people like to reverse the cycle of sleep and wakefulness.

    B. Because sleep normally coincides with the hours of darkness.

    C. Because people are required to work at night in some fields of industry.

    D. Because shift work in industry requires people to change their sleeping habits.

7. The main problem of the round-the-clock working system lies in _____.

    A. the inconveniences brought about to the workers by the introduction of automation

    B. the disturbance of the daily life cycle of workers who have to change shifts too frequently

    C. the fact that people working at night are often less effective

    D. the fact that it is difficult to find a number of good night workers

8. The best solution for implementing the 24-hour working system seems to be _____.

    A. to change shifts at longer intervals

    B. to have longer shifts

    C. to arrange for some people to work on night shifts only

    D. to create better living conditions for night workers

9. It is possible to find out if a person has adapted to the changes of routine by measuring his body temperature because _____.

    A. body temperature changes when the cycle of sleep and wakefulness alternates

    B. body temperature changes when he changes to night shift or back

    C. the temperature reverses when the routine is changed

    D. people have higher temperatures when they are working efficiently

10. Which of the following statements is NOT TRUE?

    A. Body temperature may serve as an indication of a worker's performance.

    B. The selection of a number of permanent night shift workers has proved to be the best solution to problems of the round-the-clock working system.

    C. Taking body temperature at regular intervals can show how a person adapts to the changes of routine.

    D. Disturbed sleep occurs less frequently among those on permanent night or day shifts.

Unit Three Career

Your Flexible Friends
By David Braue and Chris Bowes

If you think your next job will be in a high-rise office or factory, think again. Most new jobs will be found closer to home—in many cases in the home itself or even in your car. Welcome to the post-industrial revolution. The most dramatic result of this upheaval has been the blow to full-time jobs, the number of which has been stuck at 6.3 million since 1900, while part-time positions have burgeoned from 1.5 million to 2.1 million. But there has been another, equally far-reaching consequence: over 2.1 million Australians now do some paid work at home, while more than 344,000 work exclusively from home and the number is rising.

Gone for ever is the image of the typical worker as a male stationed at single workplace from 9 am to 5 pm. These days flexibility is the watchword, according to business trends guru Phil Ruthven, executive chairman of IBIS Business Information. "Increasingly a large proportion of [jobs] involve work from home as part or full-time options," say Ruthven. "The advent of IT&T [information technology and telecommunications] has made these things possible."

Women and to some extent men wanting to spend time close to their families are the major beneficiaries of this new workplace flexibility. But it also has huge advantages for sick and disabled people, many of whom are only able to work from home, and for those working on into partial retirement.

While the Bureau of Statistics has found that 50% more men than women work some days at home, more than twice as many

upheaval /ʌpˈhiːv ə l/ *n.* a state of violent disturbance and disorder (as in politics or social conditions generally)

burgeon /ˈbɜːdʒən/ *vi.* to develop or grow rapidly; flourish

watchword /ˈwɒtʃwɜːd/ *n.* a slogan or motto used to rally support for a cause

guru /ˈɡʊruː/ *n.* a recognized leader in some field or of some movement

advent /ˈædvənt/ *n.* arrival

beneficiary /benɪˈfɪʃəri/ *n.* one that receives a benefit

women as men work exclusively at home. Surveys show that many home workers are in their late 30s, those for whom spending time with their children is more important than maintaining social bonds at work.

outsource /'aʊtsɔːs/ vt. to send out (work, for example) to an outside provider or manufacturer in order to cut costs
congestion /kən'dʒestʃən/ n. excessive crowding
tranquility /'træŋkwɪlɪtɪ/ n. an untroubled state; free from disturbances; a state of peace and quiet
trappings /'træpɪŋz/ n. articles of dress or adornment, especially accessories; furnishing; the accessories that symbolize a condition, office, etc.
power breakfast a meeting of influential people to conduct business while eating breakfast

Unlike the industrial era, where home-based piece workers produced partly finished goods, work in the home is increasingly the preserve of white-collar professionals—and the household service industries springing up to support them. The tools of the trade for these well-educated "information workers" are their phones, faxes, computers and the Internet. While they crunch information, others are paid to mow the lawns clean the house, look after the children and cook their meals.

For women and men unafraid to outsource some of their household services and set themselves up to work from home, the benefits are proving enormous. Family was crucial to Faye and Pete Heininger's decision two years ago to trade in the ceaseless congestion of inner Sydney's Newtown for the tranquility of the beachside Wollongong suburb of Thirroul. But they didn't just move houses, they also relocated their business, Heininger Public Relations and Marketing, to the front room of their new house. The Heiningers dress causally, set their own working hours and have more time for their two young daughters.

Trappings: "We move out of Sydney to get a better life-style," says Faye Heininger. "We loved being in the city but once the kids came into the picture we needed more space." The Heiningers' Thirroul house includes a large room that now has all the trappings of a normal office including four computers, a photocopier and six phone, fax and modem lines. The office is at the front of the house with easy access for clients, leaving the rest of the house for the family.

The Heiningers, like hundreds of thousands of other small businesses, operate a so-called SOHO or small office/home office. An increasing number of professionals and former managers, many of them victims of corporate restructuring, are also setting themselves up with the latest technology to work from home.

"Since people realize they are no longer guaranteed a job for life, they're starting to ask themselves why they should get up at 6am to go to power breakfasts when they could be spending that time with their family," says Nick Hough, founding member and president of the Asia-Pacific Telework Association.

turfing /tɜːf/ *vt.* chiefly British slang, to make someone leave a place or organization, usually suddenly or roughly

quotation /kwəʊ'teɪʃən/ *n.* the prices or bids cited; an estimate of costs submitted by a contractor to a prospective client

wank /wæŋk/ *n.* something which you think is very stupid, useless, or of bad quality; rubbish

surrogate /'sʌrəgɪt/ *n.* a person or thing acting as a substitute

tactile /'tæktaɪl/ *adj.* perceptible to the sense of touch; tangible

In some cases it is the employers who are turfing their workers—usually sales staff—out of their offices and onto the road. A car, a laptop computer, a mobile phone and a desk back at head office shed on rotation with half-a-dozen other people are all the company need provide. So-called "hot desking" can save companies hundreds of thousands of dollars in rent.

Many sales professionals are more than happy taking their offices on the road. Tony Burville, sales manager with Fibreglass Material Services, works four days a week from his Landrover Discovery and one day back at head office in western Sydney. Armed with a notebook PC, wireless modem and mobile phone, he can stay in touch with clients, send and receive faxes, and prepare quotations on site. Always on the lookout for potential time-saver, Burville is evaluating speech-recognition software, which will allow him to compose correspondence hands-free while driving between appointments.

"I got my first car phone in 1986," says Burville. "People thought it was a bit of a wank , quite frankly. These days it's just another business tool—it's the same with the mobile office."

Limits: Such road warriors may miss the trappings of their own office but frequent contact with clients means they are less likely to suffer some of the problems associated with the home office environment, particularly for isolated workers. "There are limits to working from home," admits Ruthven. "The first factor is the ability to bounce ideas off fellow workers and improve your skills base. While people can and do converse over the Internet, for the majority of people that's not a very adequate surrogate to personal contact—the tactile environment you get. Then there's the loneliness factor. Some people are not equipped for working by themselves."

Such isolation can lead to lack of motivation, poor work performance and even depression. Others have the opposite problem: they are unable to switch off, leading to increased stress levels.

"Maintaining the split between home and work is important," says Brisbane graphic designer Peter Lynch. In 1995, Lynch moved his growing five-year-old firm, Peter Lynch Design, from a Fortitude Valley office space to a renovated <u>fish-and-chips</u> shop in New Farm. Lynch now rents out the street front shop, runs his five-employee business from another building on the property, and lives in his own home further back on the block.

goof off to spend time in a lazy or foolish way
retain /rɪˈteɪn/ vt. if a company retains workers, it continues to employ them for a long time

After several years working from home Lynch knows the importance of separating home and work; he intentionally designed his office and home with separate doors so that he has to step outside to go to work. "I have a mental switch inside my head that clicks from one to the other," he says. "To have to walk out onto the footpath provides an important psychological separation."

Discipline: The most critical part of successfully working from home is discipline. Fearing employees may elect to spend sunny days at the beach, corporate managers have traditionally opposed working from home. However, studies suggest workers are actually more productive away from the office. "Office workers are less productive because of distractions like unnecessary meetings, coffee breaks and talking to people in the hallway," says Hough, who estimates home workers are 15% more efficient.

For self-employed SOHO workers like Lynch and the Heiningers, motivation is rarely a problem. "When you're working for yourself you work harder than ever", say Lynch. "You do have the freedom to choose when you work, but you really have to put in the effort to get things done because nobody else is going to do it for you." Faye Heininger agrees. "It takes a particular sort of discipline. We work from 8:30 am and nothing gets in our way; we don't even take a lunch hour. But even though we might work until 11pm if we have to, we know we can take the whole weekend for quality tie with the girls. And because we set our own hours it's easy to go to the kindergarten if the girls have something going on."

Employers who have overcome their fear of home workers <u>goofing off</u> are finding that telecommuting—the connecting of home office systems into a corporate net work—pays off in other ways. "Setting up the company to allow telecommuting lets companies <u>retain</u> workers who might otherwise leave for family reasons," says Hough. "Many employees might be perfectly happy to continue working if they can start at 10 after the kids are at school. Stop from 3 to 5 to pick them up and work a few more hours at night." Making provision for home-bound staff also lets companies recruit employees who live far from the office or disabled workers who cannot easily commute.

Technologies such as faxes and electronic mail have made it easier than ever for SOHO workers to stay in the loop. "The world is going on around us and we still have to be a part of it no matter where we are working," says Heininger. "We realized the Internet was going to be the greatest freedom we could have; E-mail makes it easy to keep in touch with our clients and our Web site means we have a 24-hour shopfront open for visitors."

(approximately 1200 words)

Reading Time: _____   Reading Rate: _____

Cultural Notes

1. **The source of this article:** *Bulletin,* Nov. 4,1997

2. **SOHO or small office/home office or Small or Home Office or Single Office/ Home Office:** Beginning in the mid-1990s, the advent of the personal computer, and breakthroughs in voice and data communication, has enabled anyone working from a home office to compete globally. This leads to the emergence of a great number of small businesses that have a tiny or medium sized office. Many consultants and the members of several professions such as lawyers, real estate agents or surveyors in small and medium sized towns operate from such home offices. The 36 hour or 48 hour cycles of much of software development has led many practitioners in this domain to do their work in home offices given the difficulty of the traditional business world to adapt its "normal" hours to some of the more extreme needs of software engineering. Technology has also created a demand for larger businesses to employ individuals who work from home. Sometimes these people remain as an independent business-person, and sometimes they actually become employees of a larger company. With a global reach through the use of technology the SOHO, small office/ home office now has a better chance of emerging as a greater challenge in the world marketplace.

3. **hot desking:** originates from the definition of being the temporary physical occupation of a work station or surface by a particular employee. The term "hot desking" is thought to be derived from the naval practice, called hot racking, where sailors on different shifts share bunks. Originating as a trend in the late 1980s—early 1990s, hot desking involves one desk shared

between several people who use the desk at different times. A primary motivation for hot desking is cost reduction through space savings—up to 30% in some cases.

4. **fish-and-chips:** a popular take-away food with British origins, consists of deep-fried fish in batter or breadcrumbs with deep-fried chipped potatoes.

Comprehension Exercises

I. Answer the following questions based on the text.

1. According to the author, what features the post-industrial revolution?
2. What makes it possible for this new trend of change in workplace?
3. What equipments does a typical SOHO need?
4. What are the major causes of this new workplace flexibility?
5. What are the advantages of this new workplace flexibility?
6. What's the biggest problem confronting those who work at home?
7. Are there any effective ways to solve the problem?

II. Decide whether each of the following statements is true or false according to the text.

1. An increasing number of Australians have chose to do some paid work at home, although such tendency has exerted negative influence on a variety of industries such as primary industry, secondary industry and tertiary industry.
2. Feasibility has been the buzzword concerning the latest working-at-home mode to people from all walks of life, be s/he a man or a woman, be s/he a sick person or a disabled one, when it comes to the major advantage of such new mode.
3. According to David Braue and Chris Bowes, some salesperson have been forced to leave their offices and even their homes to work by their employers who have not yet clear idea of the benefits brought about the working-at-home style.
4. An overwhelming majority of people in Australia have preferred to work out of their offices for such possible reasons as being together with their family members, working for themselves, saving a lot of rents as well as a lot of time.
5. According to the author, information technology and telecommunications are indispensable to the successful operation of working-out-of-one's-office style although it has its potential deficiency.

III. Select the most appropriate word or phrase and use its proper form to complete each of the following sentences.

upheaval	exclusively	flexibility	watchword	burgeon
guru	beneficiary	preserve	crunching	advent
outsource	tranquility	tactile	retain	congestion
initiatively	turf	quotation	surrogate	renovate

1. Humiliating military defeat in Vietnam; two oil shocks; double-digit inflation; unlegislated tax increases as inflation drove taxpayers into higher tax brackets; bussing and racial quotas; the _____ in sexual mores; college campus insurrections—all in barely a decade—destroyed liberalism's credibility as a philosophy of government.

2. The seed of friendship and cooperation we sow today will _____ and harvest in the future and China-US partnership of cooperation will definitely enjoy a better tomorrow.

3. Talking _____ to BBC, Sinead said the hostile reception she received at the concert, in response to her tearing up a picture of the Pope on Saturday Night Live, prompted her decision to abandon her career as a singer.

4. The Science courses therefore provide a high degree of _____ with the added advantage that in a number of cases, selection of most degree courses, undergraduates are able to share in these activities by undertaking research projects in their final year.

5. "Caution" will be the _____ for retailers this holiday season, whether it comes to ordering inventory or hiring employees, analysts said.

6. Aside from Hayles, a literary theorist at UCLA who also holds an advanced degree in chemistry and reprises some ideas from her Posthumans, here are many of the usual suspects: California cyber-_____ Michael Heim, MIT's cyber-architectural theorist William Mitchell, and new-media artists Carol Gigliotti and Brenda Laurel.

7. And I think that also, as President Clinton indicated and we have all said, that with the _____ of technology, globalization, modernization, there is no question that ultimately the evolution of China has got to be in that direction, and also a realization of the importance to us and the international community about moving on the human rights issue.

8. A year later, his mother-in-law died, also mysteriously; and shortly thereafter his perfectly healthy sister-in-law took out a mass of life-insurance policies on herself with Wainewright the _____—and promptly dropped dead.

9. The making and conduct of foreign policy is largely the _____ of the president.

10. I pored over the books with great enthusiasm, often _____ the numbers until 1:00 am.

11. Meanwhile, data services companies continued expanding their horizons: corporate downsizing and the evolution of electronic commerce create myriad opportunities for companies that _____ and process transactions.

12. Inadequately controlled non-residential development will impair the public health, safety, and welfare of the residents of Palo Alto by causing increased traffic _____, associated air and noise pollution, diminution of property values, depletion of land which would otherwise contribute to the City's housing supply, and the exhaustion of the City's natural resources.

13. The early morning _____ of the picnic area is replaced by the smell of BBQ's and the sounds of conversation and children running and playing.

14. Something of the same argument might be made for books, or for the _____ pleasure of holding and reading a well-made book.

15. They make possible the breadth and depth of Stanford's educational curriculum: they enable Stanford to recruit and _____ the very best faculty; and they supply essential financial support to the young men and women who will be the world's future leaders.

IV. Try to paraphrase the following sentences, paying special attention to the underlined parts.

1. Gone for ever is the image of the typical worker as a male stationed at single workplace from 9 am to 5 pm.

   _____

   _____

2. Unlike the industrial era, where home-based piece workers produced partly finished goods, work in the home is increasingly the preserve of white-collar professionals—and the household service industries springing up to support them.

   _____

   _____

3. Family was crucial to Faye and Pete Heininger's decision two years ago to trade in the ceaseless congestion of inner Sydney's Newtown for the tranquility of the beachside Wollongong suburb of Thirroul.

   _____

   _____

4. In some cases it is the employers who are turfing their workers—usually

sales staff—out of their offices and onto the road.

5. Always <u>on the lookout for potential time-saver</u>, Burville is evaluating speech-recognition software, which will allow him to compose <u>correspondence hands-free while driving between appointments</u>.

V. Discuss with your partner about each of the three statements and write an essay in no less than 260 words about your understanding of one of them.

1. Such isolation can lead to lack of motivation, poor work performance and even depression. Others have the opposite problem: they are unable to switch off, leading to increased stress levels.

2. Technologies such as faxes and electronic mail have made it easier than ever for SOHO workers to stay in the loop. "The world is going on around us and we still have to be a part of it no matter where we are working," says Heininger. "We realized the Internet was going to be the greatest freedom we could have; E-mail makes it easy to keep in touch with our clients and our Web site means we have a 24-hour shopfront open for visitors."

3. Your profession is not what brings home your paycheck. Your profession is what you were put on earth to do. With such passion and such intensity that it becomes spiritual in calling.

VI. List four websites where we can learn more about how to keep a balance between work and family or how to keep a balance between self-development and looking after one's kid and provide a brief introduction to each of them.

1. _____

_____

_____ .

2. _____

_____ .

3. _____

_____

_____ .

4. _____

_____

_____ .

Text B

Words That Get You Hired

By Donald and Diana Stroetzel

At age 44, with no job, two kids in college and a third about to start, Jim Day of Fairfield, Conn., had fallen on rough times. Dismissed in a major cutback by The Hertz Corp., Day had talked with nearly 200 people in his search for another management position. As he arrived for his first interview with a large glass company, however, he was smiling and confident. This time, he felt, he had a job-winning strategy.

In preparation, Day had listed questions that kept coming up in earlier, unsuccessful interviews. Then he had a friend ask him the questions in front of a home video camera. *Would I hire this person*? Day wondered as he watched himself on playback. No, he decided. "I sat sternly with arms folded like a kid called to the principal's office. I rambled. What I thought was self-confidence came across as arrogance."

After more practice, Day knew he was ready. And sure enough, the glass company soon hired him as a regional vice president.

The same approach that helped Jim Day triumph over mid-life unemployment can work for others of all ages in today's tight job market. "What you want to do is simply highlight your strong points," says

cutback /ˈkʌtbæk/ *n.* a decrease or reduction in quantity or rate

ramble /ˈræmbəl/ *vi.* to move about aimlessly

Anne Weinstock, vice president of Drake, Beam, Morin, Inc., largest of the outplacement firms engaged to coach severed employees in job-finding techniques. "Almost anyone can learn to carry off a good interview," adds Kansas City outplacement consultant Evelyn Davis. "You may not be a salesperson, but you have a huge advantage. You know the product—yourself—better than anyone else."

Among applicants of equal ability, what any successful interview ultimately comes down to is giving the right answers to the right questions. We talked with job interviewers across the country and pinpointed eight key questions that, in one form or another, almost every good interviewer asks:

1. "Who are you, really?" That's what your questioner wants to know when he or she greets you with "Tell me about yourself." The interviewer has already noted whether you arrived on time and are appropriately dressed. Now you have to make sure your first words impress favorably. In a concise, two-minute reply, you might talk about your education and work experience, bridging into why you're right for the job.

You should include a sentence that will make you memorable. For one winner, it was: "I graduated from an undistinguished college, but look at my job progression in ten years." That tabbed him as smart and hard-driving, and helped him outpace elite-school competitors.

Don't fudge facts. Knowing proof of age can't legally be demanded in an interview, the front-runner for a human-resources vice presidency said he'd graduated from college five years later than really had. But his attempt to be taken for 52, not 57, backfired when the interviewer checked on his grades. He was instantly ruled out for lack of integrity.

2. "Why are you on the job market?" The interviewer will be alert for deceptions. Be direct and quick. "Longer than a minute, and you're dead," warns DBM's Weinstock. Never breaking eye contact, Jim Day said with a chuckle, "I was the victim of a downsizing plan I designed myself." A simple, straightforward answer can also work: "I had philosophical

outplacement /ˈaʊtpleɪsmənt/ *n.* the process of facilitating a terminated employee's search for a new job by providing of professional services, such as counseling, paid for by the former employer

pinpoint /ˈpɪnpɔɪnt/ *vt.* to locate or identify with precision

tab /tæb/ *usu. n.* meaning a short strip of material attached to or projecting from something in order to facilitate opening or identifying or handling it. Here it is a *vt.*, meaning to supply with a tab or tabs

fudge /fʌdʒ/ *vt.* to fake or falsify

backfire /bækˈfaɪə/ *vi.* come back to the originator of an action with an undesired effect

deception /dɪˈsepʃən/ *n.* the act of deliberately making someone believe something that is not true

downsize /ˈdaʊnsaɪz/ *n.* the reduction in number or size or the reduction of expenditures in order to become financially stable

differences with a new group of bosses." Another readily understood explanation is: "The job they put me in wasn't the one I was hired for and wasn't a good fit."

stigma /'stigmə/ *n.* a mark of social disgrace
arrogance/cockiness *n.* offensive boldness and excessive self-confidence
turnoff *n.* one that is distasteful or something that causes loss of interest
spreadsheet /'spredʃiːt/ *n.* a computer program for manipulating figures, used for financial planning

Even if you were fired, "your best answer is always the honest one," notes veteran interviewer Thomas Fay, a United Technologies Corporation senior vice president. "With so much corporate budget cutting being let go doesn't carry the stigma it used to. There's also much more tolerance of job hopping—once a no-no."

3. "What can you do for us?" The interviewer is seeking evidence that you researched his company. In a survey of 320 company recruiters, Northwestern University placement director Victor R. Lindquist found that "lack of knowledge about the company and industry" ranked with "arrogance/cockiness" and "poor oral communication" as principal job-interview turnoffs. "Failure to prepare tells me the person lacks discipline and doesn't care," says Janet Sansone, a human-resources director for General Electric.

It's easy to research a prospective employer. "Discover your library and read, read, read." Counsels executive-search researcher Margaret Phelan. Librarians can point you to annual reports, directories and sometimes even computer data banks crammed with information on potential employers.

4. "What are your strengths?" High energy level? Enthusiasm? Assertive "We look for all of the above," says Patricia Coyle, a senior vice president of a New England banking group. Back your assertions with concrete examples from work or school. "I sold more tickets for the senior play than any other student" would be good evidence for a recent high school graduate.

Don't say "I can do anything you need." The interviewer wants more focus. But don't define your scope too narrowly. "We don't want people to be just underwriters, claims adjusters or marketers," says Toni Nabholz, recruiting director for The Travelers Companies. "They must also demonstrate computer literacy and ability to communicate—skills that will help them grow."

"With managers pressed to do more with less, the age of specialization is over," notes St. Louis executive recruiter Barth Holohan. "Interviewers want a new hire to be adaptable to a fast-changing world. It's an absolute turnabout from the '80s, when the spreadsheet whiz kid was king."

5. "What are your weaknesses?" Probing for candor, honesty and good psychological balance, executive recruiter Robert Heidrick often says, "Tell me about one of your failures."

The wrong answer: "I can't think of any." It's an unrealistic egocentric who is above flopping once in a while. "But don't go to the opposite extreme and lift up the hair looking for warts ," counsels Weinstock.

Safe ground is the "weakness" that is really overuse of a strength. Example: "Sometimes people mistake my decisiveness for impatience, but I have learned to watch how I express things."

Always try to show you profited from your mistake. One young engineering student, on a wrestling scholarship, nearly flunked out of Cornell University after partying through his freshman year. But as a graduating senior, he told recruiters, "I bounced back by applying the same quality—tenacity—that I needed to pin an opponent. Now I'm getting straight A's." He received multiple job offers.

6. "What type of boss do you like?" Forget the wisecrack like "One I see once a year." And don't knock your last boss. The interviewer is probing for whether you're likely to have boss conflicts.

Here's the ideal boss as defined by one successful executive: "A competent and strong leader I can learn from, who will let me take chances, coach me and kick my butt when I need it."

7. "What are your most significant accomplishments?" Some bosses never hire anyone who can't list at least one outstanding achievement. Write down what made you proudest in each of the past five years. Wherever possible, provide numbers to show scope: "I chaired the Red Cross drive that raised $234,000—ten percent more than ever before." Or: "By introducing computerized typesetting, I saved my company $82,000 a year."

whiz /wiz/ *n. (informal)* one who has remarkable skill
candor /ˈkændə/ *n.* the quality of being honest and straightforward in attitude and speech; openness
flop /flɒp/ *vi. (informal)* to fail utterly
wart /wɔːt/ *n.* an imperfection; a flaw
flunk out to expel or be expelled from a school or course because of work that does not meet required standards
tenacity /tɪˈneɪsɪtɪ/ *n.* persistent determination
wisecrack /ˈwaɪzkræk/ *n.* a clever, amusing, sometimes unkind, remark
typesetting /ˈtaɪpˌsetɪŋ/ *n.* the job or activity of arranging types for printing

8. **"What salary are you looking for?"** Don't bring up pay in an initial interview. Your prospective employer will typically talk compensation in the second or third interview, just

low-ball *vt.* to underestimate or understate deliberately

ad-lib *n.* remark made spontaneously without prior preparation

before making an offer. If pressed, don't <u>low-ball</u>, revealing lack of confidence in your worth, or high-ball, maybe scaring off the prospect. Give a range, such as, "I'm considering opportunities between $45,000 and $60,000."

Besides these eight crucial questions, you can expect attempts to test you. The interviewer might describe an actual job problem and ask how you'd solve it. Interviewers have a variety of ways, too, of testing your integrity. Michael Miller, Monsanto's corporate vice president for administration, will sometimes drop this bait: "It's accepted practice in some foreign countries for companies to pay under-the-table fees to get business. Would you have trouble doing this?" There is only one right answer: "An American company operates under US law and ethics that prohibit bribery. I could not do it."

Job interviews often close with a question such as "Is there anything you'd like to bring up that we haven't talked about?" This is a good time to ask about job content, the boss's expectations, and why the last person who had the job left. Intelligent questions impress, reminding the interviewer that you have to be satisfied too.

As parting words, summarize why you'd be right for the job. After practicing, the correct "<u>ad-lib</u>" should come easily—and help get you hired over candidates less prepared for winning interviews.

(approximately 1460 words)

Reading Time: _____   Reading Rate: _____

Cultural Notes

1. **United Technologies Corporation (UTC):** an American multinational conglomerate based in Hartford, Connecticut and is the 20th largest US manufacturer. It researches, develops, and manufactures high-technology products in numerous areas, including aircraft engines, helicopters, heating and cooling, fuel cells, elevators and escalators, fire and security, building systems, and industrial products, among others. UTC is also a large military contractor, producing missile systems and military helicopters, most notably

the UH-60 Black Hawk helicopter. In 2005, it received over 5 billion dollars in military contracts.

2. **Northwestern University (NU):** a private, nonsectarian, coeducational research university with campuses located in Evanston, Illinois and downtown Chicago. The university is organized into eleven schools and colleges, most of which ranked highly in their respective fields. NU is a founding member of the Big Ten Conference, the United States' oldest Division I college athletic conference.

3. **Cornell University** is a private university located in Ithaca, New York, US. Its two medical campuses are in New York City and Education City, Qatar. Cornell is one of two private land grant universities and a member of the Ivy League. Cornell counts more than 240,000 living alumni and 40 Nobel laureates affiliated with the university as faculty or students. Cornell produces more graduates that go on to become doctors than any other university in the US. It also produces the largest number of graduates in the life sciences who continue for PhD degrees, and the third highest number in science and engineering.

Comprehension Exercises

I. Answer the following questions based on the text.

1. Why did Jim Day fail so many times in his search for a desired position? Why did he feel he had a job-winning strategy this time? What was his strategy?

2. What is the proper way to respond to the questions about your former job?

3. What attitude should you adopt towards your own weaknesses and accomplishments?

4. Among applicants of equal ability, what finally counts, according to the authors, in any successful interview?

5. How should you respond to the question about salary?

6. What are the proper conclusive words at the end of an interview?

II. Decide whether each of the following statements is true or false according to the text.

1. Jim Day's case has illustrated the role that preparations, self-confidence and highlighting one's strong points have played in succeeding in finding a good job in current tight job market.

2. The statement—giving the right answers to the right questions—is the ultimate guideline for any successful interview although it is hard for both the interviewer and the interviewee to follow.

3. Honesty is the best policy according to Donald and Diana Stroetzel for any falsification of facts may lead to the immediate rule-out due to lack of integrity.

4. Direct and quick answers to the question—"Why are you on the job market?"—sound rude and abrupt so that it is preferable to give a simple and straightforward answer such as "I had philosophical differences with a new group of bosses" or "The job they put me in wasn't the one I was hired for and wasn't a good fit."

5. The principle—"Always try to show you profited from your mistake."—is better than "I can't think of any." as a solution to such issues as "What are your weakness?" in job interview because "it's an unrealistic egocentric who is above flopping once in a while." according to Weinstock.

III. Select the most appropriate word or phrase and use its proper form to complete each of the following sentences.

cutback	ramble	outplacement	severe	stern
pinpoint	progression	backfire	deception	undistinguished
veteran	prospective	tenacity	compensation	stigma
typesetting	flunk	candor	flop	turnoff

1. London Underground said it may have to axe 500 signalling jobs because of government _____ in its investment.

2. It's as if, over the years, we remember our mother's _____ instructions not to boast, but completely forget her advice to put our best foot forward.

3. You could choose either to carry your own tent, stay in youth and family hostels, or _____ from cabin to cabin.

4. "After that do nothing more strenuous than to sit down with a blank sheet of paper and a drink," advises Dennis Millward, senior consultant at CEPEC, an _____ specialist.

5. When women started working in offices, they opted for _____ in dress in order to imply sobriety.

6. At NASA's Jet Propulsion Laboratory (JPL) in Pasadena, California, a team of scientists and engineers is planning to surround the planet with a constellation of at least six navigation satellites that will allow robots—or humans—on the ground to _____ their position.

7. My tasks were sometimes quite _____ (tracking attendance, writing down the blocking as Gary communicated it to the cast, erasing and writing new blocking as it changed to reflect the developing concept, checking props as opening night approached, etc.) but I had the opportunity to watch Gary coach the cast and help them bring his vision of the show to life!

8. There is a complete _____ of habitats from dry meadows through marshes and reed-beds to open water.

9. If a plan or project _____, it has the opposite result to the one that was intended.

10. The dominant story represents a convergence of two: (1) Melinda's tale of Cinderella-like service to a distant, unfeeling husband, culminating in her abandonment after she gave birth to their child; and (2) George's tale of _____ by a woman promising warmth and acceptance, who turned into a controlling, unfeeling wife who turned away from him in time of need.

11. Here, _____ runners, dreaming of breaking three or four hours in the marathon, smile happily at the thought of giving over every waking hour to the pursuit of their dream and they are not the worst.

12. We were concerned that as Elizabeth and Amy grew up they should understand why they were special rather than feel there was any _____ attached to the fact that they came from frozen embryos.

13. With the advance of the Human Genome Project, the time is approaching when _____ parents will be able to choose their favourite from a range of alternative embryos.

14. Talent, hard work and sheer _____ are all crucial to career success.

15. Someone who is awarded _____ for future loss of earnings is not entitled to receive unemployment benefit for any part of the period covered by that award falling within the first year following the end of the employment. Supplementary benefit, however, may still be payable, depending on the employee's circumstances.

IV. Try to paraphrase the following sentences, paying special attention to the underlined parts.

1. You may not be a salesperson, but you have a huge advantage. You know the product—yourself—better than anyone else.

_____

_____

2. Failure to prepare tells me the person lacks discipline and doesn't care.

_____

_____

3. With managers pressed to do more with less, the age of specialization is over.

_____

_____

4. Always try to show you profited from your mistake.

_____

_____

5. If pressed, don't low-ball, revealing lack of confidence in your worth, or high-ball, maybe scaring off the prospect.

_____

_____

V. Discuss with your partner about each of the three statements and write an essay in no less than 260 words about your understanding of one of them.

　1. Among applicants of equal ability, what any successful interview ultimately comes down to is giving the right answers to the right questions.

_____

_____

　2. Probing for candor, honesty and good psychological balance.

_____

_____

　3. Try to discover the road to success and you'll seek but never find, But blaze your own path and the road to success will trail right behind.

_____

_____

VI. List four websites where we can learn more about how to succeed in a job interview or how to write an impressive resume and provide a brief introduction to each of them.

　1._____

_____

_____.

　2._____

_____

_____.

　3._____

_____

_____.

4. _____

_____

_____ .

Twenty Minutes' Reading

You are required to read the following two sections within 20 minutes.

Section A

Many studies have identified a strong link between suicide and diagnosable mental illness, especially depression. So, because women suffer from depression at a much higher rate than men, they would seem to be at a higher risk of suicide. Yet, women actually commit suicide about one-fourth as often as men.

George E. Murphy, professor of psychiatry at Washington University School of Medicine in St. Louis, says that females may be protected because of the way they think about problems and interact with others. "Women process their experience with friends. They discuss their feelings, seek feedback, and take advice. They are much more likely to tell a physician how they feel and cooperate in the prescribed treatment. As a result, women get better treatment for their depression."

That treatment may help protect them from suicide, but Murphy suggests there is more to it. The approach to problem-solving is what often lands a woman in a psychiatrist's office in the first place, and that approach may be keeping female suicide rates lower.

Murphy believes that women are less inclined to commit suicide because their thinking is more inclusive than that of men. While a man might tend to throw aside seemingly peripheral issues to get to the core of a problem, a woman might take more things into account. She may continue to seek input and process problems long after the point where men decide on a course of action. "She'll consider not just her feelings, but also the feelings of others—her family, the children, even acquaintances—and how these people will be affected by a decision like suicide. A man is much less likely to take those things into account. He makes his decision, and it's about him, so he does not feel the need to share it with anyone else."

1. The passage is mainly concerned with _____.
   A. the relationship between depression and suicide
   B. men's higher risk of committing suicide

C. reasons for women's lower risk of committing suicide

D. causes of women's depression

2. One of the reasons that females get better treatment for their depression is that _____ .

    A. they are more concerned about their health

    B. they need physician's advice and feedback

    C. they discuss their feelings with a doctor and cooperate with him

    D. they often urge their friends to send them to a psychiatrist's office

3. The word "inclusive" in Line 2, Para. 4 probably means _____ .

    A. including many things

    B. open-minded

    C. considerate

    D. relevant to a problem

4. It is implied that a man can reduce his chance of committing suicide if he _____ .

    A. goes straight to the core of a problem

    B. does not allow himself to be influenced by his acquaintances

    C. consults a psychiatrist regularly

    D. considers more things related to a problem

5. When a man suffers from depression, it is typical of him to _____ .

    A. process his feelings and seek advice

    B. consider just his feelings when he makes a decision

    C. throw aside obviously important issues

    D. act in a hostile manner towards a psychiatrist

Section B

Since World War II, there has been a clearly discernible trend, especially among the growing group of college students, toward early marriage. Many youths begin dating in the first stages of adolescence, "go steady" through high school, and marry before their formal education has been completed. In some quarters, there is much shaking of graying locks and clucking of middle-aged tongues over the ways of "wayward youth". However, emotional maturity is no respecter of birthdays; it does not arrive automatically at twenty-one or twenty-five. Some achieve it surprisingly early, while others never do, even in threescore years and ten.

Many students are marrying as an escape, not only from an unsatisfying home life, but also from their own personal problems of isolation and loneliness. And it can almost be put down as a dictum that any marriage entered into as an escape cannot prove entirely successful. The sad fact is that marriage seldom solves one's problems; more often, it merely accentuates them. Furthermore, it is doubtful whether the home as an institution is capable of carrying all that the young are seeking to put into it; one might say in theological terms, that they are forsaking one idol only to worship another. Young people correctly understand that their parents are wrong in believing that "success" is the ultimate good, but they erroneously believe that they themselves have found the true center of life's meaning. Their expectations of marriage are essentially Utopian and therefore incapable of fulfillment. They want too much, and tragic disillusionment is often bound to follow. Shall we, then join, the chorus of "Miseries" over early marriages? One cannot generalize: all early marriages are not bad any more that all later ones are good. Satisfactory marriages are determined not by chronology, but by the emotional maturity of the partners. Therefore, each case must be judged on its own merits. If the early marriage is not an escape, if it is entered into with relatively few illusions or false expectations, and if it is economically feasible, why not? Good marriages can be made from sixteen to sixty, and so can bad ones.

6. According to this passage, the trend toward early marriages _____.
   A. can be clearly seen
   B. is the result of the Great Depression of the 30s'
   C. can't be easily determined
   D. is an outgrowth of the moral looseness brought about by World War II
7. The writer suggests that many of today's early marriages result from _____.
   A. the lack of formal education   B. idol shift
   C. escapism   D. chronology
8. More often than not, early marriage will often _____.
   A. ease one's problems   B. intensify one's problems
   C. not affect one's problems   D. solve one's problems
9. All of the following statements are true EXCEPT that _____.
   A. an early marriage should be economically feasible
   B. not all early marriages are bad
   C. bad marriages can be made from sixteen to sixty
   D. satisfactory marriages are bad
10. Younger people's expectations of marriage can be described as _____.
    A. Utopian
    B. realistic
    C. materialistic
    D. tragic

Unit Four
European Business News

European Business News

1. Eurozone Unemployment "May Have Peaked"
By Pan Pylas

The eurozone's labor market appears to have stabilized, official figures indicated Tuesday, another sign that the region's economy is recovering from its longest-ever recession.

Though Eurostat, the EU's statistics office, said the unemployment rate across the 17-member eurozone held steady at 12 percent in August, it found the number of people out of work fell for the third month running. That's the first time the region has enjoyed such a run since April 2011.

In total, the number of unemployed dipped by 5,000 to 19.18 million, triggering hopes that the 20 million threshold that many economists had been forecasting this year will not be struck and that the 12.1 percent record high booked in June may not be breached.

"The eurozone's jobless rate is past its peak for the current economic cycle," said Zach Witton, an economist at Moody's Analytics. "However, the unemployment rate will fall only gradually as the weak recovery provides limited support to profit margins, giving companies little incentive to boost hiring."

As usually happens in a recovery, the

stabilize /ˈsteɪbəlaɪz/ *v.* to become firm, steady, or unchanging, or to make something firm or steady
recession /rɪˈseʃ(ə)n/ *n.* a difficult time when there is less trade, business activity, etc. in a country than usual
steady /ˈstedɪ/ *adj.* continuing or developing gradually or without stopping, and not likely to change
dip /dɪp/ *v.* to go downwards or to a lower level
trigger /ˈtrɪɡə/ *v.* to make something, especially a series of events, happen very quickly
threshold /ˈθreʃəʊld/ *n.* **a.** the entrance to a room or building, or the area of floor or ground at the entrance; **b.** the level at which something starts to happen or have an effect
breach /briːtʃ/ *v.* to break a law, rule, or agreement
margin /ˈmɑːdʒɪn/ *n.* the difference between what it costs a business to buy or produce something and what they sell it for
incentive /ɪnˈsentɪv/ *n.* something that encourages you to work harder, start a new activity, etc.

modest improvement in the labor market has lagged behind the region's emergence from recession by a few months. The economy grew in the second quarter by a modest quarterly rate of 0.3 percent after contracting for six straight quarters, its longest recession since the euro currency was launched in 1999.

Most surveys suggest the eurozone expanded further during the summer months and that the growth won't rely only on Germany, Europe's largest economy. Even Greece, mired in recession for the best part of six years as the global financial crisis morphed into a crippling sovereign debt crisis, is expected to start growing soon.

lag /læg/ *v.* to move or develop more slowly than others

modest /ˈmɒdɪst/ *adj.* not very great, big, or expensive

contract /ˈkɒntrækt/ *v.* to become smaller or narrower

mire /maɪə/ *v.* to be in a bad or difficult situation that you cannot seem to escape from

morph /mɔːf/ *v.* to develop a new appearance or change into something else, or to make something do this

crippling /ˈkrɪplɪŋ/ *adj.* causing so much damage or harm that something no longer works or is no longer effective

sovereign /ˈsɒvrɪn/ *adj.* having the highest power in a country

gauge /ɡeɪdʒ/ *n.* a fact or an event that can be used to estimate or judge sth

cast /kɑːst/ *v.* If something casts a light or shadow somewhere, it causes it to appear there. **cast a shadow/ cloud over something** (*literary*) to make people feel less happy or hopeful about something

laggard /ˈlæɡəd/ *n.* someone or something that is very slow or late

grapple /ˈɡræp(ə)l/ *v.* to try hard to deal with or understand something difficult

Hopes for an improvement in the eurozone economy were supported by a closely-watched manufacturing survey released Tuesday.

The purchasing managers' index for the manufacturing sector—a gauge of business activity published by financial information company Markit—was 51.1 points in September. Though down on August's 26-month high of 51.4, the survey points to continuing expansion — anything above the 50 threshold indicates growth.

"This is good news for the eurozone but also for the global economy," said Chris Williamson, chief economist at Markit. "The downturn in demand caused by the region's recession and the uncertainty generated by its debt crisis had cast a shadow over economic recoveries across the globe. But we must not get too carried away."

Over the past three years, the eurozone, which has a population of around 330 million, has been the laggard of the world economy as it grappled with a debt crisis that at various times threatened the future of the euro currency itself.

Countries across the region, but mainly in the south, such as Greece, Portugal and Spain, have had to enact tough austerity measures to convince bond market investors that they could get a handle on their public finances. A combination of recession, poor management and expensive bank bailouts had caused public debt to swell in the region.

The problems afflicting the eurozone have weighed on sentiment around the world, putting a brake on the global economic recovery. Though the U.S. unemployment rate may have fallen steadily over the past two to three years to 7.3 percent in August, many economists think the decline would have been steeper were it not for Europe's problems.

The wider 28-country European Union, which includes non-euro countries such as Britain and Sweden and has a population of a little over 500 million, has also struggled in the wake of the eurozone's woes in recent years. Here, too, the unemployment rate appears to have steadied, staying unchanged in August at 10.9 percent for the fourth month running.

Olli Rehn, the EU's commissioner for economic affairs, warned that despite the indications of a rebound, the crisis in the eurozone is not yet over. He said governments should continue their economic reforms and debt cuts, lest they stymie the budding recovery.

He also lamented the shutdown of the U.S. government, but said that he thought the impact on other economies would be limited if it didn't last very long.

"But, of course, the recovery in the global economy, and also in the European economy, is so fragile that they do not need any new risks or any new elements of political instability," he told reporters in Paris.

Few economists think the eurozone's current economic growth is enough to significantly bring down unemployment,

austerity /ɒˈsterɪtɪ/ *n.* bad economic conditions in which people do not have much money to spend; austerity occurs when a government has a deliberate policy of trying to reduce the amount of money it spends, e.g. austerity programme/plan/package

bailout /ˈbeɪlaʊt/ *n.* (*informal*) financial help given to a person or a company that is in difficulty

swell /swel/ *v.* to increase in amount or number

afflict /əˈflɪkt/ *v.* to affect someone or something in an unpleasant way, and make them suffer

sentiment /ˈsentɪm(ə)nt/ *n.* **a.** (*formal*) an opinion or feeling you have about something; **b.** feelings of pity, love, sadness, etc. that are often considered to be too strong or not suitable for a particular situation

woe /wəʊ/ *n.* (*formal*) **a.** the problems and troubles affecting someone; **b.** (*literary*) great sadness

commissioner /kəˈmɪʃ(ə)nə/ *n.* someone who is officially in charge of a government department in some countries

rebound /riˈbaʊnd/ *n.* a positive reaction that happens after sth negative

stymie /ˈstaɪmɪ/ *v.* (*informal*) to prevent someone from doing what they have planned or want to do

lament /ləˈment/ *v.* to express feelings of great sadness about something

fragile /ˈfrædʒaɪl/ *adj.* a fragile situation is one that is weak or uncertain, and likely to become worse under pressure

particularly among the young. The manufacturing PMI survey, for example, showed companies in the sector were still shedding jobs in September, though at a slower rate than before.

The Eurostat figures also mask huge divergences across the eurozone: While Germany has an unemployment rate of 5.2 percent, Spain's jobless rate stood at 26.2 percent. The situation in Greece is even worse, with 27.9 percent of people out of work in June—Greek figures are compiled on a different timeframe.

shed /ʃed/ *v.* to get rid of something that you no longer need or want
divergence /daɪˈvɜːdʒ(ə)ns/ *n.* difference between two or more things, attitudes, or opinions
compile /kəmˈpaɪl/ *v.* to make a book, list, record, etc., using different pieces of information, music, etc.
acute /əˈkjuːt/ *adj.* very serious or severe
coffer /ˈkɒfə/ *n.* the money that an organization, government, etc. has available to spend
fuel /fjʊəl/ *v.* to make something, especially something bad, increase or become stronger
coalition /ˌkəʊəˈlɪʃ(ə)n/ *n.* a union of two or more political parties that allows them to form a government or fight an election together
fraud /frɔːd/ *n.* the crime of deceiving people in order to gain something such as money or goods
conviction /kənˈvɪkʃ(ə)n/ *n.* a decision in a court of law that someone is guilty of a crime, or the process of proving that someone is guilty
uphold /ʌpˈhəʊld/ *v.* if a court upholds a decision made by another court, it states that the decision was correct

The situation among the young—that is, potential workers under the age of 25—is even more acute. Greece and Spain, for example, have over half their youth unemployed. In Greece, youth unemployment stood at a stunning 61.5 percent in June.

As well as being a burden to a country's coffers, sky-high levels of youth unemployment have an additional social cost of denying potential workers skills and experience—that's a long-term cost to the region's economic potential and has also fueled an increase in social tensions.

2. Italy's Youth Unemployment Reaches New All–Time High
By Katie Harris

While euro zone unemployment maintained a steady 12% in August, Italy's jobless rate rose from 12.1% to 12.2%. But it was youth unemployment that took the worst hit in the euro zone's third largest economy, reaching a new all-time high of 40.1% from 39.7% in July, reports the Guardian.

The rise comes at a time of political instability in Italy. The Italian center-right party, headed by Silvio Berlusconi, pulled out of Prime Minister Enrico Letto's coalition government on Sept. 28 after five months of shaky cooperation. Italy's coalition government has been particularly unstable since Berlusconi's tax fraud conviction was upheld by a top Italian court on Aug. 1, reports Reuters.

In addition to its high levels of youth unemployment, Italy is also struggling to manage a two-year-long recession and a two trillion euro ($2.7 trillion) public debt.

3. Why the Europeans Don't Really Want an E.U. Budget Deal

By Bruce Crumley

Three months after failing to reach agreements on whether to slash or bolster the E.U. budget, leaders gather in Brussels to find their positions still far apart.

It's difficult to designate an obvious villain in the European Union's stalled budget negotiations. Virtually all 27 member states are advancing mostly national interests in what's supposed to be the world's largest team effort. That is why few observers expect E.U. leaders converging on Brussels Thursday for another round of budget summitry to come away with a mutually acceptable compromise. Indeed, no agreement may be the best agreement for all concerned.

The Feb. 7 and 8 summit seeks to establish the E.U.'s budget for the 2014—2020 period—a quest that went nowhere when leaders last huddled to talk finances in November. On the face of it, the cause of the impasse is fairly simple. Fiscally conservative countries like the U.K., Germany, the Netherlands and Denmark want to see Europe's budget cut in the same way that spending by national governments has been slashed to remedy debt-plagued public accounts. Countries like France, Poland, Italy and Spain, by contrast, generally seek to maintain or inch up current E.U. funding levels and redirect money saved through austerity to other economic and social programs capable of stimulating slumping growth. If that seems like déjà vu all over again, it is: those are largely the same fault lines that split northern and southern E.U. members over how to respond to Europe's financial crisis.

slash /slæʃ/ *v.* to greatly reduce an amount, price, etc.— used especially in newspapers and advertising

bolster /ˈbəʊlstə/ *v.* to improve something

designate /ˈdezɪgneɪt/ *v.* to choose someone or something for a particular job or purpose

villain /ˈvɪlən/ *n.* the main bad character in a film, play, or story

stall /stɔːl/ *v.* to deliberately delay because you are not ready to do something, answer questions, etc.

converge /kənˈvɜːdʒ/ *v.* if groups of people converge in a particular place, they come there from many different places and meet together to form a large crowd

huddle /ˈhʌd(ə)l/ *v.* to sit or stand with a small group of people in order to discuss something privately

impasse /æmˈpɑːs/ *n.* a situation in which it is impossible to continue with a discussion or plan because the people involved cannot agree

slump /slʌmp/ *v.* to suddenly go down in price, value, or number

Cultural Notes

1. **The eurozone:** a monetary union, was established in 1999 and came into full force in 2002. It is currently composed of 17 member states. Through the Common Foreign and Security Policy, the EU has developed a role in external relations and defense. Permanent diplomatic missions have been established around the world. The EU is represented at the United Nations, the WTO, the G8, and the G-20.

2. **EU (Europe Union):** an economic and political union of 28 member states that are located primarily in Europe. The EU operates through a system of supranational independent institutions and intergovernmental negotiated decisions by the member states. Institutions of the EU include the European Commission, the Council of the European Union, the European Council, the Court of Justice of the European Union, the European Central Bank, the Court of Auditors, and the European Parliament. The European Parliament is elected every five years by EU citizens. The EU's de facto capital is Brussels. The EU traces its origins from the European Coal and Steel Community (ECSC) and the European Economic Community (EEC), formed by the Inner Six countries in 1951 and 1958, respectively. In the intervening years the community and its successors have grown in size by the accession of new member states and in power by the addition of policy areas to its remit. The Maastricht Treaty established the European Union under its current name in 1993. The latest major amendment to the constitutional basis of the EU, the Treaty of Lisbon, came into force in 2009. The EU has developed a single market through a standardised system of laws that apply in all member states. Within the Schengen Area (which includes 22 EU and 4 non-EU states) passport controls have been abolished. EU policies aim to ensure the free movement of people, goods, services, and capital, enact legislation in justice and home affairs, and maintain common policies on trade, agriculture, fisheries, and regional development. With a combined population of over 500 million inhabitants, or 7.3% of the world population, the EU in 2012 generated a nominal gross domestic product (GDP) of 16.584 trillion US dollars, constituting approximately 23% of global nominal GDP and 20% when measured in terms of purchasing power parity, which is the largest nominal GDP and GDP PPP in the world. The EU was the recipient of the 2012 Nobel Peace Prize.

3. **Moody's Analytics** is a subsidiary of Moody's Corporation established in 2007 to focus on non-rating activities, separate from Moody's Investors Service. It provides economic research regarding risk, performance and financial modeling, as well as consulting, training and software services. Moody's Analytics is composed of divisions such as Moody's KMV, Moody's Economy.com, Moody's Wall Street Analytics, the Institute of Risk Standards and Qualifications, and Canadian Securities Institute Global Education Inc.

4. **Markit (Markit Group Limited)** is an international market data vendor dealing in financial information services company with over 3,000 employees. Markit was founded in 2001 as the first independent source of credit derivative pricing. Markit claimed that with its unique and "privileged relationships with 16 shareholder banks" giving them "unparalleled access to a valuable dataset spanning credit, equities, and the broader OTC derivative universe," their data, valuations, and trade processing services became the "market standard in the global financial markets" helping market participants "reduce risk and improve operational efficiency". The company provides independent data, valuations and trade processing of assets. The service aims to enhance transparency, reduce financial risk and improve operational efficiency. Its client base includes significant institutional participants in the financial marketplace. Markit is headquartered in London. Other Markit offices include New York, Dallas, Boulder, Calgary, Vancouver, Toronto, Amsterdam, Frankfurt/Main, Luxembourg, Tokyo, Singapore, Delhi and Sydney.

Comprehension Exercises

I. Answer the following questions based on the text.

1. What was the labor market like in the eurozone according to the Eurostat, the EU's statistics office?

2. Why did companies lack motivation and enthusiasm to recruit employees?

3. What would have happened to the U.S. unemployment rate were it not for Europe's problems according to the news excerpt?

4. What is exceptional in Italy when it comes to the unemployment rate?

5. Why do few observers expect E.U. leaders may reach mutually acceptable compromise at the budget summitry?

II. Decide whether each of the following statements is true or false according to the text.

1. The unemployment rate has been on the rise in eurozone countries since April 2011 because they have experienced the stagflation.

2. More than 20 million people have been out of work although European countries have taken a great variety of measures to prevent the economy from declining.

3. The 17-member eurozone had once witnessed the longest sluggish economic situation since the euro currency was launched in 1999.

4. Non-euro countries in the European Union have experienced the worse economic depression than eurozone members with unsteady unemployment rates and higher inflation since August.

5. Olli Rehn, the EU's commissioner for economic affairs, maintained that the worst economic problems in eurozone countries exerted a profound and everlasting impact on the U.S. economy. The shutdown of many of the local U.S. governments is a good case in point.

III. Select the most appropriate word or phrase and use its proper form to complete each of the following sentences.

shed	margin	breach	recession	trigger
incentive	crippling	sovereign	gauge	grapple
cast	swell	lament	afflict	bailout
threshold	contract	sentiment	commissioner	austerity

1. If she noticed it at all, it was with a sense of relief that she'd _____ that particular delusion.

2. If it is true as many commentators, including Americans, believe that the share of profits in national income has now hit an unsustainable cyclical peak, then the present rebound in the US economy will soon fizzle out in a struggle between labour and capital, a burst of inflation, a tightening of monetary policy and another _____.

3. This suggests that, in the absence of further remarkable productivity improvements, the strengthening of the pound may now be reaching the point at which it could do the British economy serious—and lasting— economic damage and _____ a balance of payments crisis.

4. On the buses, which represents the other half of its business, there are few signs of _____ growth slowing, while the firm's ambitious expansion plans in America also appear to be paying off.

5. Wildlife campaigners insist that the extension to the hunting season is in _____ of the EU Birds Directive and fear that if the French get their way, Spanish and Italian hunters will follow suit and weaken the whole system of bird protection laws.

6. The Olympia Fair overlaps with The Grosvenor House Antiques Fair and The International Ceramics Fair, a rich combination which gives the serious collector and the individual connoisseur a(n) _____ and the opportunity to comb London at its most varied, enticing and rewarding.

7. He contends that the writings of Tolstoy offer answers to some difficult cultural, political and philosophical questions the Russian people face as they _____ with forces and events taking place in their country—including questions of identity simultaneously as citizens of a great nation and members of a larger world community.

8. Who would his successor be...and how long before he could achieve the heights of popularity enjoyed by Jones? But no-one ever did replace Jones who remains, in my opinion, a golfing hero without equal. Despite a _____ disability, he was to remain an inspiring figure throughout his life. The Masters tournament each year is his fitting memorial.

9. Actually, it came down to common sense. A New Political Weapon at the turn of the century, when city neighborhoods were viewed as virtual _____ states, residents typically voted for the party that provided the best prospects for improving the neighborhood.

10. Unless there is some consideration of the effectiveness and efficiency of various methods of trial, Lord Justice Auld will not be able fully to _____ whether justice is being delivered fairly in the two basic methods of trying accused persons.

11. I can't believe that after bowling his heart out on that tour and helping set up that famous victory in Bridgetown with his best ever Test bowling performance, Angus Fraser was over-pleased when, instead of praising his efforts, Illy _____ public doubts over his fitness.

12. Yes, of course the congressional Democrats deserve obloquy for prolonging the savings and loan spree and raising the cost of the final _____ from the $ 100 billion that would have been incurred as late as 1985—by which time the magnitude of the savings and loan collapse was clear to anyone who cared to know—to whatever the final reckoning will prove to be.

13. Within hours of that respectable auctioneer's naughty daydream, would you believe it but the house's contents begin to _____, multiply, increase, until finally on auction day the colonel's antiques overflow into the garden,

where the respectable auctioneer has thoughtfully hired numerous elegant marquees for the purpose.

14. Seeing these deft works again at the Whitechapel made me _____ television's unwillingness to let artists' film and video work invade its channels today.

15. Here was a tale of how an honourable man pursuing honourable goals was _____ with hubris and led his nation towards catastrophe.

IV. Try to paraphrase the following sentences, paying special attention to the underlined parts.

1. In total, the number of unemployed <u>dipped</u> by 5,000 to 19.18 million, <u>triggering</u> hopes that the 20 million <u>threshold</u> that many economists had been forecasting this year will not be <u>struck</u> and that the 12.1 percent <u>record high booked</u> in June may not be breached.

2. As usually happens in a recovery, the modest improvement in the labor market has <u>lagged</u> behind the region's <u>emergence from recession</u> by a few months. The economy grew in the second quarter by a <u>modest</u> quarterly rate of 0.3 percent after <u>contracting</u> for six <u>straight</u> quarters, its longest recession since the euro currency was <u>launched</u> in 1999.

3. Even Greece, <u>mired in recession</u> for the best part of six years as the global financial crisis <u>morphed into a crippling sovereign debt crisis</u>, is expected to start growing soon.

4. A combination of recession, poor management and expensive bank <u>bailouts</u> had caused public debt to <u>swell</u> in the region.

5. Italy's coalition government has been particularly unstable since Berlusconi's tax <u>fraud conviction was upheld</u> by a top Italian court on Aug. 1, reports Reuters.

V. Discuss with your partner about each of the three statements and write an essay in no less than 260 words about your understanding of one of them.

1. As usually happens in a recovery, the modest improvement in the labor market has lagged behind the region's emergence from recession by a few months.

   _____

   _____

2. The downturn in demand caused by the region's recession and the uncertainty generated by its debt crisis had cast a shadow over economic recoveries across the globe.

   _____

   _____

3. Business underlies everything in our national life, including our spiritual life, witness the fact that in the Lord's prayer the first petition is for daily bread, No one can worship God or love his neighbor on an empty stomach.

   _____

   _____

VI. List four websites where we can learn more about euro or eurozone and provide a brief introduction to each of them.

1. _____

   _____

   _____ .

2. _____

   _____

   _____ .

3. _____

   _____

   _____ .

4. _____

   _____

   _____ .

Text B

Is Higher Inflation the Most Painless Way to Escape Current Economic Troubles?

1. A new policy rule is needed, rather than a temporary expedient
By Scott Sumner

THERE have recently been a number of calls for a higher inflation target. The proponents claim that this would stimulate economic growth and also ease sovereign-debt crises. I have mixed feelings about these proposals. There are clear advantages to adopting more expansionary monetary policies in the US, Europe, and Japan, but it's a mistake to target inflation directly, or even to describe the advantages of monetary stimulus in terms of higher inflation.

Inflation can rise due to either supply or demand-side factors. Because most consumers visualize inflation as a supply-side phenomenon (implicitly holding their own nominal income constant) they see inflation as a problem, not a solution. Thus any calls for a higher inflation target are likely to be highly controversial, which makes it unlikely they would be adopted by conservative central bankers.

A much better solution to frankly admit what a growing number of economists are saying; inflation targeting was a mistake from the beginning, and the major central banks should instead be targeting nominal income growth (preferably level targeting). All of the advantages of higher inflation (economic stimulus, lower real debt loads, etc.) are actually more closely linked to rising nominal incomes. A switch to NGDP targeting would not require the major central banks to adopt a new and higher inflation target, with the associated loss of credibility. Instead they should estimate an NGDP target likely to produce 2% inflation in the long run, that is, an NGDP growth rate target of perhaps 4.5% per year in the US, 4% in Europe, and 2.5% in Japan. If the central bank believes there is a need for some "catch-up growth" (and surely that's the case in the US and Europe), then they should start the trend line from 2008 or 2009, to allow for higher NGDP growth for the next several years.

Some might argue that this is just a back door way of raising the inflation target. Not

proponent /prəˈpəʊnənt/ *n.* someone who supports something or persuades people to do something
expansionary /ɪkˈspænʃ(ə)n(ə)rɪ/ *adj.* encouraging a business or economy to become bigger and more successful
nominal /ˈnɒmɪn(ə)l/ *adj.* a very small sum of money, especially when compared with what something would usually cost or what it is worth
controversial /kɒntrəˈvɜːʃ(ə)l/ *adj.* causing a lot of disagreement, because many people have strong opinions about the subject being discussed
credibility /kredɪˈbɪlɪtɪ/ *n.* the quality of deserving to be believed and trusted

so. Inflation targeting is what got us into this mess. If we had been targeting NGDP in 2008, level targeting, then monetary policy would have been far more stimulative, the recession would have been much milder, and the sovereign debt crisis would have been confined to Greece and perhaps one other country. We don't need an expedient like a temporarily higher inflation target, which will further erode central bank credibility. Rather we need an entirely new policy rule, a rule that will be so robust that it doesn't have to be abandoned every time we face a recession or a debt crisis. A rule that is consistent with 2% inflation in the long run. Nominal income targeting is the policy rule that is most likely to fit that description.

2. More inflation would help, but probably won't be forthcoming

By Mark Thoma

BOTH the US and Europe could benefit from temporary period of above-normal inflation. In Europe, a temporary increase in inflation would help countries struggling with sovereign-debt problems. It would also facilitate needed adjustments within the eurozone that are difficult to achieve when countries share a common currency. In the US, a period of above-normal inflation would provide needed stimulus to the economy by lowering real interest rates, making US exports more attractive, and reducing household debt loads.

Along with these benefits there are, of course, potential costs. As at the top of this page notes, these include both efficiency costs and the possibility that inflation expectations will become "de-anchored". However, the efficiency costs of a temporary increase in the inflation rate are relatively low—an extra percent or two for a period of time followed by a return to normal in the long-run won't do much damage.

And there is very little reason to think that inflation expectations would begin to drift upward as a consequence of pursuing such a policy. Both the Federal Reserve and the ECB have sufficient credibility to announce that they are going to target a higher rate of inflation, continue to pursue such a policy until unemployment falls below a predetermined level, and then return inflation to normal. So long as they are believed to be credible—and they are—inflation expectations should track the announced path for actual inflation.

confine /kənˈfaɪn/ *v.* to keep someone or something within the limits of a particular activity or subject

expedient /ɪkˈspiːdɪənt/ *n.* a quick and effective way of dealing with a problem

erode /ɪˈrəʊd/ *v.* to gradually reduce something such as someone's power or confidence

robust /rə(ʊ)ˈbʌst/ *adj.* a robust system, organization, etc. is strong and not likely to have problems

facilitate /fəˈsɪlɪteɪt/ *v.* to make it easier for a process or activity to happen

address /əˈdres/ *v.* to think about a problem or a situation and decide how you are going to deal with it

exploit /ɪkˈsplɔɪt/ *v.* to try to get as much as you can out of a situation, sometimes unfairly; to use something fully and effectively

deflate /dɪˈfleɪt/ *v.* to change economic rules or conditions in a country so that prices fall or stop rising

plunge /plʌn(d)ʒ/ *v.* to move, fall, or be thrown suddenly forwards or downwards; to suddenly experience a difficult or unpleasant situation, or to make someone or something do this

So the expected benefits from providing even modest help to economies struggling to escape the recession are large, and the expected costs are relatively low. Thus, the answer to the question "Should the rich world use above-normal inflation as a way to address economic ills?" is a clear yes.

As to the question of "Will the rich world use above-normal inflation as a way to address economic ills?" that's not likely in the US or Europe. The Fed would probably tolerate, nervously, a short-run period of inflation above 2% during the recovery, though not much over 2%. But while the Fed may tolerate a temporary increase in inflation if it happens, it is not likely to announce and then pursue a higher inflation target. And although Europe could surely use the help—this is the time to exploit the hard-earned credibility that was earned in the past—it's even less likely that the ECB would tolerate a burst of inflation.

That's too bad, because with fiscal policy all but off the table in both the US and Europe, we need all the help from monetary authorities that we can get.

3. Higher inflation might provide Europe a short but costly reprieve
By Gilles Saint-Paul

INFLATION would certainly deflate the real value of public debt in most countries. It would also reduce real interest rates, inducing people to spend more so as to get rid of their nominal assets, and may also reduce the cost of labor to the extent that workers have nominal wage contracts.

Yet this would be just a short-term fix and it would not address the structural problems. We have learned in the seventies that inflation only works if it is unanticipated. Otherwise it is reflected in higher nominal interest rates (notably on public debt) and in indexed wage contracts. As it is difficult to fool people more than once, after such a surprise inflation can they easily crawl into the two-digit zone and disinflation may be quite costly: to stop inflation the Fed had to plunge the US economy into a recession in the late seventies/early eighties.

The structural problems are that most European welfare states are trying to finance themselves by running a Ponzi game and that markets are finally realizing it, and that labor market rigidities generate upward pressure in real wages that can only be tamed at high rates of unemployment. Clearly a shot of inflation would do nothing to address those problems. Real wage losses would be made up for quite quickly, and markets will ask for a premium on the rate of return on public debt as soon as they realize we have reached a new inflationary regime.

During the early part of the crisis, when in the name of stimulus government let budget deficits slip to 8-10% of GDP, few people believed that some countries might face a sovereign-debt crisis. Such events were supposedly confined to middle-income countries. Now, instead of having an intended temporary burst of inflation, European countries may find themselves permanently in the "banana republic" category, in which case they will face the choice between validating expectations of high inflation by indeed having it, or trying to restore their credibility at great pains. As of now, this sounds implausible, but so was the idea of a sovereign-debt crisis in the euro-zone four years ago.

Indeed, fears of deflation have not materialized during the current recession and inflation in Europe is at around 2% despite the low level of economic activity. This was the same rate as during the booming years, suggesting the output/inflation trade-off has shifted out and that inflationary pressure will resume whenever growth picks up. It will be interesting to see whether the ECB will swiftly restore its credibility or bow to political pressure to inflate away the large sovereign debts that were accumulated during the crisis.

Also, inflation is an opaque and undemocratic way of allocating the burden of adjustment. Austerity plans force elected officials to make explicit choices and are generally subject to parliamentary scrutiny. Instead, inflation is a government-led soft wave of invalidation of private and public contracts, with a diffuse allocation of gains and losses (with the most trusting and virtuous people bearing most of the losses). Of course this is made even worse when such inflation is

tame /teɪm/ *v.* to reduce the power or strength of something and prevent it from causing trouble

regime /reɪˈʒiːm/ *n.* a particular system—used especially when talking about a previous system, or one that has just been introduced

validate /ˈvælɪdeɪt/ *v.* **a.** to validate something such as a claim or statement means to prove or confirm that it is true or correct; **b.** to validate a person, state, or system means to prove or confirm that they are valuable or worthwhile

restore /rɪˈstɔː/ *v.* to make something return to its former state or condition

implausible /ɪmˈplɔːzɪb(ə)l/ *adj.* difficult to believe and therefore unlikely to be true

accumulate /əˈkjuːmjʊleɪt/ *v.* to gradually get more and more money, possessions, knowledge, etc. over a period of time

opaque /ə(ʊ)ˈpeɪk/ *adj.* difficult to understand; not clear

allocate /ˈæləkeɪt/ *v.* to use something for a particular purpose, give something to a particular person, etc., especially after an official decision has been made

scrutiny /ˈskruːtɪnɪ/ *n.* careful and thorough examination of someone or something

diffuse /dɪˈfjuːz/ *adj.* using a lot of words and not explaining things clearly and directly

virtuous /ˈvɜːtjʊəs/ *adj.* behaving in a very honest and moral way

implement /ˈɪmplɪm(ə)nt/ *v.* to take action or make changes that you have officially decided should happen

conceivably /kənˈsiːvəb(ə)lɪ/ *adv.* able to be believed or imagined

mandate /ˈmændeɪt/ *n.* an official instruction given to a person or organization, allowing them to do something

implemented by a non-elected transnational body such as the ECB, although conceivably member states could officially agree to change its mandate before it can go ahead with a higher target for inflation.

Comprehension Exercises

I. Answer the following questions based on the text.

1. Why does Scott Sumner have mixed feelings about the proponent's proposal?
2. What kind of new policy rule do we need according to Scott Sumner?
3. How does the US benefit from temporary period of above-normal inflation according to Mark Thoma?
4. Why is the answer of "Should the rich world use above-normal inflation as a way to address economic ills?" a clear yes?
5. What are the structural problems according to Gilles Saint-Paul?

II. Decide whether each of the following statements is true or false according to the text.

1. According to Scott Sumner, few consumers regarded inflation as a solution to tackle the current economic problems although many proponents claimed it would stimulate economic growth.
2. The central banks in the U.S. and Europe have already realized the necessity of some "catch-up growth", thereby allowing for higher NGDP automatically since the year 2008.
3. Scott Sumner has denounced the claim of inflation targeting as a way to handle the economic problems.
4. According to Mark Thoma, a temporary period of above-normal inflation would help in both the U.S. and Europe, but with potential risks.
5. Gilles Saint-Paul pointed out that although the inflation once worked in the 1970s as an approach to handing the economic problems, it turned out to be ineffective, even troublesome with a variety of negative impacts on such aspects as the allocation of burden adjustment, the private and public contracts, as well as the allocations of gain and losses.

III. Select the most appropriate word or phrase and use its proper form to complete each of the following sentences.

mandate	virtuous	diffuse	scrutiny	implement
allocate	implausible	proponent	controversial	accumulate
expedient	validate	expansionary	nominal	robust
erode	opaque	facilitate	address	restore

1. Are there instructions that need to go out to be very explicit about what the consequences are, because we're talking about a voluntary test that, in some cases, the state may _____ for everyone, but in other cases the state will let them be a local option and local schools and local school districts will make their decisions about this thing.

2. But you want to think carefully about how much specification you want to make because test developers have to figure out how to _____ your instructions and you have to hope that they remain true to your intent here.

3. It is social conditions that form character, as another conservative hero, Alexis de Tocqueville, demonstrated, and if our characters are now less _____ than formerly, we must identify in what way our social conditions have changed in order to understand why.

4. His writing is so _____, obscure, and overwrought that it is difficult to make out what he is trying to say.

5. On the contrary, the very acuteness of his _____ serves to drive any hint of sickly sentimentality from the compassion with which he imbues his characters, mankind and life itself.

6. And then, within that list as we discuss the open-ended, you know, balance of items and so forth, then we come back to say within that, how do we _____ those resources, that we start to look at, you know, to develop some items and move closer to a set of specifications because I think all of us around— especially I think it was Pat.

7. If the welfare state is unstable, if its costs must outrun its revenues and if debts _____ in ways that rile society's constituent groups against one another, yes, then the thing will collapse.

8. Money is tough to earn and hard to save, but without it home-buying is _____.

9. Halsey was identified as a leading _____ of the values of progressive education.

10. Although they were all regarded as edgy and _____ for mainstream TV in the Seventies, satirising a war in which the US was floundering, they now

represent just the sort of everyday issues—homosexuality, interracial marriage, adultery, the foolishness of hospital administrators—that ER so loves to plunge its plots into.

11. First, the weapons should be intended for use only in retaliation after a nuclear attack. Second, the possession of the weapons must be a temporary _____ .

12. The goal of the system is to standardize and _____ the document creation and maintenance process for fifteen documentation departments which are comprised of approximately 150 technical writers.

13. Establish and explain relationships using geometrics, make conjectures, _____ and justify conclusions, use informal induction and deduction, that's in geometry.

14. It was only after his colleagues sold out unconditionally to the government by agreeing to suspend all attacks against non-military targets and by proposing future negotiations with the government representatives to further _____ the democratic rights of our organization that he walked out of the talks and returned home to resume the armed struggle.

15. The driver closed the door behind them, quickly retreating behind the wheel and the protection of the _____ bulletproof windows and chassis which encased Dennison's white Mercedes.

IV. Try to paraphrase the following sentences, paying special attention to the underlined parts.

1. <u>A switch to</u> NGDP targeting would not require the major central banks to adopt a new and higher inflation target, with the associated loss of <u>credibility</u>.

_____

_____

2. Some might argue that this is just <u>a back door way</u> of raising the inflation target. Not so. Inflation targeting is <u>what got us into this mess</u>.

_____

_____

3. We don't need an <u>expedient</u> like a temporarily higher inflation target, which will further <u>erode</u> central bank credibility. Rather we need an entirely new policy rule, a rule that will be so <u>robust</u> that it doesn't have to be abandoned every time we face a recession or a debt crisis.

_____

_____

4. And although Europe could surely use the help—this is the time to <u>exploit</u> the <u>hard-earned credibility</u> that was earned in the past—it's even less likely that the ECB would <u>tolerate a burst of inflation</u>.

_____

5. Clearly <u>a shot of inflation</u> would do nothing to <u>address</u> those problems. Real wage losses would be <u>made up for</u> quite quickly, and markets will ask for a <u>premium</u> on the rate of return on public debt as soon as they realize we have reached a new inflationary <u>regime</u>.

_____

_____

V. Discuss with your partner about each of the three statements and write an essay in no less than 260 words about your understanding of one of them.

1. Inflation can rise due to either supply or demand-side factors.

_____

2. Inflation is as violent as a mugger, as frightening as an armed robber and as deadly as a hit man.

_____

3. Also, inflation is an opaque and undemocratic way of allocating the burden of adjustment.

_____

VI. List four websites where we can learn more about how to control inflation or economic crisis and provide a brief introduction to each of them.

1. _____

_____

_____

2. _____

_____

3. _____

_____

4. _____

_____

_____.

Twenty Minutes' Reading

You are required to read the following two sections within 20 minutes.

Section A

What has the telephone done to us, or for us, in the hundred years of its existence? A few effects suggest themselves at once. It has saved lives by getting rapid word of illness, injury, or fire from distant places. By joining with the lift to make possible the multi-story building or office building, it has made possible—for better or worse—the modem city. By bringing about a great leap in the speed and ease with which information moves from place to place, it has greatly sped up the rate of scientific and technological changes and growth in industry. Beyond doubt it has seriously weakened, if not killed, the ancient art of letter writing. It has made living alone possible for persons with normal desires; by so doing, it has played a role in one of the greatest social changes of this century, the breakup of the multi-generational household. It has made the war more efficient than before. Perhaps though not provably, it has prevented wars that might have arisen out of international misunderstanding caused by written communication. Or perhaps—again not probably—by magnifying and extending irrational personal disagreement based on voice contact, it has caused wars. Certainly it has extended the scope of human conflicts, since it fairly spreads the useful knowledge of scientists and the nonsense of the ignorant, the affection of the affectionate and the malice (恶意) of the malicious.

1. What is the main idea of the passage?
   A. The telephone has helped to save people from illness and fire.
   B. The telephone has helped to prevent wars and conflicts.
   C. The telephone has made the modern city ncither better nor worse.
   D. The telephone has had positive as well as negative effects on us.
2. According to the passage, it is the telephone that _____.
   A. has made letter writing an art
   B. has prevented wars by avoiding written communication

C. has made the world different from what it was

D. has caused wars by extending human conflicts

3. The telephone has intensified conflicts among people because _____.

A. it increases the danger of war

B. it provides services to both the good and the malicious

C. it makes distant communication easier

D. it breaks up the multi-generational household

4. The author describes the telephone as impartial because it _____.

A. saves lives of people in distant places

B. enables people to live alone if they want to

C. spreads both love and ill will

D. replaces much written communication

5. The writer's attitude towards the use of the telephone is _____.

A. affectionate

B. disapproving

C. approving

D. neutral

Section B

I had an experience some years ago which taught me something about the ways in which people make a bad situation worse by blaming themselves. One January, I had to officiate at two funerals on successive days for two elderly women in my community. Both had died "full of years," as the Bible would say; both yielded to the normal wearing out of the body after a long and full life. Their homes happened to be near each other, so I paid condolence calls on the two families on the same afternoon.

At the first home, the son of the deceased woman said to me, "If only I had sent my mother to Florida and gotten her out of this cold and snow, she would be alive today. It's my fault that she died." At the second home, the son of the other deceased woman said, "If only I hadn't insisted on my mother's going to Florida, she would be alive today. That long airplane ride, the abrupt change of climate, was more than she could take. It's my fault that she's dead."

When things don't turn out as we would like them to, it is very tempting to assume that had we done things differently, the story would have had a happier ending. Priests know that any time there is a death, the survivors will feel guilty. Because the course of action they took turned out badly, they believe that the opposite course—keeping Mother at home, postponing the operation—would have turned out better. After all, how could it have turned out any worse?

There seem to be two elements involved in our readiness to feel guilty. The first is our pressing need to believe that the world makes sense, that there is a cause for every effect and a reason for everything that happens. That leads us to find patterns and connections both where they really exist and where they exist only in our minds.

The second element is the notion that we are the cause of what happens, especially the bad things that happen. It seems to be a short step from believing that every event has a cause to believing that every disaster is our fault. The roots of this feeling may lie in our childhood. Psychologists speak of the infantile myth of omnipotence. A baby comes to think that the world exists to meet his needs, and that he makes everything happen in it. He wakes up in the morning and summons the rest of the world to its tasks. He cries, and someone comes to attend to him. When he is hungry, people feed him, and when he is wet, people change him. Very often, we do not completely outgrow that infantile notion that our wishes cause things to happen.

6. What is said about the two deceased elderly women?
   A. They lived out a natural life.
   B. They died of exhaustion after the long plane ride.
   C. They weren't accustomed to the change in weather.
   D. They died due to lack of care by family members.
7. The author had to conduct the two women's funerals probably because _____.
   A. he wanted to console the two families
   B. he was an official from the community
   C. he had great sympathy for the deceased
   D. he was priest of the local church
8. People feel guilty for the deaths of their loved ones because _____
   A. they couldn't find a better way to express their grief
   B. they believe that they were responsible
   C. they had neglected the natural course of events
   D. they didn't know things often turn out in the opposite direction
9. In the context of the passage, "... the world makes sense" probably means that _____.
   A. everything in the world is predetermined
   B. the world can be interpreted in different ways
   C. there's an explanation for everything in the world
   D. we have to be sensible in order to understand the world

10. People have been made to believe since infancy that _____.
   A. everybody is at their command
   B. life and death is an unsolved mystery
   C. every story should have a happy ending
   D. their wishes are the cause of everything that happens

Unit Five
The Familiar Essay (I)

Text A

Solve That Problem—With Humor

Anonymous

A lot of us lose life's tougher confrontations by mounting a frontal attack—when a touch of humor might well enable us to chalk up a win. Consider the case of a young friend of mine, who hit a traffic jam en route to work shortly after receiving an ultimatum about being late on the job. Although there was a good reason for Sam's chronic tardiness—serious illness at home—he decided that this by-now-familiar excuse wouldn't work any longer. His supervisor was probably already pacing up and down with a dismissal speech rehearsed.

He was. Sam entered the office at 9:35. The place was as quiet as a locker room; everyone was hard at work. Sam's supervisor approached him. Suddenly, Sam forced a grin and shoved out his hand. "How do you do!" he said. "I'm Sam Maynard. I'm applying for a job which I understand became available just 35 minutes ago. Does the early bird get the worm?"

The room exploded with laughter. The supervisor clamped off a smile and walked back to his office. Sam Maynard had saved his job—with the only tool that could win, a laugh.

Humor is a most effective, yet frequently neglected, means of handling the difficult situations in our lives. It can be used for patching up differences, apologizing, saying "no," criticizing, getting the other fellow to do

route /ruːt/ *adv.* on or along the way
ultimatum /ˌʌltɪˈmeɪtəm/ *n.* a final statement of terms made by one party to another
tardiness /ˈtɑːdɪnɪs/ *n.* the quality or habit of not adhering to a correct or usual or expected time
clamp off release
patch up reconcile; come to terms

what you want without his losing face. For some jobs, it's the only tool that can succeed. It is a say to discuss subjects so sensitive that serious dialog may start a riot. For example, many believe that comedians on television are doing more today for racial and religious tolerance than are people in any other forum.

escalate /ˈeskəleɪt/ *vi.* to increase in intensity or extent
intone /ɪnˈtəʊn/ *vi.* to speak with a singing tone or with a particular intonation
twinkling /ˈtwɪŋklɪŋ/ *n.* an instant
enlist /ɪnˈlɪst/ *vi.* to participate actively in a cause or an enterprise
de rigueur *adj.* required by the current fashion or custom
studied /ˈstʌdɪd/ *adj.* resulting from deliberation and careful thought
enunciate /ɪˈnʌnsieɪt/ *vi.* to pronounce
one-liner *n.* a short joke or witticism, usually expressed in a single sentence
conspiracy /kənˈspɪrəsi/ *n.* a plan by a group intent usually on a treacherous purpose
truculent /ˈtrʌkjulənt/ *adj.* expressing bitter opposition
line /laɪn/ *n.* a line or procession of people picketing a place of business or otherwise staging a public protest （工会组织的）罢工纠察线

Humor is often the best way to keep a mal misunderstanding from escalating into a big deal. Recently a neighbor of mine had a squabble with his wife as she drove him to the airport. Airborne, he felt miserable, and he knew she did, too. Two hours after she returned home, she received a long-distance phone call. "Person-to-person for Mrs. I. A. Pologize," intoned the operator. "That's spelled 'P' as in..." In a twinkling, the whole day changed from grim to lovely at both ends of the wire.

An English hostess with a quick wit was giving a formal dinner for eight distinguished guests whom she hoped to enlist in a major charity drive. Austerity was de rigueur in England at the time, and she had drafted her children to serve the meal. She knew that anything could happen—and it did, just as her son, with the studied concentration of a tightrope walker, brought in a large roast turkey. He successfully elbowed the swinging dining-room door, but the backswing deplattered the bird onto the dining-room floor.

The boy stood rooted; guests stared at their plates. Moving only her head, the hostess smiled at her son. "No harm, Daniel," she said. "Just pick it up and take him back to the kitchen"—she enunciated clearly so he would think about what she was saying—"and bring in the other one."

A wink and a one-liner instantly changed the dinner from a red-faced embarrassment to a conspiracy of fun.

The power of humor to dissolve a hostile confrontation often lies in its unspoken promise "You let me off the hook, my friend, and I'll let you off." The trick is to assign friendly motives to your opponent, to smile just a little—but not too much. Canada's Governor-General Roland Michener, master of the technique, was about to inspect a public school when he was faced with a truculent picket line of striking maintenance personnel. If he backed away from the line, he would seriously diminish his office's image; if he crossed it, he might put the government smack into a hot labor issue.

While he pondered the matter, more strikers gathered across his path. Suddenly, the graying pencil-line mustache on Michener's face stretched a little in Cheshirean complicity. "How very nice of you all to turn out to see me!" he boomed. "Thank you. Shall we go in?" The line parted and, by the time the pickets began to chuckle, the governor-general was striding briskly up the school steps.

Next time you find yourself in an ethnically awkward situation, take a lesson from the diplomatic delegates to Europe's Common Market. In the course of history nearly every member nation has been invaded or betrayed by at least one of the others, and the Market's harmony must be constantly buttressed. One method is the laugh based on national caricatures. Recently, a new arrival at Market headquarters in Brussels introduced himself as a Minister for the Swiss Navy. Everybody laughed. The Swiss delegate retorted, "Well, why not? Italy has a Minister of Finance."

Of course, humor is often more than a laughing matter. In its more potent guises, it has a Trojan-horse nature: no one goes on guard against a gag; we let it in because it looks like a little wooden toy. Once inside, however, it can turn a city to reform, to rebellion, to resistance. Some believe, for instance, that, next to the heroic British RAF, British humor did the most to fend off a German takeover in the World War II. One sample will suffice: that famous story of the woman who was finally extracted from the rubble of her house during the London blitz. Asked, "Where is your husband?" she brushed brick dust off her head and arms and answered, "Fighting in Libya, the bloody coward!"

Similarly, whenever we Americans start taking ourselves a bit too seriously, a grassroots humor seems to rise and strew banana peels in our path. The movement is usually led by professionals: Mark Twain penlancing the boils of pomposity

smack /smæk/ *n.* an enthusiastic kiss
complicity /kəm'plɪsɪti/ *n.* aiding another in the planning or commission of a crime
boom /buːm/ *vi.* to utter or give forth with a deep, resonant sound
briskly /briskli/ *adv.* quickly and energetically
buttress /'bʌtres/ *vt.* to support or reinforce
caricature /'kærɪkətjʊə/ *n.* a representation, especially pictorial or literary, in which the subject's distinctive features or peculiarities are deliberately exaggerated to produce a comic or grotesque effect
potent /'pəʊtənt/ *adj.* highly effective
gag /gæg/ *n.* a comic effect or remark
extract /ɪk'strækt/ *vt.* to draw or pull out, using great force or effort
grassroots *adj.* of or involving the common people
penlancing a word coined by the author meaning "lancing (cutting into) with pen"
pomposity /pɒm'pɒsɪti/ *n.* full of high-sounding phrases

("Man was made at the end of the week's work, when God was tired."); Will Rogers <u>deflating</u> out law-makers ("The oldest boy became a Congressman, and the second son turned out no good, too."); Bill Mauldin needling <u>fatuous</u> officers (one 2nd lieutenant to another, on observing a beautiful sunset: "Is there one for enlisted men, too?"). Such masters of comic deflation restore the balance. They bring us back to ourselves.

deflate /diːˈfleɪt/ *vi.* to reduce or lessen the size or importance of
fatuous /ˈfætjuəs/ *adj.* foolish or silly, especially in a self-satisfying way
unlipped a word coined by the author meaning "part one's lips"
psychiatrist /saɪˈkaɪətrɪst/ *n.* a physician who specializes in psychiatry
citadel /ˈsɪtədəl/ *n.* a base area

When life has us in a tight corner, one of the first questions we might ask is, "Can I solve this with a laugh?" Men with giant responsibilities have frequently used this approach to giant problems—often with sweeping effect. As Gen. George C, Marshall, US Army Chief of Staff, labored to prepare this then-unready nation to enter World War II, he met stiff opposition from his Commander-in-Chief regarding the elements that called for the most bolstering. Marshall felt that what we needed most were highly developed ground forces. President Roosevelt was a navy man who believed that our principal need was for a powerful navy, plus a large air force. In increasingly tense debates with the President, Marshall pushed his argument so hard that he began to foster ever stronger resistance. Finally, during a particularly hot session, the usually stonefaced Marshall forced a grin. "At least, Mr. President," he said, "You might stop referring to the Navy as 'us' and the Army as 'them'."

Roosevelt studied Marshall over his glasses, then <u>unlipped</u> a great show of teeth and laugher. Shortly thereafter, he made a more objective study of Marshall's recommendations and eventually bought the ground-force concept.

Occasionally, humor goes beyond saving arguments, saving face or saving jobs; it can save life itself. Victor E. Frankl was a <u>psychiatrist</u> imprisoned in a German <u>concentration camp</u> during World War II. As the shrinking number of surviving prisoners descended to new depths of hell, Frankl and his closest prisoner friend sought desperately for ways to keep from dying. Piled on top of malnutrition, exhaustion and disease, suicidal despair was the big killer in these <u>citadels</u> of degradation.

As a psychiatrist, Frankl knew that humor was one of the soul's best

aloofness /əˈluːfnɪs/ *n.* indifference by personal withdrawal

contagion /kənˈteɪdʒən/ *n.* the tendency to spread, as of a doctrine, influence, or emotional state

protocol /ˈprəʊtəkɒl/ *n.* a code of correct conduct

implore /ɪmˈplɔː/ *vt.* beg

ladle /ˈleɪdl/ *vt.* to lift out or serve with a long-handled spoon

survival weapons, since it can create, if only for moments, aloofness from horror. Therefore, Frankl made a rule that once each day he and his friend must invent and tell an amusing anecdote, specifically about something which could happen after their liberation.

Others were caught up in the contagion of defiant laughter. One starving prisoner forecast that in the future he might be at a prestigious formal dinner, and when the soup was being served, he would shatter protocol by imploring the hostess, "Ladle it from the bottom!"

If humor can be used successfully against such odds, what can't you and I do with it in daily life?

(approximately 1450 words)

Reading Time: _____   Reading Rate: _____

Cultural Notes

1. **Trojan-horse:** from Greek mythology, a giant hollow horse was containing Greek soldiers, used to overtake the city of Troy during the Trojan War. It has since become a metaphor for any person or thing that appears innocent or benign, but actually presents danger or harmful intent.

2. **The Royal Air Force (RAF):** the air arm of the British Armed Forces. Formed on 1 April 1918, the RAF has taken a significant role in British military history ever since, playing a large part in World War II and in more recent conflicts.

3. **The London Blitz:** the sustained bombing of Britain by Nazi Germany between 7 September 1940 and 10 May 1941, in World War II. While the "Blitz" hit many towns and cities across the country, it began with the bombing of London for 57 nights in a row. By the end of May 1941, over 43,000 civilians, half of them in London, had been killed by bombing and more than a million houses destroyed or damaged in London alone.

4. **concentration camp:** Prior to and during World War II, Nazi Germany under Hitler maintained **concentration camps** throughout the territories it

controlled. They grew rapidly through the 1930s as political opponents and many other groups of people were incarcerated without trial or judicial process.

Comprehension Exercises

I. Answer the following questions based on the text.

1. What examples did the author present respectively to prove that humor can save arguments, save face, save jobs and even save life itself?

2. Can you interpret the humorous message of the long-distance call the lady received from her husband?

3. In paragraph 9, how did the Governor-General Roland Michener dissolve a hostile confrontation by humor?

4. In paragraph 18, the starving prisoner said: "Ladle it from the bottom!" Can you explain why this sentence is comic?

5. Where do the charms of humor lie? Can you cite some personal examples to illustrate?

II. Decide whether each of the following statements is true or false according to the text.

1. Sam might come up with many excuses for his being late again that day, but he failed to do so for he had a clear picture of what his supervisor would do if he dared to do so.

2. The author has illustrated the vital importance of humor in dealing with such sensitive subjects as racial and religious tolerance by citing an example of comedians on television who have done more than people in any other forum.

3. An English hostess handled the embarrassment with a quick wit at a formal dinner to enlist eight prestigious guests in a major charity drive when the roast turkey fell onto the ground from the large shallow plate.

4. Roland Michener succeeded in tackling the tough situation when opponents gathered in front of him by pretending that they all turned out to welcome him.

5. The anonymous author of this article reminded the reader of the fact that men with giant responsibilities may be out of dilemma in life with a laugh, also with sweeping effect.

III. Select the most appropriate word or phrase and use its proper form to complete each of the following sentences.

protocol	aloof	bolster	fatuous	contagion
potent	buttress	brisk	ponder	caricature
ultimatum	escalate	enunciate	conspiracy	tardy
clamp	patch	enlist	dissolve	implore

1. From that day on imperial _____ required her parents to use a formal honorific language towards her and they instructed her younger brother and sister to think of her no longer as "one of us".

2. You can use _____ to refer to the spreading of ideas, or attitudes, or feelings that you consider to be bad or unacceptable from one group of people to another.

3. The chairman and president of Nintendo of America has none of his father-in-law's _____; instead, he laughs easily, takes time from business during the day to watch game players.

4. He helped the players' association secure radio and television revenue to _____ the new pension plan and supported a player's minimum salary of $ 5,000.

5. Syndrome Word used by journalists in a non-medical context to make some _____ conclusion sound plausible.

6. But whatever the spirit with which the voting levers were pulled, the vote total's effect was to convince Buchanan and his allies that their nationalist conservatism was not marginal, not futile, but potentially a _____, even dominant, force in American public life.

7. She wore awful grey suits and thick stockings with laced-up shoes: a _____ of the spinster school-teacher, in fact.

8. Lapham uses this quotation to _____ his own argument that Americans have been too compliant, too willing to go along with politicians who would reduce their liberties, not expand them.

9. A warm-up should be 5—10 minutes of very gentle exercise, including a jog or _____ walk to increase the body temperature and then specific stretching exercises concentrating on the muscles and joints to be used in the activity.

10. I found myself constantly _____ the question: "How could anyone do these things?".

11. She told me that she just wasn't happy living with me and she issued an _____ and decided to bid me farewell forever.

12. Companies which are _____ in embracing mobile computing will be left

behind by more nimble competitors.

13. It is a day like no other: The last Armistice Day of the 20th Century—a century which saw war _____ from hand-to-hand combat to nuclear bombs.

14. Perhaps in years to come those who can speak clearly and _____ properly will grow rich because they can make themselves more easily understood by the computers that surround us all, and do not have to waste time persuading recalcitrant software to do what they want.

15. There are awesomely detailed tales of crime and _____ among the British secret services, eye-witness accounts of the hideous excesses of Our Boys in Northern Ireland, alarming tales of ecological vandalism in a feature on Greenpeace, and an investigation into the bloodstained history of Australian Aborigines.

IV. Try to paraphrase the following sentences, paying special attention to the underlined parts.

1. A lot of us lose life's tougher confrontations by mounting a frontal attack—when a touch of humor might well enable us to chalk up a win.

2. It can be used for patching up differences, apologizing, saying "no," criticizing, getting the other fellow to do what you want without his losing face.

3. A wink and a one-liner instantly changed the dinner from a red-faced embarrassment to a conspiracy of fun.

4. The power of humor to dissolve a hostile confrontation often lies in its unspoken promise "You let me off the hook, my friend, and I'll let you off."

5. Piled on top of malnutrition, exhaustion and disease, suicidal despair was the big killer in these citadels of degradation.

V. Discuss with your partner about each of the three statements and write an essay in no less than 260 words about your understanding of one of them.

1. Humor is a most effective, yet frequently neglected, means of handling the difficult situations in our lives.

2. Of course, humor is often more than a laughing matter.

3. Imagination was given to man to compensate him for what he is not; a sense of humor to console him for what he is.

VI. List four websites where we can learn more about how to be humorous in our daily life or how to be flexible in dealing with tough situation and provide a brief introduction to each of them.

1.

2.

3.

4.

Text B

The Crooked Streets

By Hilaire Belloc

Why do they pull down and do away with the Crooked Streets, I wonder, which are my delight, and hurt no man living? Every day the wealthier nations are pulling down one or another in their capitals and their great towns: they do not know why they do it; neither do I.

It ought to be enough, surely, to drive the great broad ways which commerce

needs and which are the life-channels of a modern city, without destroying all the history and all the humanity in between: the islands of the past. For, note you, the Crooked Streets are packed with human experience and reflect in a lively manner all the chances and misfortunes and expectations and domesticity and wonderment of men. One marks a boundary, another the kennel of an ancient stream, a third the track some animal took to cross a field hundreds upon hundreds of years ago; another is the line of an old defence, another shows where a rich man's garden stopped long before the first ancestor one's family can trace was born; a garden now all houses, and its owner who took delight in it turned to be a printed name.

Leave men alone in their cities, pester them not with futilities of great governments, nor with the fads of too powerful men, and they will build you Crooked Streets of their very nature as moles throw up the little mounds or bees construct their combs. There is no ancient city but glories, or has gloried, in a whole foison and multitude of Crooked Streets. There is none, however, wasted and swept by power, which, if you leave it alone to natural things, will not breed Crooked Streets in less than a hundred years and keep them for a thousand more.

I know a dead city called Timgad, which the sand or the barbarians of the Atlas overwhelmed fourteen centuries ago. It lies between the desert and the Algerian fields, high up upon a mountainside. Its columns stand. Even its fountains are apparent, though their waterways are choked. It has a great forum or marketplace, all flagged and even, and the ruined walls of its houses mark its emplacement on every side. All its streets are straight, set out with a line, and by this you may judge how a Roman town lay when the last order of Rome sank into darkness.

Well, take any other town which has not thus been mummified and preserved but has lived through the intervening time, and you will find that man, active, curious, intense, in all the fruitful centuries of Christian time has endowed them with Crooked Streets, which kind of streets are

domesticity /ˌdɒmesˈtɪsɪti/ *n.* home life or devotion to it
kennel /ˈkenl/ *n.* a gutter along a street
futility /fjuːˈtɪlətɪ/ *n.* the quality of having no useful result; uselessness
mole /məʊl/ *n.* a small furry almost blind animal that digs passages under ground to live in 鼹鼠
mound /maʊnd/ *n.* a raised mass
foison /ˈfɔɪzn/ *n.* abundance
emplacement /ɪmˈpleɪsmənt/ *n.* position; location
mummify /ˈmʌmɪfaɪ/ *vt.* to cause to shrivel and dry up

the most native to Christian men. So it is with Arles, so it is with Nîmes, so it is with old Rome itself, and so it is with the City of London, on which by a special Providence the curse of the Straight Street has never fallen, so that it is to this day a labyrinth of little lanes. It was intended after the Great Fire to set it all out in order with "piazzas" and bou-

labyrinth /'læbərɪnθ/ *n.* an intricate structure of interconnecting passages through which it is difficult to find one's way; a maze
piazza /pi'ætsə/ *n.* square in an Italian town
vistas /'vɪstə/ *n.* a distant view or prospect, especially one seen through an opening, as between rows of buildings or trees
exchequer /ɪks'tʃekə/ *n.* financial resources; funds
regal /'riːgəl/ *adj.* magnificent; splendid
gabled /'geɪbəld/ *adj.* having one or more gables

levards and the rest—but the English temper was too strong for any such nonsense, and the streets and the courts took to the natural lines which suit us best.

The Renaissance indeed everywhere began this plague of vistas and of avenues. It was determined three centuries ago to rebuild Paris as regular as a chessboard, and nothing but money saved the town—or rather the lack of money. You may to this day see in a square called the "Place des Vosges" what was intended. But when they had driven their Straight Street two hundred yards or so the exchequer ran dry, and thus was old Paris saved. But in the last seventy years they have hurt it badly again. I have no quarrel with what is regal and magnificent, with splendid ways of a hundred feet or more, with great avenues and lines of palaces; but why should they pull down my nest beyond the river—Straw Street and Rat Street and all those winding belts round the little Church of St Julien the Poor, where they say that Dante studied and where Danton in the Madness of his grief dug up his dead love from the earth on his returning from the wars?

Crooked Streets will never tire a man, and each will have its character, and each will have a soul of its own. To proceed from one to another is like traveling in a multitude or mixing with a number of friends. In a town of Crooked Streets it is natural that one should be the Moneylender's Street and another that of the Burglars, and a third that of the Politicians, and so forth through all the trades and professions.

Then also, how much better are not the beauties of a town seen from Crooked Streets! Consider those old Dutch towns where you suddenly come round a corner upon great stretches of salt water, or those towns of Central France which from one street and then another show you're the Gothic in a hundred ways.

It is as it should be when you have the back of Chartres Cathedral towering up above you from between and above two houses gabled and almost meeting. It is what the builders meant when one comes out from such <u>fissures</u> into the great Place, the <u>parvis</u> of the cathedral, like a sailor from a river into the sea. Not that certain buildings were not made particularly for wide approaches and splendid roads, but that these, when they are the rule, sterilize and kill a town. Napoleon was wise enough when he designed that there should lead up all beyond the Tiber to St Peter's a vast imperial way. But the modern nondescript <u>horde</u>, which has made Rome its prey, is very ill advised to drive those new Straight Streets foolishly, emptily, with mean <u>façades</u> of plaster and great gaps that will not fill.

You will have noted in your travels how the Crooked Streets gather names to themselves which are as individual as they, and which are bound up with them as our names are with all our own human reality and humour. Thus I bear in mind certain streets of the town where I served as a soldier. There was the Street of the Three Little Heaps of Wheat, the Street of the Trumpeting Moor, the Street of the False Heart, and an exceedingly pleasant street called "Who Grumbles at It?" and another short one called "The Street of the Devil in his Haste", and many others.

From time to time those modern town councilors from whom Heaven has wisely withdrawn all immoderate sums of money, and who therefore have not the power to take away my Crooked Streets and put Straight ones in their places, change old names to new ones. Every such change indicates some snobbery of the time: some little battle exaggerated to be a great thing; some public fellow or other in Parliament or what not; some fad of the learned or of the important in their day.

Once I remember seeing in an obscure corner a twist of dear old houses built before George III was king, and on the corner of this row was painted "Kipling Street: late Nelson Street".

Upon another occasion I went to a little Norman market town up among the hills, where one of the smaller squares was called "The Place of the Three Mad Nuns", and when I got there after so many years and was beginning to renew my youth I was struck all of a heap to see a great <u>enameled</u> blue and white affair upon the walls. They had renamed the triangle. They had called it "The Place <u>Victor Hugo</u>"!

However, all you who love Crooked Streets, I bid you lift up your hearts. There is no power on earth that can make man build Straight Streets for long. It is a bad thing, as

fissure /ˈfɪʃə/ *n.* a long, narrow opening; a crack or cleft
parvis /ˈpɑːvɪs/ *n.* an enclosed courtyard or space at the entrance to a building, especially a cathedral
horde /hɔːd/ *n.* a nomadic tribe or group
façade /fəˈsɑːd/ *n.* generally one side of the exterior of a building, especially the front
enamel /ɪˈnæməl/ *vt.* to give a glossy or brilliant surface to

a general rule, to prophesy good or to make men feel comfortable with the vision of a pleasant future; but in this case I am right enough. The Crooked Streets will certainly return.

prophesy /ˈprɒfisaɪ/ *vt.* to predict with certainty

scansion /ˈskænʃən/ *n.* the analysis of a poem's meter

Let me boldly borrow a quotation which I never saw until the other day, and that in another man's work, but which having once seen it I shall retain all the days of my life.

"*O passi gravora, dabit Deus his quoque finem*", or words to that effect. I can never be sure of a quotation, still less of scansion, and anyhow, as I am deliberately stealing it from another man, if I have changed it so much the better.

(*approximately 1470 words*)

Reading Time: _____   Reading Rate: _____

Cultural Notes

1. **Hilaire Belloc** (27 July 1870—16 July 1953): a Frenchborn writer who became a naturalised British subject in 1902. He was one of the most prolific writers in England during the early twentieth century.

2. **Arles:** a city in the south of France.

3. **Nîmes:** a city and commune of southern France. Nîmes has a rich history, dating back to the Roman Empire, and is a popular tourist destination.

4. **The Great Fire (of London):** a major conflagration that swept through the central parts of London from Sunday, 2 September to Wednesday, 5 September 1666, was one of the major events in the history of England. The social and economic problems created by the disaster were overwhelming. Evacuation from London and settlement elsewhere were strongly encouraged by Charles II, who feared a London rebellion amongst the dispossessed refugees. Despite numerous radical proposals, London was reconstructed on essentially the same street plan used before the fire.

5. **Danton** (Georges Jacques Danton) (October 26, 1759—April 5, 1794): a leading figure in the early stages of the French Revolution and the first President of the Committee of Public Safety.

6. **the Gothic** (Gothic architecture): a style of architecture which flourished during the high and late medieval period. Originating in 12th-century France and lasting into the 16th century, Gothic architecture was known

during the period as "the French Style". Its characteristic features include the pointed arch, the ribbed vault and the flying buttress. Gothic architecture is most familiar as the architecture of many of the great cathedrals, abbeys and parish churches of Europe. It is also the architecture of many castles, palaces, town halls, guild halls, universities, and to a less prominent extent, private dwellings.

7. **Victor Hugo** (February 26, 1802—May 22, 1885): a French poet, playwright, novelist, essayist, visual artist, statesman, human rights campaigner, and perhaps the most influential exponent of the Romantic movement in France.

 Comprehension Exercises

I. Answer the following questions based on the text.

1. Why are the Crooked Streets "my delight"? Do you personally like the Crooked Streets?

2. In paragraph 2, what does "the islands of the past" refer to?

3. What does the author want to illustrate by the example about the dead city called Timgad?

4. For what reasons didn't the author like the new names of some Crooked Streets?

5. What does this sentence mean?—"*Then also, how much better are not the beauties of a town seen from Crooked Streets!*"

II. Decide whether each of the following statements is true or false according to the text.

1. The Crooked Streets once played a variety of roles such as a boundary, the kennel of an ancient stream, a track, the line of an old defense.

2. Hilaire Belloc cited analogy of moles throwing up the little mounds and bees constructing their combs in order to demonstrate his point that the Crooked Streets would be built by men themselves and be kept as they were without negative influence by governments or the fads of too powerful men.

3. In paragraph 5, Hilaire Belloc emphasized the fact that the Crooked Streets are typical of towns unless they have not been mummified or preserved with but have lived through the intervening time in all the fruitful centuries of Christian time.

4. In paragraph 6, the author gave us an example of streets in Paris to show us

that the Crooked Streets would be preserved if local governments were lacking in money in both Renaissance time and contemporary time.

5. A man seems to meet many a friend with different features, experience diverse trades and professions when strolling along various Crooked Streets with peculiar features in different towns.

III. Select the most appropriate word or phrase and use its proper form to complete each of the following sentences.

prophesy	façade	sterilize	multitude	exaggerate
regal	labyrinth	overwhelm	futility	vista
misfortune	retain	mummify	endow	humanity
enamel	snobbery	exchequer	domesticity	kennel

1. He _____ that within five years his opponent would either be dead or in prison.

2. But the question is meant to provoke a discussion about whether writers always mean literally what they say, or whether they sometimes _____ to make a point, and, if they do, whether that's (a) always, (b) sometimes, or (c) never proper.

3. The drab grey _____ was in desperate need of a fresh coat of paint, and when she stepped inside it only confirmed her initial gut feeling—it was a dive.

4. If a person or an animal is _____, they have a medical operation that makes it impossible for them to have or produce babies.

5. One of the major problems of older women living alone is that the _____ of physical chores involved in just keeping the house together soon becomes onerous, especially if your husband did most of the outside physical work like mowing the lawn, cleaning the gutters, raking leaves, and doing other yard work.

6. Queen Margrethe is tall, blonde, deeply _____ and a decent artist—she illustrated *Lord of the Rings* under a pseudonym and studied in Paris, Cambridge and the LSE.

7. As she looked out over the _____, illuminated only by the sporadic flickering lights of the tiny settlements in the valley below, she found herself thinking back to what Rick had said about the gorge having once been a dumping ground for the bodies of those who'd dared to oppose the repressive rule of the gun.

8. Rats scurry through this gloomy Swiss cheese of a _____ as fleetly as Harry

Lime, aka Orson Welles.

9. He has found that careful application and choice of herbicides can check annual weeds and grasses that might otherwise _____ the less competitive wild flowers.

10. He has little to give Coffey in return for what he asks of him, and it is this sense of _____ and frustration which still haunts him as an old man.

11. But don't be malicious, don't tell lies, and don't derive pleasure from someone else's _____, no matter how much you dislike the subject of the gossip.

12. Although not long afterwards his father's career as an accountant took him to London, he never regarded himself as anything other than a Wearsider, nor lost those northern qualities of shrewdness and straight talking, a short way with affectation and pretence, and a warm but undemonstrative _____.

13. A tree planting programme ensures that the campus will _____ its "greenness" for succeeding generations of students.

14. In America, people are paying up to $150,000 to be _____ after death.

15. He became professor of nutrition at Queen Elizabeth College, London University, from 1954 to 1971. The collection is being sold by his son Michael to _____ a scholarship.

IV. Try to paraphrase the following sentences, paying special attention to the underlined parts.

1. ...the Crooked Streets are packed with human experience and reflect in a lively manner all the chances and misfortunes and expectations and domesticity and wonderment of men.

2. Crooked Streets will never tire a man, and each will have its character, and each will have a soul of its own.

3. It is what the builders meant when one comes out from such fissures into the great Place, the parvis of the cathedral, like a sailor from a river into the sea. Not that certain buildings were not made particular for wide approaches and splendid roads, but that these, when they are the rule, sterilize and kill a town.

4. Every such change indicates some snobbery of the time: some little battle

exaggerated to be a great thing; some public fellow or other in Parliament or what not; some fad of the learned or of the important in their day.

_____

5. It is a bad thing, as a general rule, to prophesy good or to make men feel comfortable with the vision of a pleasant future...

_____

_____

V. Discuss with your partner about each of the three statements and write an essay in no less than 260 words about your understanding of one of them.

1. It ought to be enough, surely, to drive the great broad ways which commerce needs and which are the life-channels of a modern city, without destroying all the history and all the humanity in between: the islands of the past.

_____

_____

2. The past reminds us of timeless human truths and allows for the perpetuation of cultural traditions that can be nourishing; it contains examples of mistakes to avoid, preserves the memory of alternatives ways of doing things, and is the basis for self-understanding...

_____

_____

3. Leave men alone in their cities, pester them not with futilities of great governments, nor with the fads of too powerful men, and they will build you Crooked Streets of their very nature as moles throw up the little mounds or bees construct their combs.

_____

_____

VI. List four websites where we can learn more about how to preserve places of historical interest or scenic spots and provide a brief introduction to each of them.

1. _____

_____

_____.

2. _____

_____

_____.

3. _____
_____
_____
_____.

4. _____
_____
_____.

Twenty Minutes' Reading

You are required to read the following two sections within 20 minutes.

Section A

To say that the child learns by imitation and that the way to teach is to set a good example oversimplifies. No child imitates every action he sees. Sometimes, the example the parent wants him to follow is ignored while he takes over contrary patterns from some other example. Therefore we must turn to a more subtle theory than "Monkey see, monkey do".

Look at it from the child's point of view. Here he is in a new situation, lacking a ready response. He is seeking a response which will gain certain ends. If he lacks a ready response for the situation, and cannot reason out what to do, he observes a model who seems able to get the right result. The child looks for an authority or expert who can show what to do.

There is a second element at work in this situation. The child may be able to attain his immediate goal only to find that his method brings criticism from people who observe him. When shouting across the house achieves his immediate end of delivering a message, he is told emphatically that such a racket is unpleasant, that he should walk into the next room and say his say quietly. Thus, the desire to solve any objective situation is overlaid with the desire to solve it properly. One of the early things the child learns is that he gets more affection and approval when his parents like his response. Then other adults reward some actions and criticize others. If one is to maintain the support of others and his own self-respect, he must adopt responses his social group approves.

In finding trial responses, the learner does not choose models at random. He imitates the person who seems a good person to be like, rather than a person whose social status he wishes to avoid. If the pupil wants to be a good violinist, he will observe and try to copy the techniques of capable players; while some other person may most influence his approach to books.

Admiration of one quality often leads us to admire a person as a whole, and he becomes an identifying figure. We use some people as models over a wide range of situations, imitating much that they do. We learn that they are dependable and rewarding models because imitating them leads to success.

1. The statement that children learn by imitation is incomplete because _____.
   A. they only imitate authorities and experts
   B. they are not willing to copy their parents
   C. the process of identification has been ignored
   D. the nature of their imitation as a form of behavior has been neglected
2. For a child the first element in his learning by imitation is _____.
   A. the need to find an authority
   B. the need to find a way to achieve the desired result
   C. the need for more affection from his parents
   D. the desire to meet the standards of his social group
3. Apart from achieving his desired results, a child should also learn to _____.
   A. behave properly
   B. attain his goal as soon as possible
   C. show his affection for his parents
   D. talk quietly
4. Children tend to imitate their models _____.
   A. who do not criticize them
   B. who bring them unexpected rewards
   C. whom they want to be like
   D. whose social status is high
5. "An identifying figure" refers to a person who _____.
   A. who serves as a model for others
   B. who is always successful
   C. who can be depended upon
   D. who has been rewarded for his success

Section B

Frustrated with delays in Sacramento, Bay Area officials said Thursday they planned to take matters into their own hands to regulate the region's growing pile of electronic trash.

A San Jose councilwoman and a San Francisco supervisor said they would propose local initiatives aimed at controlling electronic waste if the California law-making body fails to act on two bills stalled in the Assembly—They are among a growing number of California cities and counties that have expressed the same intention.

Environmentalists and local governments are increasingly concerned about the toxic hazard posed by old electronic devices and the cost of safely recycling those products. An estimated 6 million televisions and computers are stocked in California homes, and an additional 6,000 to 7,000 computers become outdated every day. The machines contain high levels of lead and other hazardous substances, and are already banned from California landfills.

Legislation by Senator Byron Sher would require consumers to pay a recycling fee of up to $30 on every new machine containing a cathode ray tube. Used in almost all video monitors and televisions, those devices contain four to eight pounds of lead each. The fees would go toward setting up recycling programs, providing grants to non-profit agencies that reuse the tubes and rewarding manufacturers that encourage recycling.

A separate bill by Los Angeles-area Senator Gloria Romero would require high-tech manufacturers to develop programs to recycle so-called e-waste.

If passed, the measures would put California at the forefront of national efforts to manage the refuse of the electronic age.

But high-tech groups, including the Silicon Valley Manufacturing Group and the American Electronics Association, oppose the measures, arguing that fees of up to $30 will drive consumers to online, out-of-state retailers.

"What really needs to occur is consumer education. Most consumers are unaware they're not supposed to throw computers in the trash," said Roxanne Gould, vice president of government relations for the electronics association.

"Computer recycling should be a local effort and part of residential waste collection programs," she added.

Recycling electronic waste is a dangerous and specialized matter, and environmentalists maintain the state must support recycling efforts and ensure that the job isn't contracted to unscrupulous junk dealers who send the toxic parts overseas.

"The graveyard of the high-tech revolution is ending up in rural China," said Ted Smith, director of the Silicon Valley Toxics Coalition. His group is pushing for an amendment to Sher's bill that would prevent the export of e-waste.

6. What step were Bay Area officials going to take regarding e-waste disposal?
   A. Exert pressure on manufacturers of electronic devices.
   B. Lay down relevant local regulations themselves.

C. Lobby the lawmakers of the California Assembly.

D. Rally support to pass the stalled bills.

7. The two bills stalled in the California Assembly both concern _____.

A. regulations on dumping hazardous substances into landfills

B. the sale of used electronic devices to foreign countries

C. the funding of local initiatives to reuse electronic trash

D. the reprocessing of the huge amounts of electronic waste in the state

8. Consumers are not supposed to throw used computers in the trash because _____.

A. they contain large amounts of harmful substances

B. this is banned by the California government

C. some parts may be recycled for use elsewhere

D. unscrupulous dealers will retrieve them for profit

9. High-tech groups believe that if an extra $30 is charged on every TV or computer purchased in California, consumers will _____.

A. abandon online shopping

B. buy them from other states

C. strongly protest against such a charge

D. hesitate to upgrade their computers

10. We learn from the passage that much of California's electronic waste has been _____.

A. collected by non-profit agencies

B. dumped into local landfills

C. exported to foreign countries

D. recycled by computer manufacturers

Unit Six Gender

Text A

When Bright Girls Decide That Math Is "a Waste of Time"

By Susan Jacoby

Susannah, a 16-years-old who has always been an A student in every subject from <u>algebra</u> to English, recently informed her parents that she intended to drop physics and calculus in her senior year of high school and replace them with a drama seminar and a work-study program. She expects a major in art or history in college, she explained, and "any more science or math will just be a waste of my time."

Her parents were neither concerned by nor opposed to her decision. "Fine, dear," they said. Their daughter is, after all, an outstanding student. What does it matter if, at age 16, she had taken a step that may limit her understanding of both machines and the natural world for the rest of her life?

This kind of decision, in which girls turn away from studies that would give them a sure footing in the world of science and technology, is a self-inflicted female disability that is, regrettably, almost as common today as it was when I was in high school. If Susannah had announced that she had decided to stop taking English in her senior year, her mother and father would have been horrified. I also think they would have been a good deal less <u>sanguine</u> about her decision if she were a boy.

In saying that scientific and mathematical ignorance is a self-inflicted female wound, I do not, obviously, mean that cultural expectations play no role in the process. But the world does not <u>conspire</u> to

algebra /ˈældʒɪbrə/ *n.* a branch of mathematics in which signs and letters are used to represent numbers and values [数] 代数

sanguine /ˈsæŋgwɪn/ *adj.* cheerfully confident; optimistic

conspire /kənˈspaɪə/ *vt.* to join or act together; combine

deprive modern women of access to science as it did in the 1930s, when Rosalyn S. Yalow, the Nobel Prize-winning physicist, graduated from Hunter College and was advised to go to work as a secretary because no graduate school would admit her to its physics department. The current generation of adolescent girls—and their parents, bred on old expectations about women's interests—are active conspirators in limiting their own intellectual development.

deprive /dɪˈpraɪv/ *vt.* to take something away from
eliminate /ɪˈlɪmɪneɪt/ *vt.* to leave out or omit from consideration; reject
syndrome /ˈsɪndrəʊm/ *n.* a group of symptoms that collectively indicate or characterize a disease, psychological disorder, or other abnormal condition
akin /əˈkɪn/ *adj.* having a similar quality or character; analogous
phobia /ˈfəʊbɪə/ *n.* a strong fear, dislike, or aversion
epitomize /ɪˈpɪtəmaɪz/ *vt.* to make an epitome of; sum up
brainy /ˈbreɪnɪ/ *adj.* intelligent; smart

It is true that the proportion of young women in science-related graduate and professional school, most notably medical schools, has increased significantly in the past decade. It is also true that so few women were studying advanced science and mathematics before the early 1970s that the percentage increase in female enrollment does not yet translate into large numbers of women actually working in science.

The real problem is that so many girls eliminate themselves from any serious possibility of studying science as a result of decisions made during the vulnerable period of midadolescence, when they are most likely to be influenced—on both conscious and subconscious levels—by the traditional belief that math and science are "masculine" subjects.

During the teen-age years the well-documented phenomenon of "math anxiety" strikes girls who never had any problem handling numbers during earlier schooling. Some men, too experience this syndrome—a form of panic, akin to a phobia, at any task involving numbers—but women constitute the overwhelming majority of sufferers. The onset of acute math anxiety during the teen-age years is, as Stalin was fond of saying, "not by accident."

In adolescence girls begin to fear that they will be unattractive to boys if they are typed as "brains." Science and math epitomize unfeminine braininess in a way that, say, foreign languages do not. High-school girls who pursue an advanced interest in science and math (unless they are students at special institutions like the Bronx High School of Science where everyone is a brain) usually find that they are greatly outnumbered by boys in their classes. They are, therefore, intruding on male turf at a time when their sexual confidence, as well as that of the boys, is most fragile.

A 1981 assessment of female achievement in mathematics, based on research conducted under a National Institute for Education Grant, found significant differences in the mathematical achievements of 9th and 12th graders. At age 13 girls were equal to or slightly better than boys in tests involving algebra, problem solving and spatial ability; four years later the boys had outstripped the girls.

It is not mysterious that some very bright high-school girls suddenly decide that math is "too hard" and "a waste of time." In my experience, self-sabotage of mathematical and scientific ability is often a conscious process. I remember deliberately pretending to be puzzled by geometry problems in my sophomore year in high school. A male teacher called me in after class and said, in a baffled tone, "I don't see how you can be having so much trouble when you got straight A's last year in my algebra class."

The decision to avoid advanced biology, chemistry, physics and calculus in high school automatically restricts academic and professional choices that ought to be wide open to anyone beginning college. At all coeducational universities women are overwhelmingly concentrated in the fine arts, social sciences and traditionally female departments like education courses leading to degrees in science-and-technology-related fields are filled mainly by men.

In my generation, the practical consequences of mathematical and scientific illiteracy are visible in the large number of special programs to help professional women overcome the anxiety they feel when they are promoted into jobs that require them to handle statistics.

The consequences of this syndrome should not, however, be viewed in narrowly professional terms. Competence in science and math does not mean one is going to become a scientist or mathematician any more than competence in writing English means one is going to become a professional writer. Scientific and mathematical illiteracy—which has been cited in several recent critiques by panels studying American education from kindergarten through college—produces an incalculably impoverished vision of human experience.

turf /tɜːf/ n. the area claimed by a gang, as of youths, as its personal territory

sabotage /ˈsæbətɑːʒ/ n. destruction of property or obstruction of normal operations, as by civilians or enemy agents in time of war

impoverished /ɪmˈpɒvərɪʃt/ adj. deprived of natural richness or strength; limited

Scientific illiteracy is not, of course, the exclusive province of women. In certain intellectual circles it has become fashionable to proclaim a willed, aggressive ignorance about science and technology. Some female writers specialize in ominous, uninformed diatribes against genetic research as a plot to remove control of childbearing from women, while some well-known men of letters proudly announce that they understand absolutely nothing about computers, for that matter, about electricity. This lack of understanding is nothing in which women or men ought to take pride.

proclaim /prəˈkleɪm/ *vt.* to announce officially and publicly; declare
ominous /ˈɒmɪnəs/ *adj.* of or being an omen, especially an evil one
diatribe /ˈdaɪətraɪb/ *n.* a bitter, abusive denunciation
chromosome /ˈkrəʊməsəʊm/ *n.* a threadlike linear strand of DNA and associated proteins in the nucleus of cells that carries the genes and functions in the transmission of hereditary information [生]染色体
acquiesce /ˌækwɪˈes/ *vi.* to consent or comply passively or without protest
accede /ækˈsiːd/ *vt.* to give one's consent, often at the insistence of another; concede
stereotype /ˈsterɪətaɪp/ *n.* a conventional, formulaic, and oversimplified conception, opinion, or image

Failure to comprehend either computers or chromosomes leads to a terrible sense of helplessness, because the profound impact of science on everyday life is evident even to those who insist they don't, won't, can't understand why the changes are taking place. At this stage of history women are more prone to such feelings of helplessness than men because the culture judges their ignorance less harshly and because women themselves acquiesce in that indulgence.

Since there is ample evidence of such feelings in adolescence, it is up to parents to see that their daughters do not accede to the old stereotypes about "masculine" and "feminine" knowledge. Unless we want our daughters to share our intellectual handicaps, we had better tell them no, they can't stop taking mathematics and science at the ripe old age of 16.

(approximately 1160 words)

Reading Time: _____   Reading Rate: _____

Cultural Notes

1. **Susan Jacoby** has worked as an educator and as a reporter for *The Washington Post*. As a free-lance journalist in the former Soviet Union (from 1969 to 1971), she produced two books about her experiences. Jacoby now contributes to *The Nation and Macall's*; her books include *The Possible She* (1979), a collection of autobiographical essays. In this essay from *The New York Times*, Jacoby examines the reasons why girls are often deficient in math and science.

2. Rosalyn S. Yalow: American medical physicist and joint recipient (with Andrew V. Schally and Roger Guillemin) of the 1977 Nobel Prize for Physiology or Medicine, awarded for her development of the radioimmunoassay (RIA), an extremely sensitive technique for measuring minute quantities of biologically active substances.

Comprehension Exercises

I. Answer the following questions based on the text.

1. Why did Susannah decide to drop physics and calculus in her senior year of high school?
2. What's the author's attitude towards Susannah's decision mentioned above?
3. What's the author's opinion on the approval of Susannah's parents? What suggestion(s) might the author give to them?
4. How did the author drop her math when she was in middle school?
5. What might be the consequences of a girl's dropping math at the age of 16?

II. Decide whether each of the following statements is true or false according to the text.

1. Susannah's parents were indifferent to her decision to substitute drama seminar and a work-study program for physics and calculus for she expected a major in art or history in college.
2. According to Susan Jacoby, girl students are always inclined to focus their attention on subjects that may help them feel secure in the world of science and technology, which is almost as common today as it was.
3. In the view of Susan Jacoby, both adolescent girls and their parents are responsible for hindering their intellectual development due to the fact that they are all brought up in the old expectations about women's interests.
4. Although more and more female students were enrolled in the field of science such as medicine, it didn't indicate that large numbers of women were actually working in science.
5. The author, in the concluding part of the essay, called on readers not to yield to the stereotypes that subjects in adolescent girls' school life are labeled as "masculine" or "masculine" so that teenage girls can develop intellectually by taking mathematics and science at their ripe old age of 16.

III. Select the most appropriate word or phrase and use its proper form to complete each of the following sentences.

aggressive	deprive	conspire	sanguine	ominous
inflict	stereotype	diatribe	proclaim	accede
impoverish	sabotage	vulnerable	eliminate	syndrome
acquiesce	accede	brainy	phobia	epitomize

1. Governments in that region in particular that have dealt with the reality of his _____ behavior and yet have also dealt with the crosswinds that blow across that region, in terms of the political dynamic that they face, make their analysis and judgments based on a number of complicated factors.

2. Her defeat, Kilberg warned, was not merely the rejection of a too-left candidate associated with a failed administration; no, it was an _____ signal that the Virginia Republican Party was in danger of falling under the sway of a dangerous band of fanatics.

3. No State shall make or enforce any law which shall abridge the privileges or immunities of citizens of the United States; nor shall any State _____ any person of life, liberty, or property, without due process of law; nor deny to any person within its jurisdiction the equal protection of the laws.

4. They _____ to defraud the federal government of millions of dollars in income taxes in 1958.

5. Some, like Frank Wilczek of the Institute for Advanced Study in Princeton, are _____ about the chances of solving this problem. They felt confident and optimistic so that they went to Starbuck to enjoy the holiday.

6. Quotas, affirmative action, race norming, civil rights legislation, multicultur-alism in schools and universities, welfare, busing, and unrestricted immigra-tion from Third World countries are all symbols of that attack and of the ra-cial, cultural, and political dispossession they promise to _____ upon the white post-bourgeois middle class.

7. The Prime Minister would have to _____ to any request by the opposition to recall parliament.

8. If someone is _____ as something, people form a fixed general idea or image of them, so that it is assumed that they will behave in a particular way.

9. And came the most dangerous part of this inflammatory _____, capable of the most sinister interpretations, and grist for the mill of those violent racist bodies, which strike against us at the dead of night.

10. With many baby boomers now having families, 28 percent of all U.S. households have children under 18, the growing minority of women putting

family ahead of career has led observers to _____ a renaissance in the old-fashioned family.

11. Nineteenth-and early-twentieth-century political leaders of what were then called liberal views opposed interference in the market for two stern reasons—because intervention would only wreck the economy and _____ ordinary people even more deeply, and because tampering with contracts and property rights was intrinsically wicked.

12. During the last five years have you had heart trouble, high blood pressure, albumin or sugar in your urine, liver disorder, acquired immune deficiency _____, cancer, tumor, uclers, lung disease, mental or nervous disorder?

13. Or you can take a day or two to familiarize yourself with the charts and stock your kitchen with foods that are high in Nutripoints, while you discard those that could _____ your score.

14. Recent reports disturb me greatly and result in my passionate call to all—particularly our readers and supporting constituency—to link together for justice, for fairness, for what is just common-sense decency and effective support of very _____ and needy people.

15. One feature of our assistance to all of the emerging states coming out of totalitarianism and communism has been an effort to push this money to the place where it does the best—at the grass roots, to _____ as much as possible the administrative diversion of funds or to ensure, as best we can, as methodically as we can, that there's any inappropriate diversion of this funding, and we are pretty scrupulous in the way we administer that.

IV. Try to paraphrase the following sentences, paying special attention to the underlined parts.

1. This kind of decision, in which girls turn away from studies that would give them a sure footing in the world of science and technology, is a self-inflicted female disability that is, regrettably, almost as common today as it was when I was in high school.

_____

_____

2. It is also true that so few women were studying advanced science and mathematics before the early 1970s that the percentage increase in female enrollment does not yet translate into large numbers of women actually working in science.

_____

_____

3. Science and math <u>epitomize unfeminine braininess</u> in a way that, say, foreign languages do not.

_____

_____

4. They are, therefore, <u>intruding</u> on male <u>turf</u> at a time when their sexual confidence, as well as that of the boys, is most <u>fragile</u>.

_____

_____

5. Scientific and mathematical <u>illiteracy</u>—which has been cited in several recent <u>critiques</u> by <u>panels</u> studying American education from kindergarten through college—<u>produces an incalculably impoverished vision of human experience</u>.

_____

_____

V. Discuss with your partner about each of the three statements and write an essay in no less than 260 words about your understanding of one of them.

1. Most men are very attached to the idea of being male, and usually experience a lot of fear and insecurity around the idea of being a man. Most women are very identified with their gender, and also experience a tremendous amount of fear and insecurity.

_____

_____

2. The current generation of adolescent girls—and their parents, bred on old expectations about women's interests—are active conspirators in limiting their own intellectual development.

_____

_____

3. In adolescence girls begin to fear that they will be unattractive to boys if they are typed as "brains."

_____

_____

VI. List four websites where we can learn more about how to handle gender(sexual) discrimination or to keep equality between man and woman and provide a brief introduction to each of them.

1. _____

_____

2. _____

_____

3. _____

_____ .

4. _____

_____

Text B

Escaping the Daily Grind for Life
as a House Father

By Rick Greenberg

"You on vacation?" my neighbor asked.

My 15-month-old son and I were passing her yard on our daily hike through the neighborhood. It was a weekday afternoon and I was the only working- age male in sight.

"I'm uh... working out of my house now," I told her.

Thus was born my favorite euphemism for house fatherhood, one of those new lifestyle occupations that is never merely mentioned. Explained, yes. Defended. Even rhapsodized about. I was tongue-tied then, but no longer. People are curious and I've learned to oblige.

I joined up earlier this year when I quit my job—a dead-end, ulcer-producing affair that had dragged on interminably . I left to be with my son until something better came along. And if nothing did, I'd be with him indefinitely.

This was no simple transition. I had never known a house father, never met one. I'd only read about them. They were another news magazine trend. Being a traditionalist, I never dreamed I'd take the plunge.

But as the job got worse, I gave it serious thought. And more thought. And in the end, I still felt ambivalent. This

euphemism /ˈjuːfɪmɪzəm/ *n.* the act or an example of substituting a mild, indirect, or vague term for one considered harsh, blunt, or offensive

rhapsodize /ˈræpsədaɪz/ *vi.* to express oneself in an immoderately enthusiastic manner

ulcer /ˈʌlsə/ *n.* a sore place appearing on the skin inside or outside the body which may bleed or produce poisonous matter [医]溃疡

interminably /ɪnˈtɜːmɪnəbəlɪ/ *adv.* being or seeming to be without an end; endless

ambivalent /æmˈbɪvələnt/ *adj.* having or showing both good and bad feelings about sb/sth

was a radical change that seemed to carry as many drawbacks as benefits. My dislike for work finally pushed me over the edge. That, and the fact that we had enough money to get by.

Escaping the treadmill was a bold stroke. I had shattered my lethargy and stopped whining , and for that I was proud.

Some friends said they were envious. Of course they weren't quitting one job without one waiting—the ultimate in middle-class taboos. That ran through my mind as I triumphantly, and without notice, tossed the letter of resignation on my boss's desk. Then I walked away wobbly-kneed.

treadmill /ˈtredmɪl/ *n.* a monotonous task or set of tasks seeming to have no end
lethargy /ˈleθədʒɪ/ *n.* sluggishness or dullness
whine /waɪn/ *vi.* to complain or protest in a childish fashion
trauma /ˈtrɔːmə/ *n.* a mental condition caused by severe shock, especially when the harmful effects last for a long time
mitigate /ˈmɪtɪgeɪt/ *vt.* to moderate (a quality or condition) in force or intensity; alleviate
therapeutic /ˌθerəˈpjuːtɪk/ *adj.* having or exhibiting healing powers
subside /səbˈsaɪd/ *vi.* to sink to a lower or normal level
obnoxious /əbˈnɒkʃəs/ *adj.* very annoying or objectionable; offensive or odious
heresy /ˈherəsɪ/ *n.* any belief thought to be contrary to official or established theory
gypsy /ˈdʒɪpsi/ *n.* an opinion or a doctrine at variance with established religious beliefs
benchmark /ˈbentʃmɑːk/ *n.* a standard by which something can be measured or judged
proxy /ˈprɒksi/ *n.* a person authorized to act on behalf of someone else

The initial trauma of quitting, however, was mitigated by my eagerness to raise our son. Mine was the classic father's lament: I felt excluded. I had become "the man who got home after dark," that other person besides Mama. It hurt when I couldn't quiet his crying.

I sensed that staying home would be therapeutic. The chronic competitiveness and aggressiveness that had served me well as a daily journalist would subside. Something better would emerge, something less obnoxious. My ulcer would heal. Instead of beating deadlines, I'd be doing something important for a change. This was heresy coming from a newspaper gypsy, but it rang true.

There was unease, too. I'd be adrift, stripped of the home-office-home routine that had defined my existence for more than a decade. No more earning a living. No benchmarks. Time would be seamless. Would Friday afternoons feel the same?

The newness of it was scary.

Until my resignation, my wife and I typified today's baby boomer couples, the want-it-all generation. We had two salaries, a full-time nanny and guilt pangs over practicing parenthood by proxy.

Now, my wife brings home the paychecks, the office problems and thanks for good work on the domestic front. With me at home, her work hours are more flexible. Nanny-less, I change diapers, prepare meals and do all the rest. And I wonder what comes next.

What if I don't find another job? My field is tight. At 34, I'm not getting any more marketable and being out of work doesn't help.

As my father asked incredulously: "Is this going to be what you do?"

Perhaps. I don't know. I wonder myself. It's even more baffling to my father, the veteran of a long and traditional 9-to-5 career. For most of it, my mother stayed home. My father doesn't believe in trends. All he knows is that his only son—with whom he shares so many traits—has violated the natural order of men providing and women raising children. In his view, I've shown weakness and immaturity by succumbing to a bad job.

But he's trying to understand, and I think he will.

I'm trying to understand it myself. House fatherhood has been humbling, rewarding and unnerving.

"It's different," I tell friends. "Different."

Imagine never having to leave home for the office in the morning. That's how different. No dress-up, no commute. Just tumble out of bed and you're there. House fathering is not for claustrophobics.

I find myself enjoying early morning shopping. My son and I arrive right after the supermarket opens. The place is almost empty. For the next hour we glide dreamily, cruising the aisles to a Muzak accompaniment. This is my idyll. My son likes it, too; he's fascinated by the spectacle.

Housekeeping still doesn't seem like work, and that's by design. I've mastered the art of doing just enough chores to get by. This leaves me enough free time. Time to read and write and daydream. Time with my son. Time to think about the structure.

So much time, and so little traditional

succumb /səˈkʌm/ *vi.* to submit to an overpowering force or yield to an overwhelming desire; give up or give in

claustrophobic /ˈklɔːstrəˈfəʊbik/ *n.* persons who suffer from claustrophobia, abnormally afraid of closed-in places 幽闭恐惧症患者

structure, that the days sometimes blur together. I remember on Sunday nights literally dreading the approaching work week, the grind. Today, the close of the weekend still triggers a shiver of apprehension; I now face the prospect of a week without tangible accomplishments, a void.

On our hikes to the playground, I can feel my old identity fading. All around are people with a mission, a sense of purpose. Workers. And then, there's the rest of us—the stroller and backpack contingent. The moms, the nannies, and me. I wonder if I've crossed over a line never to return.

contingent /kənˈtɪndʒənt/ *n.* a group of people at a meeting or an event who have sth in common, especially the place they come from, that is not shared by other people at the event

pamper /ˈpæmpə/ *vt.* to treat with excessive indulgence

errand /ˈerənd/ *n.* a short trip taken to perform a specified task, usually for another

drudgery /ˈdrʌdʒəri/ *adj.* tedious, menial, or unpleasant work

mellow /ˈmeləʊ/ *vt.* to become mature as time passes

mundane /ˈmʌndeɪn/ *adj.* of, relating to, or typical of this world; secular

anathema /əˈnæθɪmə/ *n.* a formal ecclesiastical ban, curse, or excommunication

shtick /ʃtɪk/ *n.* a characteristic attribute, talent, or trait that is helpful in securing recognition or attention

Still, the ulcer seems to be healing. I take pride in laying out a good dinner for the family and in pampering my wife after a tough day at the office. I love reading to my son. Running errands isn't even so bad. A lot of what had been drudgery or trivia is taking on new meaning; maybe I'm mellowing.

Which is ironic. To be a truly committed and effective at-home parent, there must be this chance—a softening, a contentment with small pleasures, the outwardly mundane. This is a time of reduced demands and lowered expectations. Progress is gradual, often agonizingly so. Patience is essential. Ambition and competitiveness are anathema. Yet eliminating these last two qualities—losing the edge—could ruin my chances of resurrecting my career. I can't have it both ways.

The conflict has yet to be resolved. And it won't be unless I make a firm commitment and choose one lifestyle over the other. I'm not yet ready for that decision.

In the meantime, a wonderful change is taking place in our home. Amid all the uncertainties, my son and I have gotten to know each other. He can't put a phrase together, but he confides in me. It can be nothing more than a grin or a devilish look. He tries new words on me, new shtick. We roll around a lot; we crack each other up. I'm no longer the third wheel, the man who gets home after dark. Now, I'm as much a part of his life as his mother is. I, too, can stop his crying. So far, that has made the experiment worthwhile.

(approximately 1200 words)

Reading Time: ＿＿＿＿＿＿＿　　　　　　Reading Rate: ＿＿＿＿＿＿＿

Cultural Notes

1. **baby boomer:** a North American-English term used to describe a person who was born between 1946 and 1964. Following World War II, these countries experienced an unusual spike in birth rates, a phenomenon commonly known as the baby boom. The term is iconic and more properly capitalized as *Baby Boomers*. The terms "baby boomer" and "baby boom" along with others (e.g., "goomies" or "goomers") are also used in countries with demographics that did not mirror the sustained growth in American families over the same interval.

2. **Muzak:** a registered trademark of Muzak LLC. The word "Muzak" has, in popular usage, broken free from its corporate parent and become a catchall generic term (often pejoratively applied) for easy listening, Middle of the road, or elevator music—or, indeed, for any type of banal, derivative, or repetitive music, usually as instrumentals without lyrics.

Comprehension Exercises

I. Answer the following questions based on the text.

1. Why did the author quit his job as a daily journalist and become a housefather?
2. What are the reactions of his family members to his change of life role?
3. How did he feel at first to be a housefather?
4. What changes have taken place after he began his fatherhood?
5. What was the most important in his fatherhood, according to the author himself?

II. Decide whether each of the following statements is true or false according to the text.

1. According to Rick Greenberg, "I", in the essay, was determined to be a "full-time father" partially because his job was demanding, exhausting and ulcer-producing.
2. After experiencing endless house chores, boredom and sluggishness in

housekeeping, "I" came to be proud of his "hours at home".

3. Before "I" decided to resign, "I" thought over this point—to quit one job means to another one coming—a point that was popular among middle-classes.

4. In the beginning of my fatherhood, my trauma was lessened because I was eager to take good care of my son although "I" was no more a typical one of the working middle-class men.

5. In the view of the author, a compromise must be made because this is a time of reduced demands and lowered expectations, a time when progress is gradual and patience is essential, a time when one has to resolve the conflict between ambition, competitiveness and idealism.

III. Select the most appropriate word or phrase and use its proper form to complete each of the following sentences.

euphemism	interminable	transition	plunge	rhapsodize
ambivalent	lethargy	whine	trauma	treadmill
mitigate	subside	obnoxious	contingent	therapeutic
heresy	benchmark	proxy	succumbing	errand

1. We total out bank account, grateful for "overdraft protection," a _____ that allows us to spend more than we save, and sometimes more than we earn.

2. If you _____ about someone or something, you express great delight or enthusiasm about them.

3. He was exhausted by their _____ arguments—some calm, some whipped into the slashing words of anguished souls—while they tried to resolve the predicament that had suddenly appeared six months ago.

4. To guide students through this _____ and bring sophomores into closer contact with faculty mentors, we've developed some special programs.

5. Helen decided to take the _____ and turned professional in 1991, joining the Women's Professional European Tour the same year. She won the hearts of the galleries as she finished in 6th place at the Weetabix Women's British Open. It came as no great surprise to the golfing world when Helen was voted Rookie of the Year 1991.

6. If one partner has become more assertive, for example, the therapist might wonder how the other, who has been _____ about this change, would like to respond, and encourage a response.

7. On other occasions I have smoked simply in order to relax—to get off the sometimes fearful _____ of being an international celebrity, trying to forget for a moment the pressures which were on me all the time.

8. Get your body moving to boost energy, stay supple and shake off winter _____.

9. If I had to give some good general advice for widows, it would be this: Don't _____; don't complain; don't let anyone but your very closest friends know how unhappy you are (and even with them, don't dwell on it often); and don't think of yourself as a poor, unlucky person who has suffered the greatest tragedy in the world.

10. The doctor found that Mr. Timpson had developed the problems because of his new job, running the corruption investigation codenamed Operation Lancet and domestic difficulties that resulted in "emotional _____ affecting his judgment and work".

11. But developments elsewhere in the economy, not least deflation in the high street, should help to _____ the impact of earnings growth on inflation.

12. Follow our landlubber's guide to water therapy at home, using a combination of tap water, sea salt and products which capture the _____ effects of minerals and marine extracts.

13. At dusk, when the humidity increases and the temperature cools, the brightness of the fire dims, and the flames _____ to a flicker.

14. With a(n) _____ personality totally incongruous with his musical genius, Mozart died neglected and impoverished while the mediocre Salieri lived in a blaze of fame and praise.

15. All property sales should be _____ on a title examination conducted by the purchaser's attorney or title company showing that the seller owns the property, has clear title, and that all unwanted liens and claims have been eliminated by closing.

IV. Try to paraphrase the following sentences, paying special attention to the underlined parts.

1. That ran through my mind as I triumphantly, and without notice, tossed the letter of resignation on my boss's desk. Then I walked away wobbly-kneed.

_____

2. House fatherhood has been humbling, rewarding and unnerving.

_____

3. To be a truly committed and effective at-home parent, there must be this chance—a softening, a contentment with small pleasures, the outwardly mundane. This is a time of reduced demands and lowered expectations.

Progress is gradual, often <u>agonizingly</u> so. <u>Patience is essential. Ambition and competitiveness are anathema.</u>

___

4. The conflict has yet to be <u>resolved</u>. And it won't be unless I make a firm <u>commitment</u> and choose one lifestyle over the other. I'm not yet ready for that decision.

___

V. Discuss with your partner about each of the three statements and write an essay in no less than 260 words about your understanding of one of them.

1. Henry James once defined life as that predicament which precedes death, and certainly nobody owes you a debt of honor or gratitude for getting him into that predicament. But a child does owe his father a debt, if Dad, having gotten him into this peck of trouble, takes off his coat and buckles down to the job of showing his son how best to crash through it.

___

2. But as the job got worse, I gave it serious thought. And more thought. And in the end, I still felt ambivalent. This was a radical change that seemed to carry as many drawbacks as benefits. My dislike for work finally pushed me over the edge.

___

3. I sensed that staying home would be therapeutic. The chronic competitiveness and aggressiveness that had served me well as a daily journalist would subside. Something better would emerge, something less obnoxious.

___

VI. List four websites where we can learn more about how to be a qualified fater or mother in modern time and provide a brief introduction to each of them.

1. ___

___

___

2. _____
   _____
   _____ .

3. _____
   _____
   _____ .

4. _____
   _____
   _____ .

Twenty Minutes' Reading

You are required to read the following two sections within 20 minutes.

Section A

When imaginative men turn their eyes towards space and wonder whether life exist in any part of it, they may cheer themselves by remembering that life need not resemble closely the life that exists on Earth. Mars looks like the only planet where life like ours could exist, and even this is doubtful. But there may be other kinds of life based on other kinds of chemistry, and they may multiply on Venus or Jupiter. At least we cannot prove at present that they do not.

Even more interesting is the possibility that life on their planets may be in a more advanced stage of evolution. Present-day man is in a peculiar and probably temporary stage. His individual units retain a strong sense of personality. They are, in fact, still capable under favorable circumstances of leading individual lives. But man's societies are already sufficiently developed to have enormously more power and effectiveness than the individuals have.

It is not likely that this transitional situation will continue very long on the evolutionary time scale. Fifty thousand years from now man's societies may have become so close-knit that the individuals retain no sense of separate personality. Then little distinction will remain between the organic parts of the multiple organism and the inorganic parts (machines) that have been constructed by it. A million years further on man and his machines may have merged as closely as the muscles of the human body and the nerve cells that set them in motion.

The explorers of space should be prepared for some such situation. If they arrive on a foreign planet that has reached an advanced stage (and this is by no means impossible), they may find it being inhabited by a single large organism composed of many closely cooperating units.

The units may be "secondary" — machines created millions of years ago by a previous form of life and given the will and ability to survive and reproduce. They may be built entirely of metals and other durable materials. If this is the case, they may be much more tolerant of their environment, multiplying under conditions that would destroy immediately any organism made of carbon compounds and dependent on the familiar carbon cycle.

Such creatures might be relics(遗物) of a past age, many millions of years ago, when their planet was favorable to the origin of life, or they might be immigrants from a favored planet.

1. What does the word "cheer" imply?
   A. Imaginative men are sure of success in finding life on other planets.
   B. Imaginative men are delighted to find life on other planets.
   C. Imaginative men are happy to find a different kind of life existing on other planets.
   D. Imaginative men can be pleased with the idea that there might exist different forms of life on other planets.

2. Humans on Earth today are characterized by _____.
   A. their existence as free and separate beings
   B. their capability of living under favorable conditions
   C. their great power and effectiveness
   D. their strong desire for living in a close-knit society

3. According to this passage, some people believe that eventually _____.
   A. human societies will be much more cooperative
   B. man will live in a highly organized world
   C. machines will replace man
   D. living beings will disappear from Earth

4. Even most imaginative people have to admit that _____.
   A. human societies are as advanced as those on some other planets
   B. planets other than Earth are not suitable for life like ours to stay
   C. it is difficult to distinguish between organic parts and inorganic parts of the human body
   D. organism are more creative than machines

5. It seems that the writer _____.
   A. is interested in the imaginary life forms
   B. is eager to find a different form of life

C. is certain of the existence of a new life form

D. is critical of the imaginative people

Section B

Throughout the nation's more than 15,000 school districts, widely differing approaches to teaching science and math have emerged. Though there can be strength in diversity, a new international analysis suggests that this variability has instead contributed to lackluster achievement scores by U.S. children relative to their peers in other developed countries.

Indeed, concludes William H. Schmidt of Michigan State University, who led the new analysis, "no single intellectually coherent vision dominates U.S. educational practice in math or science." The reason, he said, "is because the system is deeply and fundamentally flawed."

The new analysis, released this week by the National Science Foundation in Arlington, Va., is based on data collected from about 50 nations as part of the Third International Mathematics and Science Study.

Not only do approaches to teaching science and math vary among individual U.S. communities, the report finds, but there appears to be little strategic focus within a school district's curricula, its textbooks, or its teachers' activities. This contrasts sharply with the coordinated national programs of most other countries.

On average, U.S. students study more topics within science and math than their international counterparts do. This creates an educational environment that "is a mile wide and an inch deep," Schmidt notes.

For instance, eighth graders in the United States cover about 33 topics in math versus just 19 in Japan. Among science courses, the international gap is even wider. U.S. curricula for this age level resemble those of a small group of countries including Australia, Thailand, Iceland, and Bulgaria. Schmidt asks whether the United States wants to be classed with these nations, whose educational systems "share our pattern of splintered visions" but which are not economic leaders.

The new report "couldn't come at a better time," says Gerald Wheeler, executive director of the National Science Teachers Association in Arlington. "The new National Science Education Standards provide that focused vision," including the call "to do less, but in greater depth."

Implementing the new science standards and their math counterparts will be the challenge, he and Schmidt agree, because the decentralized responsibility for education in the United States requires that any reforms be tailored and instituted one community at a time.

   In fact, Schmidt argues, reforms such as these proposed national standards "face an almost impossible task, because even though they are intellectually coherent, each becomes only one more voice in the babble."

   6. According to the passage, the teaching of science and math in America is _____.
      A. focused on tapping students' potential
      B. characterized by its diversity
      C. losing its vitality gradually
      D. going downhill in recent years
   7. The fundamental flaw of American school education is that _____.
      A. it lacks a coordinated national program
      B. it sets a very low academic standard for students
      C. it relies heavily on the initiative of individual teachers
      D. it attaches too much importance to intensive study of school subjects
   8. By saying that the U.S. educational environment is "a mile wide and an inch deep", the author means U.S. educational practice _____.
      A. lays stress on quality at the expense of quantity
      B. offers an environment for comprehensive education
      C. encourages learning both in depth and in scope
      D. scratches the surface of a wide range of topics
   9. The new National Science Education Standards are good news in that they will _____.
      A. provide depth to school science education
      B. solve most of the problems in school teaching
      C. be able to meet the demands of the community
      D. quickly dominate U.S. educational practice
   10. Putting the new science and math standards into practice will prove difficult because _____.
      A. there is always controversy in educational circles
      B. not enough educators have realized the necessity for doing so
      C. school districts are responsible for making their own decisions
      D. many schoolteachers challenge the acceptability of these standards

Unit Seven   Education

A Matter of Degrees
By Clive Crook

It is unusual nowadays to venture more than five minutes into any debate about the American economy—about widening income inequality, say, or threats to the country's global competitiveness, or the squeeze on the middle class—without somebody invoking the great economic cure-all: education. We must improve it. For a moment, partisan passions subside and everybody nods.

But only for a moment. How, exactly, do we improve education? Where does the problem reside—in elementary schools, high schools, or colleges? Is the answer to recruit better teachers, or to get more students moving from high school to university? Should we spend more public money? Change the way schools are organized and paid for (supporting charter schools and vouchers, perhaps)? In no time, correctly orthogonal positions are laid down, and the quarreling resumes. But nobody challenges the importance of the issue. The centrality of education as a driver of the nation's economic prospects appears beyond dispute.

Yet the connections between education and economics are not as they seem. To rest the case for improving schools and colleges largely on economic grounds is a mistake. It distorts education policy in unproductive ways. And though getting education right surely matters, more is at stake than a slight increase in economic growth.

venture /ˈventʃə/ *vi.* to proceed somewhere despite the risk of possible dangers
invoke /ɪnˈvəʊk/ *vt.* to bring about; to resort to
partisan /pɑːtɪˈzæn/ *adj.* devoted to or biased in support of a party, group, or cause
subside /səbˈsaɪd/ *vi.* to become less loud, excited, or violent; to wear off or die down
reside /rɪˈzaɪd/ *vi.* to be inherent in; exist
recruit /rɪˈkruːt/ *vt.* to supply with new members or employees
orthogonal /ɔːˈθɒɡənl/ *adj.* having a set of mutually perpendicular axes; meeting at right angles
prospect /ˈprɒspekt/ *n. (pl.)* chances or opportunities for future success
distort /dɪsˈtɔːt/ *vt.* to twist out of shape; deform
at stake if something that you value very much is at stake, you will lose it if a plan or action is not successful

Everybody understands that, as a rule of thumb, more school means a bigger paycheck. On average, having a college degree, rather than just a high-school degree, increases your earnings by about two-thirds. A problem arises, however, if you try to gross up these gains across the whole population. If an extra year of education equipped students with skills that increased their productivity, then giving everybody another year of school or college would indeed raise everybody's income. But take the extreme case, and suppose that the extra year brought no gain in productive skills. Suppose it merely sorted people, signaling "higher ability" to a would-be employer. Then giving an extra year of school to everybody would raise nobody's income, because nobody's position in the ordering would change. The private benefit of more education would remain, but the social benefit would be zero.

rule of thumb a useful principle having wide application but not intended to be strictly accurate or reliable in every situation

gross up (*rare*) add up the entire amount of income before any deductions are made

premium /'prɪmɪəm/ *a. n.* a sum of money or bonus paid in addition to a regular price, salary, or other amount **b.** *adj.* of superior quality or value

scale up to increase the amount or size of something

impart /ɪm'pɑːt/ *vt.* to grant a share of; to give (a specified quality)

presumably /prɪ'zjuːməbli/ *adv.* used to say that you think something is probably true

feudal /'fjuːdl/ *adj.* of or relating to or characteristic of feudalism

aggregate /'æɡrɪɡɪt/ *vt.* to gather into a mass, sum, or whole

tot up to add (numbers) together

matriculation /mətrɪkjuˈleɪʃən/ *n.* admission to a group (especially a college or university)

Would sending everybody to Harvard raise everybody's future income by the full amount of the "Harvard premium"? Yes, if the value of a degree from Harvard resided in the premium skills you acquired there (and if the college's classrooms could be scaled up a little). Well, ask any Harvard graduate about the teaching. The value of a degree from Harvard lies mainly in the sorting that happens during the application process. So the answer is no: if everybody went to Harvard, the Harvard premium would collapse.

In the case of an extra year of education, it need not be all or nothing; another year of study usually does impart *some* productivity-enhancing skill. But how much? A year of extra training in computer programming presumably has a direct material value. An extra year spent learning medieval history might improve a student's intellectual self-discipline and ability to think analytically, but has lower material utility: nobody studies feudal land grants for the boost to lifetime earnings. So aggregated figures such as the proportion of high-school graduates going on to college—a number that is constantly cited and compared internationally—tell you very little.

Totting up college matriculations as a way of measuring national success is doubly ill-conceived if the signaling function flips over, so that a college education becomes the norm, and college nonattendance is taken to mean "unfit for most jobs."

In 2004, 67 percent of American high-school graduates went straight on to college, compared with just under half in 1972. This is widely applauded. It looks like progress—but is it really? Failing to go to college did not always mark people out as rejects, unfit for any kind of well-paid employment. But now, increasingly, it does. In a cruel paradox, this may be one reason why parental incomes better predict children's incomes in the United States than they used to—in other words, one reason why America is becoming less meritocratic. A college degree has become an expensive passport to good employment, one for which drive and ability less often can substitute, yet one that looks unaffordable to many poor families.

Many occupations are suffering from chronic entry-requirement inflation. Hotels, for instance, used to appoint junior managers from among the more able, energetic, and presentable people on their support or service staff, and give them on-the-job training. Today, according to the Bureau of Labor Statistics, around 800 community and junior colleges offer two-year associate degrees in hotel management. In hotel chains, the norm now is to require a four-year bachelor's or master's degree in the discipline.

For countless other jobs that once required little or no formal academic training—preschool teacher, medical technician, dental hygienist, physical-therapy assistant, police officer, paralegal, librarian, auditor, surveyor, software engineer, financial manager, sales manager, and on and on—employers now look for a degree. In some of these instances, in some jurisdictions, the law requires one. All of these occupations are, or soon will be, closed to nongraduates. At the very least, some of the public and private investment in additional education needs to be questioned.

flip over turn upside down

paradox /ˈpærədɒks/ n. (logic) a statement that contradicts itself

meritocratic /merɪˈtɔːkrætɪk/ adj. based on demonstrated ability (merit) and talent rather than by wealth, family connections, class privilege, popularity or other historical determinants of social position and political power

presentable /prɪˈzentəbəl/ adj. that can be given, displayed, or offered; fit for introduction to others; acceptable

hygienist /ˈhaɪdʒiːnɪst/ n. a medical specialist in hygiene (practices that serve to promote or preserve health)

physical-therapy n. the treatment of physical disease

paralegal /pærəˈliːgəl/ n. a person with specialized training who assists lawyers

auditor /ˈɔːdɪtə/ n. a qualified accountant who inspects the accounting records and practices of a business or other organization

surveyor /səˈveɪə/ n. someone who conducts a statistical survey

jurisdiction /dʒʊərɪsˈdɪkʃən/ n. (law) the territory within which power can be exercised; authority in general

To be sure, today's IT-driven world is creating a genuine need for some kinds of better-educated workers. It is the shortage of such people, according to most politicians and many economists, that is causing the well-documented rise in income inequality. Both to spur the economy and to lessen inequality, they argue, the supply of college graduates needs to keep rising.

It seems plausible, but this theory too is often overstated, and does not fit the facts particularly well. The college wage premium rose rapidly for many years, up to the late 1990s. Since then it has flattened off, just when the pace of innovation would have led you to expect a further acceleration. An even more awkward fact is that especially in the past decade or so, rising inequality has been driven by huge income increases at the very top of the distribution. In the wide middle, where differences in educational attainment ought to count, changes in relative earnings have been far more subdued. During the 1990s, CEO salaries roughly doubled in inflation-adjusted terms. But median pay actually went up more slowly than pay at the bottom of the earnings distribution, and even pay at the 90th percentile (highly educated workers, mostly, but not CEOs) increased only a little faster than median wages. Today, shortages of narrowly defined skills *are* apparent in specific industries or parts of industries—but simply pushing more students through any kind of college seems a poorly judged response.

The country will continue to need cadres of highly trained specialists in an array of technical fields. In many cases, of course, the best place to learn the necessary skills will be a university. For many and perhaps most of us, however, university education is not mainly for acquiring directly marketable skills that raise the nation's productivity. It is for securing a higher ranking in the labor market, and for cultural and intellectual enrichment. Summed across society, the first of those purposes cancels out. The second does not. That is why enlightenment, not productivity, is the chief social justification for four years at college.

Shoving ever more people from high school to college is not only of dubious

spur /spɜː/ *vt.* to stimulate

plausible /ˈplɔːzəbəl/ *adj.* seemingly or apparently reasonable or true

acceleration /ækˌseləˈreɪʃən/ *n.* an increase in rate of change or speed

attainment /əˈteɪnmənt/ *n.* an achievement or the act of achieving something

median /ˈmiːdiən/ *adj.* relating to, located in, or extending toward the middle

an array of a group of people or things, especially one that is large or impressive

cancel out *(usu.)* wipe out the effect of something, but here it means "to say that an event that was planned will not happen"

enlightenment /ɪnˈlaɪtnmənt/ *n.* education that results in understanding and the spread of knowledge

shove /ʃʌv/ *vt.* to push forward or along; to push rudely or roughly

dubious /ˈdjuːbiəs/ *adj.* arousing doubt; doubtful; of doubtful quality or worth

economic value, it is unlikely to serve the cause of intellectual enrichment if the new students are reluctant or <u>disinclined</u>. Yet there are still large prizes to be had through educational reform—certainly in enlightenment and perhaps in productivity. They simply <u>lurk</u> farther down the educational ladder.

disinclined /dɪsɪnˈklaɪnd/ *adj.* unwilling because of mild dislike or disapproval
lurk /lɜːk/ *vi.* to lie in wait; to exist unobserved or unsuspected
preeminently /prɪˈemɪnəntli/ *adv.* with superiority or distinction above others
numeracy /ˈnjuːmərəsɪ/ *n.* skill with numbers and mathematics
consolation /kɒnsəˈleɪʃən/ *n.* the comfort you feel when someone or something makes you feel better in times of disappointment
address /əˈdres/ *vt.* to deal with
assorted /əˈsɔːtɪd/ *adj.* consisting of a number of different kinds
stagnation /stægˈneɪʃən/ *n.* a state of inactivity (in business or art, etc.)
terrain /ˈtereɪn/ *n.* an area of land; ground; region
consensus /kənˈsensəs/ *n.* general or widespread agreement
blind itself to to blind sb to: make someone lose their good sense or judgment and be unable to see the truth about something

The most valuable attribute for young people now entering the workforce is adaptability. This generation must equip itself to change jobs readily, and the ability to retrain, whether on the job or away from the job, will be crucial. The necessary intellectual assets are acquired long before college, or not at all. Aside from self-discipline and the capacity to concentrate, they are <u>preeminently</u> the core-curriculum skills of literacy and <u>numeracy</u>.

Illiteracy has always cut people off from the possibility of a prosperous life, from the <u>consolations</u> of culture, and from full civic engagement. In the future, as horizons broaden for everybody else, people lacking these most basic skills will seem even more imprisoned. The most recent National Assessment of Adult Literacy found that 30 million adult Americans have less than basic literacy (meaning, for instance, that they find it difficult to read mail, or address an envelope). Three out of ten seniors in public high schools still fail to reach the basic-literacy standard. Progress on literacy would bring great material benefits, of course, for the people concerned and some benefits for the wider economy—but those benefits are not the main reason to make confronting illiteracy the country's highest educational priority.

In <u>addressing</u> the nation's <u>assorted</u> economic anxieties—over rising inequality, the <u>stagnation</u> of middle-class incomes, and the fading American dream of economic opportunity—education is not the longed-for cure-all. Nor is anything else. The debate about these issues will have to range all across the more bitterly disputed <u>terrains</u> of public policy—taxes, public spending, health care, and more. It is a pity, but in the end a <u>consensus</u> that <u>blinds itself to</u> the complexity of the issues is no use to anyone.

(approximately 1550 words)

Reading Time:_____   Reading Rate: _____

Cultural Notes

1. **Clive Crook** is a senior editor of *The Atlantic Monthly,* a columnist for *National Journal* and a commentator for the *Financial Times*. He was formerly on the staff of *The Economist*, latterly (from 1993 to 2005) as deputy editor. A graduate of Oxford and the London School of Economics, he has served as a consultant to the World Bank and worked as an official in the British Treasury.

2. **charter schools:** publicly funded elementary or secondary schools in the United States that have been freed from some of the rules, regulations, and statutes that apply to other public schools in exchange for some type of accountability for producing certain results, which are set forth in each school's charter. Their founders are often teachers, parents, or activists who feel restricted by traditional public schools. They are attended by choice. State-run charter schools (schools not affiliated with local school districts) are often established by non-profit groups, universities, and some government entities.

3. **vouchers:** a school voucher also called an education voucher, a certificate by which parents are given the ability to pay for the education of their children at a school of their choice, rather than the public school to which they were assigned.

4. **junior colleges:** a junior college is a two-year post-secondary school whose main purpose is to provide academic, vocational and professional education. The highest certificate offered by such schools is usually an associate's degree, although many junior college students continue their education at a university or college, transferring some or all of the credit earned at the junior college toward the degree requirements of the four-year school.

5. **associate degrees:** an associate degree is an academic degree awarded by community colleges, junior colleges, business colleges and some bachelors degree-granting colleges/ universities upon completion of a course of study usually lasting two years.

Comprehension Exercises

I. Answer the following questions based on the text.

1. What's the public consensus about education in the US?
2. In what case an extra year of education will be worthwhile according to the author?
3. What does a college degree mean nowadays in the US?
4. Why does keeping the supply of college graduates rising not necessarily lessen income inequality according to the author?
5. What is the chief social justification for the four-year college education, productivity or enlightenment?
6. What are the valuable attributes and intellectual assets this generation of young people should equip themselves with?

II. Decide whether each of the following statements is true or false according to the text.

1. The role of education in pushing forward the nation's economy is undisputed.
2. Higher degree means more salary.
3. Failing to go to college does increasingly mean unfit for any kind of well-paid employment.
4. The supply of college graduates should keep rising to spur the economy and to less inequality.
5. As a rule of thumb, university education is not necessarily for acquiring directly marketable skills that raise the nation's productivity.

III. Select the most appropriate word or phrase and use its proper form to complete each of the following sentences.

premium	aggregate	dubious	preeminent	invoke
subside	attainment	median	presentable	blind
plausible	spur	address	consolation	paradox
shove	disinclined	assort		

1. The judge _____ an international law that protects refugees.
2. I promise once you start eating a whole food plant-based diet that your cravings for junk will almost completely _____.
3. I also have to wonder about what Yahoo gets out of the deal — other than a _____ for its depressed stock.

4. Different economies, with different currencies, should not be _____ to produce uniform policies.

5. "He is _____ and charismatic although he still has a distance to go from Apple's Steve Jobs," said an analyst who covers the company.

6. There is a _____ theory of what it might be, and a reasonable chance of testing that theory to see if it is right.

7. The administration may put more emphasis on _____ economic growth.

8. Improving graduation rates would help the country reach President Barack Obama's goal of once again making the U.S. the leader in college _____ by 2020.

9. Trends in arithmetical average incomes and _____ household incomes have differed in the US for a variety of reasons.

10. I _____ forward one more time and, incredibly, the slab comes loose, and I tumble forward over it, caught in my own momentum.

11. The current porn panic is just like all sex panics before it: championed by the white, bourgeoisie, Christian reformers and shrouded in _____ "science" claims.

12. Any way you look at it, Brian Eno is one of the _____ producers and thinkers of our time.

13. If patients are _____ to take a tablet they consider bitter or sour or because they simply do not like the color, then a change of aesthetics might be needed.

14. This kind of community participation following the state-owned enterprises, involving multi-stakeholders, leads to many difficulties to _____ with.

15. The method is based on "the friendship _____" — the counterintuitive idea is that your friends have more friends than you do.

IV. Try to paraphrase the following sentences, paying special attention to the underlined parts.

1. And though getting education right surely matters, more is at stake than a slight increase in economic growth.

2. A college degree has become an expensive passport to good employment, one for which drive and ability less often can substitute, yet one that looks unaffordable to many poor families.

3. In the wide middle, where differences in educational attainment out to count, changes in relative earnings have been far more subdued.

_____

4. Illiteracy has always cut people off from the possibility of a prosperous life, form the consolations of culture, and from full civic engagement.

_____

5. It is a pity, but in the end a consensus that blinds itself to the complexity of the issues is no use to anyone.

_____

_____

V. Discuss with your partner about each of the three statements and write an essay in no less than 260 words about your understanding of one of them.

1. Many occupations are suffering from chronic entry-requirement inflation.

_____

2. For many and perhaps most of us, however, university education is not mainly for acquiring directly marketable skills that raise the nation's productivity. It is for securing a higher ranking in the labor market, and for cultural and intellectual enrichment.

_____

3. The most valuable attribute for young people now entering the workforce is adaptability.

_____

_____

VI. List four websites where we can learn more about Clive Crook or American university education and provide a brief introduction to each of them.

1. _____

_____

_____.

2. _____

_____

_____.

3. _____
_____
_____.

4. _____
_____
_____.

Text B

How to Build a Student for the 21st Century

By Claudia Wallis and *Sonja Steptoe*

There's a dark little joke exchanged by educators with a dissident streak: Rip Van Winkle awakens in the 21st century after a hundred-year snooze and is, of course, utterly bewildered by what he sees. Men and women dash about, talking to small metal devices pinned to their ears. Young people sit at home on sofas, moving miniature athletes around on electronic screens. Older folk defy death and disability with metronomes in their chests and with hips made of metal and plastic. Airports, hospitals, shopping malls—every place Rip goes just baffles him. But when he finally walks into a schoolroom, the old man knows exactly where he is. "This is a school," he declares. "We used to have these back in 1906. Only now the blackboards are green."

American schools aren't exactly frozen in time, but considering the pace of change in other areas of life, our public schools tend to feel like throwbacks. Kids spend much of the day as their great-grandparents once did: sitting in rows, listening to teachers lecture, scribbling notes by hand, reading from text-books that are out of date by the time they are printed. A yawning chasm (with an emphasis on yawning) separates the world inside the schoolhouse from the world outside.

dissident/'dɪsɪdənt/ *adj.* characterized by departure from accepted beliefs or standards
streak/striːk/ *n.* a quality or characteristic
defy/dɪ'faɪ/ *vt.* to refuse to submit to or cooperate with; to resist openly and boldly
metronome/'metrənəʊm/ *n.* an instrument (esp. for marking time in music) that produces regular ticking sounds for a variety of rhythmic settings
baffle/'bæfəl/ *vt.* to frustrate (a person) as by confusing or perplexing
throwback/'θrəʊbæk/ *n.* a person or thing that is like something that existed or was common long ago
chasm/'kæzəm/ *n.* a wide difference in interests or feelings; a sudden interruption of continuity; a gap

For the past five years, the national conversation on education has focused on reading scores, math tests and closing the "achievement gap" between social classes. This is not a story about that conversation. This is a story about the big public conversation the nation is *not* having about education, the one that will ultimately determine not merely whether some fraction of our children get "left behind" but also whether an entire generation of kids will fail to make the grade in the global economy because they can't think their way through abstract problems, work in teams, distinguish good information from bad or speak a language other than English.

This week the conversation will burst onto the front page, when the New Commission on the Skills of the American Workforce, a high-powered, bipartisan assembly of Education Secretaries and business, government and other education leaders releases a blueprint for rethinking American education from pre-K to 12 and beyond to better prepare students to thrive in the global economy. While that report includes some controversial proposals, there is nonetheless a remarkable consensus among educators and business and policy leaders on one key conclusion: we need to bring what we teach and how we teach into the 21st century.

Right now we're aiming too low. Competency in reading and math—the focus of so much No Child Left Behind (NCLB) testing—is the meager minimum. Scientific and technical skills are, likewise, utterly necessary but insufficient. Today's economy demands not only a high-level competence in the traditional academic disciplines but also what might be called 21st century skills. Here's what they are:

Knowing more about the world. Kids are global citizens now and they must learn to act that way. Mike Eskew, CEO of UPS, talks about needing workers who are "global trade literate, sensitive to foreign cultures, conversant in different languages" —not exactly strong points in the US, where fewer than half of high school students are enrolled in a foreign-language class and where the social-studies curriculum tends to fixate on US history.

Quick! How many ways can you

high-powered *adj.* important, successful, or influential

bipartisan /ˌbaɪpɑːtɪˈzæn/ *adj.* consisting of or supported by two political parties

pre-K *n.* pre-kindergarten; early childhood settings focusing their goal on skill building, which could involve academic training or solely socializing activities

competency /ˈkɒmpɪt(ə)nsɪ/ *n.* the quality of being adequately or well qualified physically and intellectually

meager /ˈmiːgə/ *adj.* not enough in amount or quantity; insufficient

discipline /ˈdɪsɪplɪn/ *n.* a particular area of academic study

literate /ˈlɪtərɪt/ *adj.* knowledgeable or educated in a particular field or fields

conversant /kənˈvɜːsənt/ *adj.* familiar, as by study or experience

fixate /ˈfɪkseɪt/ *vi.* become fixed (on); to focus the eyes or attention

combine <u>nickels</u>, dimes and pennies to get 20c? That's the challenge for students in a second-grade math class at Seattle's John Stanford International School and hands are flying up with answers. The students sit at tables of four <u>manipulating</u> play money. One boy shouts "10 plus 10"; a girl offers "10 plus 5 plus 5," only it sounds like this: "*Ju, tasu, go, tasu, go*."

This public elementary school has taken the idea of global education and run with it. All students take same classes in either Japanese or Spanish. Other subjects are taught in English, but the content has an international flavor. Before opening the school seven years ago, principal Karen Kodama surveyed 1,500 business leaders on which languages to teach (plans for Mandarin were dropped for the lack of classroom space) and which skills and disciplines. "No. 1 was technology," she recalls. Even first-graders at Stanford begin to use PowerPoint and Internet tools. "Exposure to world cultures was also an important trait cited by the executives," says Kodama, so that instead of circling back to the <u>Pilgrims</u> and Indians every autumn, children at Stanford do social-studies units on Asia, Africa, Australia, Mexico and South America. Students actively apply the lessons in foreign language and culture by <u>video- conferencing</u> with sister schools in Japan, Africa and Mexico, by exchanging messages, gifts and joining in charity projects.

Dozens of US school districts have found ways to <u>orient</u> some of their students toward the global economy. Schools that offer the international <u>baccalaureate</u> (I.B.) program are growing in the US—from about 350 in 2000 to 682 today. The US Department of Education has a pilot effort to bring the program to more low-income students.

Thinking outside the box. Kids need to learn how to leap across disciplines because that is how breakthroughs now come about. It's <u>interdisciplinary</u> combinations—design and technology, mathematics and art—"that produce <u>YouTube</u> and Google" says Thomas Friedman, the best-selling author of *The World Is Flat.*

Depth over breadth (Teaching focuses on the most powerful and generative ideas instead of <u>galloping</u>

nickel /ˈnɪkəl/ *n.* a US or Canadian coin worth five cents
manipulate /məˈnɪpjʊleɪt/ *vt.* to move, arrange, operate, or control by the hands or by mechanical means, especially in a skillful manner
Ju, tasu, go, tasu, go in Japanese "10 plus 5 plus 5"
video-conferencing *n.* a system that enables people in different parts of the world to have a meeting by watching and listening to each other using video screens
orient /ˈɔːrient/ *v.* to direct sb/sth towards sth; to make or adapt sb/sth for a particular purpose
baccalaureate /bækəˈlɔːrɪet/ *n.* an academic degree given to someone who has successfully completed undergraduate studies; bachelor's degree
interdisciplinary /ˌɪntə(ː)ˈdɪsɪplɪnəri/ *adj.* involving more than one branch of learning
gallop /ˈgæləp/ *vi.* to move or progress swiftly

through a mind-numbing stream of topics and subtopics) and the ability to leap across disciplines are exactly what teachers aim for at the Henry Ford Academy, a public charter school in Dearborn, Mich. This fall, 10th-graders in Charles Dershimer's science class began a project that combines concepts from earth science, chemistry, business and design. After reading about Nike's efforts to develop a more environmentally friendly sneaker, students had to choose a consumer product, analyze and explain its environmental impact and then develop a analyze and explain its environmental impact and then develop a plan for reengineering it to reduce pollution costs without sacrificing its commercial appeal. Says Dershimer: "It's a challenge for them and for me."

sneaker /'sni:kə/ n. sports shoe usually made of canvas and having a soft rubber sole

media-drenched adj. a compound coined by the author, meaning abundantly covered or supplied with media

pilot /'paɪlət/ adj. serving as a test or trial or a tentative model for future experiment or development

EQ n. intelligence regarding the emotions, especially in the ability to monitor one's own or others' emotions and to interact effectively with others

into (in) line with if something changes in line with something else, it changes in the same way and at the same rate as it

Becoming smarter about new sources of information. In this media-drenched era of Blogs and Podcasts, Google searches and instant messages, young people need to acquire a new set of literacy skills that allows them to locate information, sort through it quickly and, most important, determine which sources are reliable and which ones aren't.

A pilot study of the test conducted by the Educational Testing Service last year, with 6,200 high school seniors and college freshmen found that only half could correctly judge the objectivity of a website. "Kids tend to go to Google and cut and paste a research report together," says Terry Egan, who led the team that developed the new test. "We kind of assumed this generation was so comfortable with technology that they know how to use it for research and deeper thinking," says Egan. "But if they're not taught these skills, they don't necessarily pick them up."

Developing good people skills. EQ, or emotional intelligence, is as important as IQ for success in today's workplace. "Most innovations today involve large teams of people," says former Lockheed Martin CEO Norman Augustine. "We have to emphasize communication skills, the ability to work in teams and with people from different cultures."

Feeling increasing pressure to bring their methods—along with the curriculum—into line with the way the modern world works, teachers will put

17 greater emphasis on teaching kids to collaborate and solve problems in small groups and apply what they've learned in the real world. Besides, research shows that kids learn better that way than with the old chalk-and-talk approach.

collaborate /kəˈlæbəreɪt/ *vi.* to work together, especially in a joint intellectual effort

calculus /ˈkælkjʊləs/ *n.* the branch of mathematics that deals with limits and the differentiation and integration of functions of one or more variables 微积分

cacophony /kəˈkɒfəni/ *n.* a harsh, loud unpleasant mixture of sounds

punctual /ˈpʌŋktjʊəl/ *adj.* acting or arriving exactly at the time appointed; prompt

superintendent /ˌsuːpərɪnˈtendənt/ *n.* a person who directs and manages an organization or office

deportment /dɪˈpɔːtmənt/ *n.* a manner of personal conduct; behavior

At suburban Farmington High in Michigan, the engineering-technology department functions like an engineering firm, with teachers as project managers, a Ford Motor Co. engineer as a consultant and students working in teams. The principles of calculus , physics, chemistry and engineering are taught through activities that fill the hallways with a cacophony of nailing, sawing and chattering. The result: the kids learn to apply academic principles to the real world, think strategically and solve problems.

Such lessons also teach students to show respect for others as well as to be punctual , responsible and work well in teams. Those skills were badly missing in recently hired high school graduates, according to a survey of over 400 human-resource professionals conducted by the Partnership for 21st Century Skills. "Kids don't know how to shake your hand at graduation," says Rudolph Crew, superintendent of the Miami-Dade school system. Deportment , he notes, used to be on the report card. Some of the nation's more forward-thinking schools are bringing it back. It's one part of 21st century education that sleepy old Rip would recognize.

Reading Time:_____   Reading Rate: _____

Cultural Notes

1. **Claudia Wallis** is editor-at-large at *TIME*. She has been both a writer and editor specializing in stories about health and science, women's and children's issues, education and lifestyle. She was the founding editor of *TIME for Kids*, which debuted in September of 1995 and now has a circulation of over 4 million. She is also responsible for editing *TIME*'s bonus "Connections" section for women subscribers, as well as a broad range of other projects.

And Sonja Steptoe is a national correspondent for CNN/*Sports Illustrated*. As a national correspondent, she focuses on investigative and long-term assignments, as well as provides coverage of major news stories.

2. **Rip Van Winkle:** "Rip Van Winkle" is a short story by the American author Washington Irving published in 1819. The story is set in the years before and after the American Revolutionary War. Rip Van Winkle, a villager of Dutch descent, lives in a nice village at the foot of New York's Catskill Mountains. An amiable man whose home and farm suffer from his lazy neglect, he is loved by all but his wife. One autumn day he escapes his nagging wife by wandering up the mountains. After encountering strangely dressed men, rumored to be the ghosts of Henry Hudson's crew, who are playing nine-pins, and after drinking some of their liquor, he settles down under a shady tree and falls asleep. He wakes up twenty years later and returns to his village. He finds out that his wife is dead and his close friends have died in a war or gone somewhere else. He immediately gets into trouble when he hails himself a loyal subject of King George III, not knowing that in the meantime the American Revolution has taken place. An old local recognizes him, however, and Rip's now grown daughter eventually puts him up. As Rip resumes his habit of idleness in the village, and his tale is solemnly believed by the old Dutch settlers, certain hen-pecked husbands especially wish they shared Rip's luck.

3. **achievement gap:** refering to the observed disparity on a number of educational measures between the performance of groups of students, especially groups defined by gender, race/ethnicity, ability, and socioeconomic status. The achievement gap can be observed on a variety of measures, including standardized test scores, grade point average, dropout rates, and college enrollment and completion rates. While most of the data presented in this article comes from the United States, similar or different gaps exist for these, and other groups in other nations.

4. **The No Child Left Behind Act of 2001:** often abbreviated in print as **NCLB**, is a controversial United States federal law (Act of Congress) that reauthorized a number of federal programs aiming to improve the performance of US primary and secondary schools by increasing the standards of accountability for states, school districts, and schools, as well as providing parents with more flexibility in choosing which schools their children will attend. Additionally, it promoted an increased focus on reading and re-authorized the Elementary and Secondary Education Act of 1965 (ESEA). The Act requires states to develop assessments in basic skills to be

given to all students in certain grades, if those states are to receive federal funding for schools. The effectiveness and desirability of NCLB's measures are hotly debated. A primary criticism asserts that NCLB could reduce effective instruction and student learning because it may cause states to lower achievement goals and motivate teachers to "teach to the test." A primary supportive claim asserts that systematic testing provides data that sheds light on which schools are not teaching basic skills effectively, so that interventions can be made to reduce the achievement gap for disadvantaged and disabled students.

5. **Pilgrims:** originally, the first British immigrants, who fled England, from religious persecution. They went to the "New World" by the ship Mayflower, and were known as the "Pilgrims".

6. **YouTube:** a video sharing where users can upload, view and share video clips.

7. **Podcast:** a series of digital-media files which are distributed over the Internet using syndication feeds for playback on portable media players and computers. The term *podcast,* like *broadcast,* can refer either to the series of content itself or to the method by which it is syndicated; the latter is also called **podcasting.** The host or author of a podcast is often called a **podcaster**. The term is a combination of the words "iPod" and "broadcast", the Apple iPod being the brand of portable media player for which the first podcasting scripts were developed. These scripts allowed podcasts to be automatically transferred to a mobile device after they are downloaded.

Comprehension Exercises

I. Answer the following questions based on the text.

1. At present, what are the issues educators generally focus on in the United States?
2. What skills are required by the global economy?
3. Why is it important to know more about the world, according to the author?
4. Why is it important to leap across disciplines?
5. Why is it important to develop good people skills?

II. Decide whether each of the following statements is true or false according to the text.

1. Educators and business and policy leaders have reached a consensus on what

and how to be taught in the 21st century.

2. Many American high school students are unwilling to learn a foreign-language rather than US history.

3. Some public elementary schools tend to be globalized in education.

4. The US Department of Education has tried bringing the international bacca-laureate program to more low-income students.

5. Present high school students have higher EQ than what old sleepy Rip thought.

III. Select the most appropriate word or phrase and use its proper form to complete each of the following sentences.

dissident	competency	gallop	meager	streak
literate	fixate	chasm	orient	defy
baffle	conversant	manipulate	high-powered	interdisciplinary
build	pilot	punctual		

1. Will we stand for the human rights of the _____ in Burma, the blogger in Iran, or the voter in Zimbabwe?

2. Many "sea turtles" have their own theories about why Chinese overseas might show a hostile _____.

3. We have this instinctual response to people who _____ social conventions in a way that threatens the group.

4. It used to _____ me why the media loved to do a hatchet job on single women, until I sensed something fishy going on.

5. So how do you "cross the _____" with an experimental technology like Node?

6. It seems the answer is yes, but success depends on the _____ and confidence of the individuals involved.

7. His _____ wage is not enough to support their five children.

8. So, one of the things that you can do is to become technically _____ so you can become part of the discussion and help formulate sensible policy.

9. You can _____ your background jobs from the command line using these labels.

10. Carbon capture and storage is not yet used in any major industrial operations, but three _____ projects are trying it out in Algeria, Canada and the North Sea.

11. The people _____ a new theatre to commemorate the birth of Cao Yu.

12. Population control is not just an innovation from the _____, however; it also has an impressive pedigree among the sages of the West.

13. The roper then flips the rope over the right side of the steer, while turning his _____ horse to the left.

14. Have you ever noticed that when you are in love, you seem instinctively affectionate, _____, admiring and willing to make love?

15. He piqued himself on being _____.

IV. Try to paraphrase the following sentences, paying special attention to the underlined parts.

1. Older folk defy death and disability <u>with metronomes in their chests</u> and <u>with hips made of metal and plastic</u>.

   _____

   _____

2. For the past five years, the national conversion on education has focused on reading scores, math tests and <u>closing the "achievement gap"</u> between social classes.

   _____

   _____

3. Scientific and technical skills are, <u>likewise</u>, utterly necessary but insufficient.

   _____

   _____

4. Mike Eskew, CEO of UPS, talks about needing workers who are "<u>global trade literate</u>, sensitive to foreign cultures, conversant in different languages"—not exactly strong points in the US, where fewer than half of high school student are enrolled in a foreign-language class...

   _____

   _____

5. Depth over breadth and the ability to <u>leap across disciplines</u> are exactly what teachers aim for at the Henry Ford Academy, a public charter school in Dearborn, Mich.

   _____

   _____

V. Discuss with your partner about each of the three statements and write an essay in no less than 260 words about your understanding of one of them.

1. Kids need to learn how to leap across disciplines because that is how breakthroughs now come about.

   _____

   _____

2. A pilot study of the test conducted by the Educational Testing Service last year, with 6,200 high school seniors and college freshmen found that only half could correctly judge the objectivity of a website.

_____

_____

3. EQ, or emotional intelligence, is as important as IQ for success in today's workplace.

_____

_____

VI. List four websites where we can learn more about Claudia Wallis or Rip Van Winkle and provide a brief introduction to each of them.

1. _____

_____

_____.

2. _____

_____

_____.

3. _____

_____

_____.

4. _____

_____

_____.

Twenty Minutes' Reading

You are required to read the following two sections within 20 minutes.

Section A

New vocational qualifications to provide an alternative to GCSE and transform school life for 14-to 16-year-olds are expected to be announced on Thursday by the Government.

Ministers have decided to run a pilot next year in 90 of 4,000 secondary schools. Courses for under-16s could be available in all schools by 1997. Vocational courses for over-16s have proved extremely popular, and hundreds of schools are thought to have volunteered for next year's pilot. The General National Vocational Qualification courses are not designed as training for a particular job. They are class-room-based, so a pupil taking, for instance, manufacturing, might do work experience in a local factory but would not have to make anything. Last week Sir Ron Dearing, chairman of the Schools Curriculum and Assessment Authority, said 40 per cent of the timetable for 14-to 16-year-olds would be freed so that some pupils could pursue vocational courses, while others do the more academic GCSEs. All will continue to do GCSEs in English, math and science, and short courses in modern languages and technology.

Critics say the arrangements will divide pupils into sheep and goats, and could lead to the creation of specialist academic and vocational schools. Supporters say the new courses will motivate non-academic pupils so that fewer leave school without qualifications. The new courses in health and social care, business and manufacturing are being introduced despite fierce criticism of present vocational qualifications for over-16s in reports from school inspectors and academics. The inspectors said the course content was too vague and that assessments, done mainly by teachers, were unreliable. However, the GNVQs will be modelled closely on those for over-16s, which have six units. Pupils will study three of the six, and will also have to reach agreed standards in three "core skills" of literacy, numeracy and information technology, which will account for 40 per cent of the marks.

David Blunkett, Labour's education spokesman, said it was vital that the new qualifications were seen as high-quality.

Don Foster, the Liberal Democrats' education spokesman, said: "There must be some concern that the recent criticism of the new GNVQs appears not to have been taken on board. It is vital that they are got right first time, given the crucial role they will play in achieving parity of esteem between academic and vocational qualifications."

  1. According to the passage, the vocational qualifications _____.
     A. constitute part of the GCSEs
     B. serve as a supplement to GCSEs
     C. are mainly for over-16s
     D. are designed as training for a particular job
  2. The phrase "to run a pilot" (Para. 2) can best be paraphrased as which of the following?
     A. To set up a vocational school.
     B. To continue a training course.
     C. To operate an experimental course.
     D. To begin a driving class.

3. The critic's view that "the arrangements will divide pupils into sheep and goats" means that pupils _____.

    A. will be fairly separated and treated

    B. will be grouped based on their vocational abilities.

    C. will be placed either in more academic or non academic groups

    D. will be treated either cruelly or indiscrimitively

4. The last two paragraphs of the passage _____.

    A. summarize the main idea of the article

    B. convey the general plan for vocational qualifications

    C. show the opposition against vocational qualifications

    D. introduce responses from other parties

5. Which of the following can NOT be found in the passage?

    A. Courses for vocational qualifications will be modelled on those for over -16s.

    B. Vocational courses will not be offered in most schools before 1997.

    C. Courses in health and social care, business and manufacturing meet fierce criticisms from school inspectors.

    D. Courses in English, math and science are required of all the pupils.

Section B

An invisible border divides those arguing for computers in the classroom on the behalf of students' career prospects and those arguing for computers in the classroom for broader reasons of radical educational reform. Very few writers on the subject have explored this distinction — indeed, contradiction — which goes to the heart of what is wrong with the campaign to put computers in the classroom.

An education that aims at getting a student a certain kind of job is a technical education, justified for reasons radically different from why education is universally required by law. It is not simply to raise everyone's job prospects that all children are legally required to attend school into their teens. Rather, we have a certain conception of the American citizen, a character who is incomplete if he cannot competently assess how his livelihood and happiness are affected by things outside of himself. But this was not always the case; before it was legally required for all children to attend school until a certain age, it was widely accepted that some were just not equipped by nature to pursue this kind of education. With optimism characteristic of all industrialized countries, we came to accept that everyone is fit to be educated. Computer-education advocates forsake this optimistic notion for a pessimism that betrays their otherwise cheery outlook. Banking on the confusion between educational and vocational reasons for bringing computers into schools, computer advocates often emphasize the job prospects of graduates over their educational achievement.

There are some good arguments for a technical education given the right kind of student. Many European schools introduce the concept of professional training early on in order to make sure children are properly equipped for the professions they want to join. It is, however, presumptuous to insist that there will only be so many jobs for so many scientists, so many businessmen, so many businessman, so many accountants. Besides, this is unlikely to produce the needed number of every kind of professional in a country as large as ours and where the economy is spread over so many states and involves so many international corporations.

But, for a small group of students, professional training might be the way to go since well-developed skills, all other factors being equal, can be the difference between having a job and not. Of course, the basics of using any computer these days are very simple. It does not take a lifelong acquaintance to pick up various software programs. If one wanted to become a computer engineer, that is, of course, an entirely different story. Basic computer skills take — at the very longest — a couple of months to learn. In any case, basic computer skills are only complementary to the host of real skills that are necessary to becoming any kind of professional. It should be observed, of course, that no school, vocational or not, is helped by a confusion over its purpose.

6. The author thinks the present rush to put computers in the classroom is _____.
   A. far-reaching   B. dubiously oriented
   C. self-contradictory   D. radically reformatory
7. The belief that education is indispensable to all children _____.
   A. is indicative of a pessimism in disguise
   B. came into being along with the arrival of computers
   C. is deeply rooted in the minds of computer-ed advocates
   D. originated from the optimistic attitude of industrialized countries
8. It could be inferred from the passage that in the author's country the European model of professional training is _____.
   A. dependent upon the starting age of candidates
   B. worth trying in various social sections
   C. of little practical value
   D. attractive to every kind of professional
9. According to the author, basic computer skills should be _____.
   A. included as an auxiliary course in school
   B. highlighted in acquisition of professional qualifications

C. mastered through a life-long course

D. equally emphasized by any school, vocational or otherwise

10. Which of the following statements is NOT true according to the passage?

A. Someone thought computers in the classroom would make students better career prospects.

B. Someone thought computers in the classroom was for radical educational reform.

C. Many people knew the differences of between the above statements A and B.

D. Few people made distinction between the above statements A and B.

Unit Eight
Emotional Life

Friendship: The Laws of Attraction

By Karen Karbo

Years ago researchers conducted a study in which they followed the friendships in a single two-story apartment building. People tended to be friends with the neighbors on their respective floors, although those on the ground floor near the mailboxes and the stairway had friends on both floors. Friendship was least likely between someone on the first floor and someone on the second. As the study suggests, friends are often those who cross paths with regularity; our friends tend to be coworkers, classmates, and people we run into at the gym.

It's no surprise that bonds form between those who interact. Yet the process is more complex: Why do we wind up chatting with one person in our yoga class and not another? The answer might seem self-evident—our friend-in-the-making likes to garden, as do we, or shares our passion for NASCAR or Tex-Mex cooking. She laughs at our jokes, and we laugh at hers. In short, we have things in common.

But there's more: Self-disclosure characterizes the moment when a pair leaves the realm of buddyhood for the rarefied zone of true friendship. "Can I talk to you for a minute?" may well be the very words you say to someone who is about to become a friend.

"The transition from acquaintanceship to

interact /ɪntərˈækt/ *vi.* act with each other
self-evident /ˈselfˈevɪdənt/ *adj.* evident without proof or argument
disclosure /dɪsˈkləʊʒə/ *n.* both the conscious and unconscious act of revealing more about ourselves to others
rarefied /ˈreərɪfaɪd/ *adj.* belonging to or reserved for a small, select group
transition /trænˈzɪʃən/ *n.* conversion: an event that results in a transformation

friendship is typically characterized by an increase in both the breadth and depth of self-disclosure," asserts University of Winnipeg sociologist Beverley Fehr, author of *Friendship Processes*. "In the early stages of friendship, this tends to be a gradual, reciprocal process. One person takes the risk of disclosing personal information and then 'tests' whether the other reciprocates."

breadth /bredθ/ *n.* width or broadness

reciprocal /rɪˈsɪprək ə l/ *adj.* concerning each of two or more persons or things

reciprocate /rɪˈsɪprəkeɪt/ *vi.* to make a return for something given or done

reciprocity /rɪsɪˈprɒsɪti/ *n.* a relation of mutual dependence on action or influence

infamously /ˈɪnfəməslɪ/ *adv.* having an exceedingly bad reputation; notoriously

camaraderie /kæːməˈrɑːdəri/ *n.* comradeship

publicist /ˈpʌblɪsɪst/ *n.* one who publicizes, especially a press or publicity agent

in lieu of in place of; instead of

divulge /daɪˈvʌldʒ/ *vt.* to make known (something private or secret)

peter out to diminish slowly and come to an end

tip over to change into

intimacy /ˈɪntɪməsɪ/ *n.* the condition of being intimate

hefty /ˈhefti/ *adj.* (*informal*) of considerable size or amount

thick and thin good and bad times

Reciprocity is key. Years ago, fresh out of film school, I landed my first job, at a literary agency. I became what I thought was friends with another assistant, who worked, as I did, for an infamously bad-tempered agent. We ate lunch together almost every day. Our camaraderie was fierce, like that of soldiers during wartime. Then she found a new job working for a publicist down the street. We still met for lunch once a week. In lieu of complaining about our bosses, I told her about my concerns that I wasn't ready to move in with my boyfriend. She listened politely, but she never divulged anything personal about her own life. Eventually our lunches petered out to once a month, before she drifted out of my life for good. I was eager to tell her my problems, but she wasn't eager to tell me hers. The necessary reciprocity was missing, so our acquaintanceship never tipped over into friendship.

Once a friendship is established through self-disclosure and reciprocity, the glue that binds is intimacy. According to Fehr's research, people in successful same-sex friendships seem to possess a well-developed, intuitive understanding of the give and take of intimacy. "Those who know what to say in response to another person's self- disclosure are more likely to develop satisfying friendships," she says. Hefty helpings of emotional expressiveness and unconditional support are ingredients here, followed by acceptance, loyalty, and trust. Our friends are there for us through thick and thin, but rarely cross the line: A friend with too many opinions about our wardrobe, our partner, or our taste in movies and art may not be a friend for long.

When someone embodies the rules—instinctually—their friendships are abundant indeed. Kathy is one of my oldest friends; we were roommates in graduate school and have been through cross-country moves, divorces, deaths, and births together. Her ability to be a friend shines during a lousy breakup. She knows when to listen and make sympathetic sounds, when to act good and outraged at your ex's bad behavior, when to give you a hug, and when to tell you to stop obsessing and enjoy a glass of wine. She knows when to offer you her couch. It's this responsiveness that accounts for her having more friends than anyone I know— certainly more than the five our mothers told us we were lucky to be able to count on one hand over the course of a lifetime.

Compared to these emotional gifts, a friend's utility paled, Fehr found in her study. Study participants judged as peripheral the ability of a friend to offer practical help in the form of, say, lending 20 bucks or allowing use of a car. This fact often turns up as a truism in movies, where the obnoxious, lonely rich kid can't understand why always picking up the tab never makes him popular. Money really can't buy love.

If anything, it's giving and not receiving that makes us value a friend more. It was the American statesman and inventor Benjamin Franklin who first observed the paradox, now called the Benjamin Franklin Effect: "He that has once done you a kindness will be more ready to do you another than he whom you yourself have obliged." In a nutshell, while material favors don't even come close to the emotional talents of our friends, we still want to validate our personal judgment by investing special qualities in those we select to help.

In one classic study, participants won "contest money" from a researcher. Later the researcher approached some of them and explained he'd actually used his own money and had little left; could he have the money back? Most agreed. Later, the researchers found, those asked to do the favor rated the researcher more favorably than those not approached. Psychologists concur that the phenomenon stems from a desire to reconcile feeling and action, and to view our instincts and investments as correct: "Why am I going out of my way to help this guy? Well, he must be pretty

abundant /əˈbʌndən/ *adj.* plentiful
lousy /ˈlaʊzi/ *adj.* very painful or unpleasant
obsess /əbˈses/ *vt.* to have the mind excessively preoccupied with a single emotion or topic
couch /kaʊtʃ/ *n.* a long comfortable seat for two or more people to sit on
utility /juːˈtɪlɪti/ *n.* the quality or condition of being useful; usefulness
peripheral /pəˈrɪfərəl/ *adj.* of minor relevance or importance
truism /ˈtruːɪzəm/ *n.* a self-evident truth
obnoxious /əbˈnɒkʃəs/ *adj.* very annoying or objectionable
pick up the tab pay the bill for others
in a nutshell in a few words; concisely
concur /kənˈkɜː/ *vt.* agree
stem /stem/ *vi.* to have or take origin or descent

nice." The fondness we feel toward our yoga class buddy will continue to grow if one day she asks for a ride home and we go out of our way to give it to her.

confide /kənˈfaɪd/ *vt.* to disclose private matters

in the doghouse in great disfavor or trouble

banishment /ˈbænɪʃmənt/ *n.* exile as a form of punishment

trump /trʌmp/ *vt.* to get the better of (an adversary or a competitor, for example) by using a key, often hidden resource

revealing /rɪˈviːlɪŋ/ *adj.* disclosing information that one did not know

fraternity /frəˈtɜːnɪti/ *n.* a group of people joined by similar backgrounds, occupations, interests, or tastes

If closeness forms the basis of friendship, it stands to reason that your best friend would be someone with whom you enjoy supersized intimacy. If I confide that money is tight or my boyfriend's in the doghouse I might detail the money worries or give a blow-by-blow of the dramathon that led to the boyfriend's banishment. We have with our best friends a "beyond-the-call-of-duty" expectation. If we suffer an emergency—real or imagined—and need to talk, we expect our best friend to drop everything and race to our side.

But according to social psychologists Carolyn Weisz and Lisa F. Wood at the University of Puget Sound, in Tacoma, Washington, there's another component to best friendship that may trump even intimacy: social-identity support, the way in which a friend understands, and then supports, our sense of self in society or the group. If we view ourselves as a mother first and a belly dancer only on Saturday mornings at the local dance studio, our best friend is likely to be another mom because she supports our primary social-identity (as opposed to our personal identity as, say, someone who loves film noir or comes from the Bronx). Our social-identity might relate to our religion, our ethnic group, our social role, or even membership in a special club.

Weisz and Wood showed the importance of social identity support by following a group of college students from freshman through senior year. Over that period, the students were asked to describe levels of closeness, contact, general supportiveness, and social identity support with same-sex friends.

The results were revealing. Overall closeness, contact, and supportiveness predicted whether a good friendship was maintained. But when the researchers controlled for these qualities, only a single factor—social-identity support—predicted whether a friend would ultimately be elevated to the position of "best." Best friends often were part of the same crowd—the same fraternity, say, or tennis team. But Weisz and Wood found that friends offering such support could also be outside the group. Sometimes all a friend needed to do to keep the best friendship going was to affirm the other person's identity as a member of the given group ("You're a real Christian") or even the status of the group itself ("It's so cool that you play sax for the Stanford band!"). Reasons for the finding, say the researchers, may range from greater levels of intimacy and understanding to assistance with pragmatic needs to enhanced self-esteem.

affirm /əˈfɜːm/ *vt.* confirm
pragmatic /præɡˈmætɪk/ *adj.* practical
self-esteem /ˈselfɪsˈtiːm/ *n.* self-respect
derive /dɪˈraɪv/ *vt.* to obtain or receive from a source
quarterback /ˈkwɔːtəbæk/ *n.* the backfield player whose position is behind the line of scrimmage and who usually calls the signals for the plays [橄榄球] 四分卫
substance abuse excessive use of drugs
sync /sɪŋk/ *n.* harmony; accord
court /kɔːt/ *vt.* to behave so as to invite or incur
corollary /kəˈrɒləri/ *n.* a natural consequence or effect; a result
impetus /ˈɪmpɪtəs/ *n.* an impelling force; an impulse

We become best friends with people who boost our self-esteem by affirming our identities as members of certain groups, and it's the same for both genders. Men who derive their most cherished identity through their role as high school quarterback, for instance, are most likely to call a former fellow teammate "best friend."

Our desire for identity support is so strong, Weisz found, that it may even make a difference for the addicted. In another study, she found people with substance abuse problems were likelier to kick their habits after three months when they had felt more conflict between drug use and their social roles and sense of self. Those who felt socially in sync with the drug use were less likely to become substance-free. Indeed, our s o c i a l identities are so important to us that we're willing to court disaster to preserve them. We stick with people who support our social identity and withdraw from those who don't. We may even switch friends when the original ones don't support our current view of ourselves.

Most of us would prefer to think that we love our friends because of who they are, not because of the ways in which they support who we are. It sounds vaguely narcissistic, and yet the studies bear it out.

A corollary for many people is the impetus to change best friends when life throws us a curveball or alters us in basic ways. There's no better example than former members of breast cancer support groups whose diseases have been cured. Though the women no longer have breast cancer and have continued with family and careers, their social identity as survivors often remains so powerful that their primary bonds of friendship are with other survivors, the only people who can understand what they've been through and grasp their perspective on life. After such major life events as marriage, parenthood, and divorce, we may easily switch up our best friend as well.

(approximately 1750 words)

Reading Time: _____   Reading Rate: _____

Cultural Notes

1. **Karen Karbo** is an American author. She is the author of three adult novels: *Trespassers Welcome Here, The Diamond Lane,* and *Motherhood Made a Man out of Me,* all of which were named *New York Times* Notable Books. She is also the author of *How to Hepburn*: *Lessons on Living from Kate the Great* and three books in the Minerva Clark mystery series for children: *Minerva Clark Gets A Clue* (2005), *Minerva Clark Goes to the Dogs* (2006), and *Minerva Clark Gives Up the Ghost* (2007). Karbo was also awarded the 2004 Sarah Winnemucca Award for Creative Nonfiction for *The Stuff of Life*.

2. **NASCAR:** The National Association for Stock Car Auto Racing (NASCAR) is the largest sanctioning body of stock cars (racing cars with the basic chassis of commercially available cars) in the United States. The three largest racing series sanctioned by NASCAR are the Sprint Cup, the Nationwide Series and the Craftsman Truck Series. It also oversees NASCAR Local Racing, the Whelen Modified Tour, and the Whelen All-American Series. NASCAR sanctions over 1,500 races at over 100 tracks in 39 states, Canada, and Mexico.

3. **Tex-Mex:** a term for a type of American food which is used primarily in Texas and the Southwestern United States to describe a regional cuisine which blends food products available in the United States and the kitchen creations of Mexican-Americans that are influenced by the cuisines of Mexico. A given Tex-Mex food may or may not be similar to Mexican cuisine, although it is common for all of these foods to be referred to as "Mexican food" in Texas, the United States and in some other countries. In many parts of the country outside of Texas this term is synonymous with Southwestern cuisine. Tex-Mex cooking is characterized by its heavy use of melted cheese, meat (particularly beef), beans, and spices, in addition to Mexican-style tortillas (maize or flour), fried or baked. A common feature of Tex-Mex is the combination plate, with several of the above on one large platter.

4. **literary agency:** an agency that represents writers and their written works to publishers, theatrical producers and film producers and assists in the sale

and deal negotiation of the same. Literary agents most often represent novelists, screenwriters and major non-fiction writers. They are paid a fixed percentage (ten to twenty percent; fifteen percent is usual) of the proceeds of sales they negotiate on behalf of their clients.

5. **Benjamin Franklin** (January 17, 1706—April 17, 1790): one of the Founding Fathers of the United States of America. A noted polymath, Franklin was a leading author and printer, satirist, political theorist, politician, scientist, inventor, civic activist, statesman and diplomat. As a scientist he was a major figure in the Enlightenment and the history of physics for his discoveries and theories regarding electricity. He invented the lightning rod, bifocals, the Franklin stove, a carriage odometer, and a musical instrument. He formed both the first public lending library in America and first fire department in Pennsylvania.

6. **film noir:** a cinematic term used primarily to describe stylish Hollywood crime dramas, particularly those that emphasize moral ambiguity and sexual motivation. Hollywood's classic film noir period is generally regarded as stretching from the early 1940s to the late 1950s. Film noir of this era is associated with a low-key black-and-white visual style that has roots in German Expressionist cinematography, while many of the prototypical stories and much of the attitude of classic noir derive from the hardboiled school of crime fiction that emerged in the United States during the Depression.

7. **the Bronx:** New York City's northernmost borough (district), located northeast of Manhattan, the only one of the city's five boroughs situated primarily on the United States mainland (the others are on islands). It has one of the highest percentages of Puerto Ricans and Dominicans in the U.S. with 24.0% and 20.0%, respectively. Based on sample data from the 2000 census, the U.S. Census Bureau estimates that 47.29% of the population five and older speak only English at home. 43.67% speak Spanish at home, either exclusively or along with English.

8. **curveball:** a breaking pitch in baseball thrown with a grip and hand movement that imparts down spin to the ball. A fastball typically has backspin, giving it relatively stable aerodynamic characteristics in flight. The spin of a curveball moves in the opposite direction. This spin causes a curveball to "break", or drop down and sweep horizontally as it approaches home plate, thus frustrating the batter.

Comprehension Exercises

I. Answer the following questions based on the text.

1. What typically characterizes the transition from acquaintanceship to friendship?

2. As suggested by the author, there are four ingredients that help to build up durable friendship, what are they? What are their respective functions?

3. What is Benjamin Franklin Effect?

4. What does friendship mean to most people? What is the most significant meaning of friendship according to the author?

5. What is our real incentive to friend-making in the author's opinion?

6. What is, for most people, the impetus to change best friends in life?

II. Decide whether each of the following statements is true or false according to the text.

1. People tend to make friends with the neighbors of the same floor according to a research.

2. Self-disclosure is more important than common interests in making friends.

3. More opinions friends give to each other, more intimate they are, and the friendship will last longer.

4. Asking for a small help from a friend may consolidate the friendship.

5. Men become best friends with those who boost their self-esteem by affirming their identities as members of certain groups.

6. Most of us would prefer to think that we love our friends because of who they are, not because of the ways in which they support who we are.

III. Select the most appropriate word or phrase and use its proper form to complete each of the following sentences.

reciprocal	infamous	breadth	abundant	peripheral
divulge	interact	obnoxious	confide	transition
reveal	trump	pick up the tab	sync	impetus
corollary	self-esteem	in the doghouse		

1. While the other children _____ and played together, Ted ignored them.

2. The _____ from a dictatorship to a multi-party democracy is proving to be difficult.

3. I've been _____ with my mom and dad ever since they saw my grades from last semester.

4. Let me _____ this time. You two treated me many times before when I was looking for a job. Now I'm making good money, so it should be my turn.

5. Although I gave him many presents, I had no _____ gifts from him.

6. He was _____ and unfairly introduced in Samuel Eliot Morison's magisterial "The Oxford History of the American People" as a kindly soul in a spineless body.

7. They refused to _____ where they had hidden the money.

8. Our country has a large population, vast territory and _____ resources.

9. Your _____ vision is better than you think.

10. If you think you sound _____ or obstinate by not answering the question, think of how he feels asking the question more than once.

11. The document provided a _____ insight into the government's priorities.

12. The impulse to be careful, to waste not, want not, has regained _____ since the earthquake.

13. A _____ about this observation on value creation is that those organizations that are able to successfully manage risky projects create the most value.

14. They argue that these are another nation's by right, because they are said to be meaningful to the claimant nation, important for its and its citizens' identity and _____ .

15. In addition, as we learn more about the world, our knowledge and beliefs _____ our powers of scientific reasoning.

IV. Try to paraphrase the following sentences, paying special attention to the underlined parts.

1. <u>Hefty helpings</u> of emotional expressiveness and unconditional support are ingredients here, followed by acceptance, loyalty, and trust.

   _____

   _____

2. When someone embodies the rules—<u>instinctually</u>—their friendships are abundant indeed.

   _____

   _____

3. If I confide that <u>money is tight</u> or my boyfriend's <u>in the doghouse</u> I might detail the money worries or give a blow-by-blow of the dramathon that led to

the boyfriend's banishment.

_____

_____

4. Those who felt <u>socially in sync</u> with the drug use were less likely to become <u>substance-free</u>.

_____

_____

5. A corollary for many people is the impetus to change best friends when <u>life throws us a curveball</u> or alters us in basic ways.

_____

_____

V. Discuss with your partner about each of the three statements and write an essay in no less than 260 words about your understanding of one of them.

1. Our friends are there for us through thick and thin, but rarely cross the line: A friend with too many opinions about our wardrobe, our partner, or our taste in movies and art may not be a friend for long.

_____

_____

2. He that has once done you a kindness will be more ready to do you another than he whom you yourself have obliged.

_____

_____

3. Most of us would prefer to think that we love our friends because of who they are, not because of the ways in which they support who we are. It sounds vaguely narcissistic, and yet the studies bear it out.

_____

_____

VI. List four websites where we can learn more about Karen Karbo and friend-ship and provide a brief introduction to each of them.

1. _____

_____

_____.

2. _____

_____

_____.

3. _____

_____

_____.

4. _____

_____

_____.

Text B

The Bond: Staying in Touch When Children Go to College
By Mary MacVean

It was not so long ago that parents drove a teenager to campus, said a tearful goodbye and returned home to wait a week or so for a phone call from the dorm. Mom or Dad, in turn, might write letters—yes, with pens. On stationery. But going to college these days means never having to say goodbye, thanks to near-saturation of cellphones, email, instant messaging, texting, Facebook and Skype. Researchers are looking at how new technology may be delaying the point at which college-bound students truly become independent from their parents, and how phenomena such as the introduction of unlimited calling plans have changed the nature of parent-child relationships, and not always for the better.

Students walking from biology class to the gym can easily fill a few minutes with a call to Mom's office to whine about a professor's lecture. Dad can pass along family news via email. Daily text messaging is not uncommon. How nice, you might think. And you might be right. Some research suggests that today's young adults are closer to their parents than their predecessors. But it's complicated. Sherry Turkle, a professor at the Massachusetts Institute of Technology whose specialty is technology and relationships, calls this a particular sort of "Huck Finn moment", in which Huck "takes his parents with him. We all sail down the Mississippi together."

From the electronic grade monitoring many high schools offer parents, it seems a small leap to keep electronic track of their (adult) children's schedules or to send reminders about deadlines or assignments. Professors have figured out that some kids

stationery /ˈsteʃənɛri/ *n.* paper, envelopes, and other materials or equipment used for writing

saturation /ˌsætʃəˈreʃən/ *n.* a condition in which a quantity no longer responds to some external influence

whine /waɪn/ *v.* to complain in an annoying, crying voice

predecessor /ˈpriːdɪsesə/ *n.* one who precedes you in time

specialty /speʃiːˈæləti/ *n.* the special line of work you have adopted as your career

are emailing papers home for parents to edit. And Skype and Facebook might be more than just chances to see a face that's missed at home; parents can peer into their little darling's messy dorm room or his messy social life.

Experts said the change dates to 9/11, which <u>upped</u> parents' anxiety over being out of touch with their children. And the rising cost of college can threaten parents' willingness to let children make mistakes as they learn how to be adults. Many of today's college students have had so much of their schedule programmed, they may not know what to do with time and <u>solitude</u>, said Barbara Hofer, a Middlebury College psychology professor and author with Abigail Sullivan Moore of the book *The iConnected Parent*.

Researchers are looking at these changing relationships, formed in the last few years after parents got smartphones and Facebook accounts too—and learned how to use them. "There's a <u>tremendous</u> diversity in how kids handle this. Some maintain old rules. But for many, many young people, they grow up essentially with the idea that they don't have to separate from their parents," Turkle said. "It's about having an <u>adolescence</u> that doesn't include the kind of separation that we used to consider part of adolescence," she added. "Something has become the norm that was considered <u>pathological</u> ."

Hofer and colleagues surveyed students at Middlebury in Vermont and at the University of Michigan, two schools different in many ways. But at both, parents and students were in contact frequently, an average of more than 13 times a week. "The one thing I've tried hard to do is not make this a helicopter story and not make it all negative," Hofer said in a telephone interview. "The quality of relationships that many students have with their parents is really quite remarkable. That's reported from parents and students." The complicated dance toward independence creates all sorts of tricky moments for both generations. The parents of today's college students were advised to get involved in the children's lives— to communicate, communicate, communicate. All that talk can signal a close, useful relationship, but it also can leave kids lacking what they need to <u>fend for</u> themselves.

"The parent is on speed dial, the parent is on favorites. It's about having an adolescence that doesn't include the kind of separation that we used to

up /ʌp/ *v.* raise or increase
solitude /ˈsɒlɪtjuːd/ *n.* a disposition toward being alone
tremendous /trɪˈmendəs/ *adj.* extraordinarily large in size or extent or amount or power or degree
adolescence /ædəˈlesəns/ *n.* the time period between the beginning of puberty and adulthood
pathological /pæθəˈlɒdʒɪkl/ *adj.* of or relating to the practice of pathology
fend for care for

consider part of adolescence," Turkle said. "It opens them up to real vulnerabilities now and later in life." Parents are not always eager for such separation, Hofer said. "We just heard so many stories, campus after campus, of parents crossing boundaries," she said. By intervening in roommate disputes or sending daily text reminders of class work to be done, parents perpetuate a feeling that the students needn't think for themselves because someone else was perfectly willing—even gleeful— to do it for them.

vulnerability /ˌvʌlnərəˈbɪlətɪ/ *n.* the state of being vulnerable or exposed
perpetuate /pəˈpetʃʊeɪt/ *v.* cause to continue or prevail
gleeful /ˈgliːfʊl/ *adj.* full of high-spirited delight
unplug /ʌnˈplʌg/ *v.* pull the plug of (electrical appliances)
unfriend /ʌnˈfrend/ *v.* remove a friend from the friends list
temptation /tempˈteɪʃən/ *n.* the desire to have or do something that you know you should avoid
provocative /prəˈvɒkətɪv/ *adj.* serving or tending to provoke, excite, or stimulate; stimulating discussion or exciting controversy

Have you seen the TV commercial in which two young women try to deal with an abundantly overflowing washing machine? In the end, one of them calls dad. His advice? Unplug it. A parent might laugh and cry at the thought that a young adult couldn't figure that out. Hofer cited a student who said she wasn't homesick freshman year, but sophomore year her mother learned to use Skype and placed the computer on the kitchen floor so her daughter could see the family dog when it walked by. "That brought me right back into my mom's kitchen" the daughter told Hofer, and the young woman said she was homesick for the first time.

One recent evening, eight Pomona students gathered around a table to talk about how "connected" they were to their parents. They were in touch through email or text or Skype—technologies that some parents learned through their kids. Several said keeping in touch made the transition to college easier. Freshman Tim Kung, from San Diego, said his parents "were actually very considerate" about his desire to "unfriend" them from Facebook. Talking less frequently makes their conversations more meaningful, he said.

It's tough for parents to avoid the temptation to step in when they learn from a Facebook post, as Edward Chuchla, whose daughter graduated in May from Pomona, put it in a telephone interview, "about how stressful it was writing version 927 of a politics thesis." Sometimes, he said, he takes the bait. "If they post something provocative , we pick up the phone," he said. "We just call back to tell them we love them, and we're here if they need us."

Jamie Garcia, a freshman from Rosemead, said she's friends with her mother on Facebook, but added, "I'm not worried because she doesn't know how it works. She has like five friends." Her mother, Susan, however, is adept at texting. "I get a text from my mom every night, saying good night. So I text her back good night,

adept /əˈdept/ *adj.* having or showing knowledge and skill and aptitude
optometrist /ɒpˈtɒmɪtrɪst/ *n.* a person skilled in testing for defects of vision in order to prescribe corrective glasses
counsel /ˈkaʊnsəl/ *n.* something that provides direction or advice as to a decision or course of action

like I'm alive, I made it through the day," Jamie said. Susan Garcia said later she's reassured by the idea that she can reach her daughter easily. Even though Jamie only moved 35 miles and her family comes to her softball games, they don't spend much time together, Susan Garcia said.

Katie Bent, a sophomore, calls home to Seattle weekly. "For me, I would love to be in contact with my parents very frequently, but I also feel like this is the time I'm supposed to be learning how to function without them," she said. "So last semester I completely destroyed my glasses at one point. That probably would have been a perfect time to deal with it, to find an optometrist in the area. What I did was call my mom, and said, 'Oh my God, Mom. What am I going to do?'" Mom found an optometrist.

Katie's father, Sam Bent, said that while he and his wife are much more in touch with Katie than he was with his own parents when he left home, he thinks it's important that they not talk too often. "I know I don't call Katie unless I think it's important. She's in college, she's really busy. I don't call her up just to tell her a joke," he said by phone. "In some sense I'm glad she's not calling every day. She's learning to solve her own problems."

Caitlyn Hynes, the youngest of three children, has a lot of contact with her family in Upland — not only by phone or text, but in person. Her father takes her to baseball lessons because she doesn't have a car. Caitlyn said her mother might call to say, "You should go to bed soon," which prompts Caitlyn to ask herself, "When am I actually going to be able to make these decisions for myself? I don't have two separate worlds, home and school. It's kind of like being in high school again. It's not like I don't want to hear from her, but more like needing a sense of independence."

Edward Chuchla wants to talk to his children, to feel close to them, to give counsel when asked. He and his wife also have tried to take the advice they got from the dean when they dropped off their daughter, Grace, at Pomona College four years ago: Back off; avoid being helicopter parents. "We're very careful to make sure communication happens on their terms," said Chuchla, whose son, Ben, is finishing his sophomore year at Dartmouth.

Once, he said, he went too far. When his daughter left Pomona for a semester at Oxford, she had trouble getting permission to check books out of the library. The problem wasn't getting solved, so Chuchla emailed the foreign study office himself. When he heard from Grace, the message was, "I'll kill you if you do that again." Both generations are finding their way through the transition to adulthood as technological advances present even more new ways to connect. "We're all in this together," MIT's Turkle said. "We're all a little disoriented by these new possibilities together."

(approximately 1590 words)

Reading Time: _____   Reading Rate: _____

Cultural Notes

1. **Mary MacVean** is a senior features writer and Mind & Body editor at *Los Angeles Times*, writing about health, fitness, gluten-free food. Her recent works include *Spinning a Love Story at Warner Bros, Rural Living Could Be an Obesity Risk Factor, Pediatricians Call for Better Protection for Cheerleaders* and others.

2. **Huck Finn:** Huckleberry "Huck" Finn is a fictional character created by Mark Twain, who first appeared in the book *The Adventures of Tom Sawyer*, which was set around 1845, and is the protagonist and narrator of its sequel, *Adventures of Huckleberry Finn*, which was set around 1835—1845, although taking place after *The Adventures of Tom Sawyer*. He is 12 or 13 years old during the former and a year older at the time of the latter. Huck also narrates *Tom Sawyer Abroad* and *Tom Sawyer, Detective,* two shorter sequels to the first two books. The author metaphorically names him "the juvenile pariah of the village" and describes Huck as "idle, and lawless, and vulgar, and bad," qualities for which he was admired by all the children in the village, although their mothers "cordially hated and dreaded" him. Huck is an archetypal innocent, able to discover the "right" thing to do despite the prevailing theology and prejudiced mentality of the South of that era.

Comprehension Exercises

I. Answer the following questions based on the text.

1. Are today's young adults closer to their parents than their predecessors?
2. What is Huck Finn moment?
3. What is missing in the growth of young adults these days in the eyes of Turkle?
4. What is the author's attitude to the technological bond between parents and teenagers?
5. What are closely related to the change of parent-children relationships according the passage?

II. Decide whether each of the following statements is true or false according to the text.

1. Not long ago parents wrote to their children who went to college with pens.
2. It is very nice for parents to have quick access to their children's campus life today.
3. Since 9/11, parents became more and more anxious over being out of touch with their children.
4. According Tim Kung, less communication with his parents made their conversation more meaningful.
5. Some parents learned to use email, text or Skype because of their children.

III. Select the most appropriate word or phrase and use its proper form to complete each of the following sentences.

fend for	perpetuate	specialty	unfriend	counsel
up	gleeful	adept	separate	lecture
solitude	sail down	whine about	form	account
tremendous	drop off	survey		

1. I could whimper and _____ all the slack I'm having to pick up, but in the end, it would all just take longer.
2. Unless your physics _____ is deeply theoretical or has to do with astrophysics, you can usually find an industry job that is related to your work.
3. Although we have our concerns as to the safety of that zoom in our pockets, there's no doubt that Sanyo has _____ the ante for this type of device.
4. The night regressed into utter silence and _____.
5. Modern technology catalyzed _____ economic growth in China.

6. We think Spain is quite strong to _____ itself because it has a low level of public debt and it could recapitalize its banks without risking its public debt.

7. And worst of all, they continue to _____ the fantasy that Israel will one day be flooded by the descendants of Palestinian refugees.

8. Here I am wishing myself to have a smooth and _____ trip tomorrow!

9. They also need to be _____ at collaborating with colleagues outside of IT.

10. He also said shipments continued on schedule, despite market concerns that shipping to China had _____ in recent weeks.

11. One of my friends walled off the living room so that he can have a _____ place to eat.

12. Neither the subject nor the title of this _____ is of my own choice.

13. By folding the paper as it is _____ to the others in the class or the game, each of the writers sees only the preceding line, but not the rest of the poem.

14. His father kidnaps him, but he manages to escape and together with a runaway slave, Jim, they _____ the Mississippi on a raft.

15. These ideas have been _____ in my mind.

IV. Try to paraphrase the following sentences, paying special attention to the underlined parts.

1. Researchers are looking at how new technology may be delaying <u>the point at which</u> college-bound students truly become independent from their parents, and how phenomena such as <u>the introduction of unlimited calling plans</u> have changed the nature of parent-child relationships, and not always for the better.

2. Experts said the change dates to 9/11, which <u>upped parents' anxiety</u> over being out of touch with their children.

3. <u>It's about having an adolescence</u> that doesn't include the kind of separation that we used to consider part of adolescence.

4. <u>The complicated dance toward independence</u> creates all sorts of tricky moments for both generations.

5. We're very careful to make sure communication happens <u>on their terms</u>.

_____

_____

V. Discuss with your partner about each of the three statements and write an essay in no less than 260 words about your understanding of one of them.

1. New technology may be delaying the point at which college-bound students truly become independent from their parents.

_____

_____

2. The parents of today's college students were advised to get involved in the children's lives—to communicate, communicate, communicate. All that talk can signal a close, useful relationship, but it also can leave kids lacking what they need to fend for themselves.

_____

_____

3. Both generations are finding their way through the transition to adulthood as technological advances present even more new ways to connect.

_____

_____

VI. List four websites where we can learn more about Mary MacVean and kinship and provide a brief introduction to each of them.

1. _____

_____

_____.

2. _____

_____

_____.

3. _____

_____

_____.

4. _____

_____

_____.

Twenty Minutes' Reading

You are required to read the following two sections within 20 minutes.

Section A

It was 1961 and I was in the fifth grade. My marks in school were miserable and, the thing was, I didn't know enough to really care. My older brother and I lived with Mom in a dingy multi-family house in Detroit. We watched TV every night. The background noise of our lives was gunfire and horses' hoofs from "Wagon Train" or "Cheyenne", and laughter from "I Love Lucy" or "Mister Ed". After supper, we'd sprawl on Mom's bed and stare for hours at the tube.

But one day Mom changed our world forever. She turned off the TV. Our mother had only been able to get through third grade. But she was much brighter and smarter than we boys knew at the time. She had noticed something in the suburban houses she cleaned—books. So she came home one day, snapped off the TV, sat us down and explained that her sons were going to make something of themselves. "You boys are going to read two books every week," she said. "And you're going to write me a report on what you read."

We moaned and complained about how unfair it was. Besides, we didn't have any books in the house other than Mom's Bible. But she explained that we would go where the books were: "I'd drive you to the library."

So pretty soon, there were these two peevish boys sitting in her white 1959 Oldsmobile on their way to Detroit Public Library. I wandered reluctantly among the children's books. I loved animals, so when I saw some books that seemed to be about animals, I started leafing through them.

The first book I read clear through was *Chip the Dam Builder*. It was about beavers. For the first time in my life I was lost in another world. No television program had ever taken me so far away from my surroundings as did this verbal visit to a cold stream in a forest and these animals building a home.

It didn't dawn on me at the time, but the experience was quite different from watching TV. There were images forming in my mind instead of before my eyes. And I could return to them again and again with the flip of a page.

Soon I began to look forward to visiting this hushed sanctuary from my other world. I moved from animals to plants, and then to rocks. Between the covers of all those books were whole worlds, and I was free to go anywhere in them. Along the way a funny thing happened I started to know things. Teachers started to notice it too. I got to the point where I couldn't wait to get home to my books.

Now my older brother is an engineer and I am chief of pediatric neurosurgery at John Hopkins Children's Center in Baltimore. Sometimes I still can't believe my life's journey, from a failing and indifferent student in a Detroit public school to this position, which takes me all over the world to teach and perform critical surgery.

But I know when the journey began: the day Mom snapped off the TV set and put us in her Oldsmobile for that drive to the library.

1. We can learn from the beginning of the passage that _____.
    A. the author and his brother had done poorly in school
    B. the author had been very concerned about his school work
    C. the author had spent much time watching TV after school
    D. the author had realized how important schooling was
2. Which of the following is NOT true about the author's family?
    A. He came from a middle-class family.
    B. He came from a single-parent family.
    C. His mother worked as a cleaner.
    D. His mother had received little education.
3. The mother was _____ to make her two sons switch to reading books.
    A. hesitant   B. unprepared   C. reluctant   D. determined
4. How did the two boys feel about going to the library at first?
    A. They were afraid.   B. They were reluctant.
    C. They were indifferent.   D. They were eager to go.
5. The author began to love books for the following reasons EXCEPT that _____.
    A. he began to see something in his mind
    B. he could visualize what he read in his mind
    C. he could go back to read the books again
    D. he realized that books offered him new experience

Section B

These days lots of young Japanese do *omiai*, literally, "meet and look." Many of them do so willingly. In today's prosperous and increasingly conservative Japan, the traditional *omiai kekkon*, or arranged marriage, is thriving.

But there is a difference. In the original *omiai*, the young Japanese couldn't reject the partner chosen by his parents and their middleman. After World War II, many Japanese abandoned the arranged marriage as part of their rush to adopt the more democratic ways of their American conquerors. The Western *ren'ai kekkon*, or love marriage, became popular; Japanese began picking their own mates by dating and falling in love.

But the Western way was often found wanting in an important respect: it didn't necessarily produce a partner of the right economic, social, and educational qualifications. "Today's young people are quite calculating," says Chieko Akiyama, a social commentator.

What seems to be happening now is a repetition of a familiar process in the country's history, the "Japanization" of an adopted foreign practice. The Western ideal of marrying for love is accommodated in a new *omiai* in which both parties are free to reject the match. "*Omiai* is evolving into a sort of stylized introduction," Mrs. Akiyama says.

Many young Japanese now date in their early twenties, but with no thought of marriage. When they reach the age—in the middle twenties for women, the late twenties for men—they increasingly turn to *omiai*. Some studies suggest that as many as 40 % of marriages each year are *omiai kekkon*. It's hard to be sure, say those who study the matter, because many Japanese couples, when polled, describe their marriage as a love match even if it was arranged.

These days, doing *omiai* often means going to a computer matching service rather than to a *nakodo*. The *nakodo* of tradition was an old woman who knew all the kids in the neighbourhood and went around trying to pair them off by speaking to their parents; a successful match would bring her a wedding invitation and a gift of money. But Japanese today find it's less awkward to reject a proposed partner if the *nakodo* is a computer.

Japan has about five hundred computer matching services. Some big companies, including Mitsubishi, run one for their employees. At a typical commercial service, an applicant pays $80 to $125 to have his or her personal data stored in the computer for two years and $200 or so more if a marriage results. The stored information includes some obvious items, like education and hobbies, and some not-so-obvious ones, like whether a person is the oldest child. (First sons, and to some extent first daughters, face an obligation of caring for elderly parents.)

6. According to the passage, today's young Japanese prefer _____.
   A. a traditional arranged marriage   B. a new type of arranged marriage
   C. a Western love marriage   D. a more Westernized love marriage
7. Which of the following statements is CORRECT?
   A. A Western love marriage tends to miss some Japanese values.
   B. Less attention is paid to the partner's qualification in arranged marriages.
   C. Young Japanese would often calculate their partner's wealth.
   D. A new arranged marriage is a repetition of the older type.

8. According to the passage, the figure 40% (Para. 5) is uncertain because _____.

   A. there has been a big increase in the number of arranged marriages

   B. Western love marriage still remains popular among young Japanese

   C. young Japanese start dating very early in their life in a Western tradition

   D. the tendency for arranged marriages could be stronger than is indicated

9. One of the big differences between a traditional *nakodo* and its contemporary version lies in the way _____.

   A. wedding gifts are presented   B. a proposed partner is refused

   C. formalities are arranged   D. the middleman/woman is chosen

10. What is the purpose of the last paragraph?

   A. To tell the differences between an old and modern *nakodo*.

   B. To provide some examples for the traditional *nakodo*.

   C. To offer more details of the computerized *nakodo*.

   D. To sum up the main ideas and provide a conclusion.

Unit Nine Science

The Biggest Extinction on Earth

By Naomi Miles

A view of the barren landscape in Karoo, South Africa (Dominic Morel)

Our planet has a troubled and turbulent past: five catastrophic natural events have caused mass extinctions of life on Earth. Perhaps the most famous one is the asteroid impact that caused the demise of the dinosaurs. But the most extensive extinction event occurred even before dinosaurs were around. In the Permian era, about 250 million years ago, a destructive volcanic eruption radically altered conditions on Earth and scientists are still piecing together evidence in an attempt to understand its devastating impact.

Clues in the earth

Paleontologist Roger Smith from the Museum of South Africa has been searching for hints about the extinction in the Karoo basin in South Africa. Today, it's hard to imagine life ever thrived in this barren, inhospitable landscape where living things struggle to survive. But by examining rock strata in the area, layers of rock that have built up over time, he has built up an impression of what existed here in the past.

Smith has been studying a layer of blue-green mud-rock laid down 300 million

troubled /ˈtrʌbl ə d/ *adj.* having a chaotic or restless character or tendency
asteroid /ˈæstərɔɪd/ *adj. (astronomy)* any of numerous small celestial bodies that revolve around the sun, with orbits lying chiefly between Mars and Jupiter [天文学] 小行星
demise /dɪˈmaɪz/ *n.* death
Permian /ˈpɜːmɪən/ *adj. (Geol.)* of the period of geological time about 280 million years ago [地] 二叠纪的
piece /piːs/ *vt.* to join or unite the pieces of
devastating /ˈdevəsteɪtɪŋ/ *adj.* bringing to ruin or reducing to complete disorder
paleontologist /pæliɒnˈtɒlədʒɪst/ *n.* a scientist who studies fossils
inhospitable /ɪnˈhɒspɪtəb ə l/ *adj.* unfavorable to life or growth
strata /ˈstreɪtə/ *n. (pl.* stratum) *(Geol.)* a bed or layer of sedimentary rock having approximately the same composition throughout [地] 地层

years ago. Analysis of the layer has revealed that it is made up of <u>sediments</u> deposited by frequent floods. "These blue-green mud rocks of the Permian represent <u>lush</u> wet flood plains. Lots of life, lots of flourishing vegetation, and many types of mammal-like <u>reptiles</u>," explains Smith. Above the lush mud-rock layer sits rock that Smith describes as the "death zone" since it is completely <u>devoid</u> of life. The rocks contain no evidence of animal life, let alone plants or even soil.

sediment /'sedɪmənt/ *n.* solid fragments of inorganic or organic material that come from the weathering of rock and are carried and deposited by wind, water, or ice 沉积物
lush /lʌʃ/ *adj.* having or characterized by luxuriant vegetation
reptile *n.* any of various cold-blooded, usually egg-laying creature, such as a snake, lizard, crocodile, turtle, or dinosaur, having an external covering of scales or horny plates and breathing by means of lungs 爬行动物
devoid /dɪ'vɔɪd/ *adj.* completely lacking
stumble /'stʌmbəl/ *vi.* to come upon accidentally or unexpectedly
lava /'lɑːvə/ *n.* molten rock that reaches the earth's surface through a volcano or fissure
basalt /'bæsɔːlt/ *n.* a hard, dense, dark volcanic rock 玄武岩
spew /spjuː/ *vt.* to send or force out in or as if in a stream
fracture /'fræktʃə/ *n. (Geol.)* a crack or fault in a rock
slash /slæʃ/ *vt.* to cut a slit or slits in
fountain /'fauntɪn/ *vi.* to flow or cause to flow like a stream
fissure /'fɪʃə/ *n.* a long, narrow opening

For over 150 years, the reason for the lifeless conditions in the Karoo basin has been a mystery. But in the early 1990s, some researchers <u>stumbled</u> on an exciting clue thousands of miles away in Siberia.

Volcanic evidence

Beneath the frozen Siberian landscape, thousands of square miles of <u>lava</u> were discovered. Known as <u>the Siberian traps</u>, these testify to the biggest and most destructive volcanic eruption the Earth has ever experienced.

The scale of the flood <u>basalt</u> is difficult to grasp. Two hundred and fifty thousand cubic miles of lava were <u>spewed</u> out over almost a million years. According to <u>UCL</u>'s disaster scientist Bill McGuire, it would have been "hell on Earth". "You would have had huge <u>fractures slashing</u> the crust open, and very fluid lava more than 1,000 degrees in temperature, <u>fountaining</u> out and pouring off in all directions. Any life around there would be burnt," he says.

Widespread consequences

But how did the Siberian traps affect life in the Karoo basin, on the other side of the world? The lava was certainly deadly, but scientists believe that the far-reaching effects of the Siberian traps lie in their ability to alter the Earth's climate.

Examples of some fossils from the Permian era.

To understand the impact of this ancient flood basalt, it's helpful to look at a more recent example: the Laki eruption of 1783. In this year, a 20-mile-long fissure spilled lava over 200 square miles of Iceland for a period of 8 months. Although no one actually died as a direct result of the lava flow, the flood basalt caused widespread destruction over the whole of Europe.

Along with red-hot lava, the Laki eruption spewed out 122 million tons of sulphur compounds. These combined with water vapour in the stratosphere to form tiny droplet clouds of sulphur dioxide. Acting like mirrors, the light-coloured droplets reflected sunlight back into space. Deprived of the sun's heat and light, the entire northern hemisphere cooled. Temperatures dropped to 7℃ below the average in Iceland and in the western United States they dropped by 5℃. The sulphur dioxide eventually fell to the Earth as acid rain which poisoned the struggling crops and eroded the soil. As a result, 50% of Iceland's cattle perished and 20% of its population starved.

The Siberian traps were 250,000 times bigger than Laki. "The Laki eruption actually covered a relatively small area, about a third the size of greater London. If we look at the Siberian flood basalts they covered a huge area. The deposits cover an area almost the size of the whole central part of Russia, something like the size of the United States," says McGuire.

Imagine the effects of Laki amplified two-and-a-half million times. The deadly belch of the Laki traps lasted for 8 months, but 250 million years ago, the massive slashes in the Earth's crust let out their noxious gases for hundreds of thousands of years. The Siberian traps are the likely culprit for the extreme global climate change behind the mass extinction. A huge sulphuric sun-block brought darkness and savage cold. Many species perished from the sudden glaciation. Voracious acid rain gnawed

stratosphere /ˈstrætəsfɪə/ *n.* the atmospheric layer between about 15 and 50 km above the earth 平流层
droplet /ˈdrɒplɪt/ *n.* a tiny drop
sulphur dioxide a colorless toxic gas (SO₂) that occurs in the gases from volcanoes 二氧化硫
amplify /ˈæmplɪfaɪ/ *vi.* to make larger or more powerful
belch /beltʃ/ *n.* eruption
noxious /ˈnɒkʃəs/ *adj.* harmful to living things
culprit /ˈkʌlprɪt/ *n.* one guilty of a fault or crime
sun-block *n.* a physical sunscreen or a barrier against the sun's ultraviolet rays
glaciation /gleɪsɪˈeɪʃən/ *n.* the covering of a landscape or larger region by ice
voracious /vəˈreɪʃəs/ *adj.* having or marked by an insatiable appetite for an activity or a pursuit; greedy
gnaw /nɔː/ *vt.* to cause erosion or gradual diminishment

vegetation for centuries on end.

Yet the late Permian era suffered a second affliction. Over thousands of years, greenhouse gases belched out by the traps accumulated in deadly quantities. Carbon dioxide, water vapor and methane shrouded the earth, trapping heat. It is estimated that levels of carbon dioxide were up to six times higher than today. All this translates to a 10℃ temperature rise in the Karoo basin.

affliction /əˈflɪkʃən/ n. a condition of pain, suffering, or distress
methane /ˈmeθeɪn/ n. an odorless, colorless, flammable gas, CH₄, the major constituent of natural gas [化] 甲烷, 沼气
shroud /ʃraʊd/ vt. to shut off from sight; screen
floodplain /ˈflʌdpleɪn/ n. the area on the sides of a stream, river, or watercourse that is subject to periodic flooding
oasis /əʊˈeɪsɪs/ n. a fertile or green spot in a desert or wasteland, made so by the presence of water
parched /pɑːtʃt/ adj. dried out by heat or excessive exposure to sunlight
pyrite /ˈpaɪəraɪt/ n. a brass-colored mineral [矿]黄铁矿
poles /pəʊls/ n. here refers to the North and South poles of the earth
akin /əˈkɪn/ adj. having a similar quality or character

Its effect can be read in the Karoo rock strata. Above the blues, grays and greens of the floodplain mud sits a layer of fiery red rock. This represents the moment that iron minerals in the mud and soil oxidized as they became exposed to the air. It marks the time that the lush oasis became the parched, dead land that we see today.

Effects in the oceans

The oceans also suffered. Geologist Paul Wignall from the University of Leeds in the UK examined the marine fossil record in Iceland from the Permian era. He found that the number of fossils gradually diminished, until there were none at all. At this point, Wignall analysed the rock and found that it contained many pyrite crystals. He points out that pyrite, also known as fools' gold, cannot form in the presence of oxygen.

If pyrite was forming in the ocean, there couldn't have been much oxygen. Normally, the deep ocean gets its oxygen from the poles: cold water absorbs oxygen from the atmosphere. This cold, dense, oxygenated water then sinks and moves along the sea floor towards the equator.

Two hundred and fifty million years ago, the oceans, like the land, heated up. Wignall has calculated that around the equator, temperatures would have approached 38℃, about the temperature of bath water. Near the poles, temperatures were more akin to what we experience in California today.

With no cold water at the poles, the oceans' circulation system shut down. Life

debris /'debri:/ *n. (Geol.)* an accumulation of relatively large rock fragments [地] 岩屑
decompose /ˌdiːkəmˈpəʊz/ *vi.* to separate into components or basic elements
bog /bɒg/ *n.* wet spongy ground 沼泽
swamp /swɒmp/ *n.* a seasonally flooded bottomland 沼泽地
putrid /'pjuːtrɪd/ *adj.* in an advanced state of decomposition and having a foul odor
measly /'miːzli/ *adj. (slang)* small
obliteration /əˌblɪtəˈreɪʃən/ *n.* the complete destruction of every trace of something
colossal /kəˈlɒsəl/ *adj.* enormous

in the oceans began to die. Without oxygen, organic debris can't decompose properly, and the bacteria that breaks down this dead matter produces toxic hydrogen sulphide. Today, this deadly, rotten-egg smelling gas is found in low oxygen environments like bogs and swamps. Back then, it devastated the oceans, making them stinking and poisonous.

These putrid oceans released vast amounts of hydrogen sulphide into the atmosphere, marking the final death toll for the few remaining species on land already battling drought and famine. A measly 5% of species escaped obliteration.

It took around 6 million years for biodiversity to return to normal. Today, it's been 65 million years since the last major extinction event. Life is thriving, and it's easy for us to forget that the world around us has been fundamentally shaped by colossal natural disasters. Our existence is more fragile than we imagine. Huge flood basalts, asteroid impacts, gamma ray bursts... they do happen. And they will happen again.

(approximately 1750 words)

Reading Time: _____   Reading Rate: _____

Cultural Notes

1. **the Karoo:** a semi-desert region of South Africa. It has two main sub-regions—the *Great Karoo* in the north and the *Little Karoo* in the south. The "High" Karoo is one of the distinct physiographic provinces of the larger South African Platform division.

2. **the Siberian traps:** the remnants of widespread volcanic activity that occurred in today's Siberian area, about 250 million years ago. The most common rock type is basalt, which usually erupts effusively rather than explosively, but the eruptions can be prolonged, lasting for years or even decades, and producing vast flows.

3. **UCL (University College, London):** the largest college of the University of London, and is larger than most other universities in the United Kingdom.

4. **gamma ray bursts (GRBs):** the most luminous electromagnetic events are occurring in the universe since the Big Bang. They are flashes of gamma rays

emanating from seemingly random places in deep space at random times. The duration of a gamma ray burst is typically a few seconds, but can range from a few milliseconds to minutes. Most observed GRBs appear to be collimated emission caused by the collapse of the core of a rapidly rotating, high-mass star into a black hole.

Gamma Ray Burst GRB990123
Hubble Space Telescope · STIS

The image above shows the optical after-glow of gamma ray burst GRB-990123 taken on January 23, 1999. The burst is seen as a bright dot denoted by a square on the left, with an enlarged cutout on the right. The object above it with the finger-like filaments is the originating galaxy. This galaxy seems to be distorted by a collision with another galaxy.

A nearby gamma ray burst could possibly cause mass extinctions on Earth. Though the short duration of a gamma ray burst would limit the immediate damage to life, a nearby burst might alter atmospheric chemistry by reducing the ozone layer and generating acidic nitrogen oxides. These atmospheric changes could ultimately cause severe damage to the biosphere.

Comprehension Exercises

I. Answer the following questions based on the text.

1. What has caused the most extensive extinction event that ever occurred on the earth?
2. Describe the scale of the massive eruption.
3. How did the Siberian traps affect life in the Karoo basin, on the other side of the world?
4. What are its chain effects in the ocean? Using an arrow diagram.
5. What conclusion has the author drawn from his report?

II. Decide whether each of the following statements is true or false according to the text.

1. The blue-green mud-rocks contain no evidence of animal life, plants or soil.
2. The reason for the lifeless conditions in the Karoo basin has still been a mystery.
3. The lifeless conditions in the Karoo basin were affected by the Siberian traps

according to some researches.

4. Temperatures, because of the Laki eruption, dropped by 7℃ below the average in the Iceland and in the western United States they dropped by 5℃.

5. Huge flood basalts, asteroid impacts, gamma ray bursts had happened and will happen soon.

III. Select the most appropriate word or phrase and use its proper form to complete each of the following sentences.

devastate	lush	piece	slash	fountain
stumble	akin	colossal	noxious	spew
trouble	amplify	culprit	shroud	trap
voracious	devoid	hospitable		

1. It was how I felt at the time, as a young man deeply _____ and conflicted about the war.

2. We managed to _____ together the truth from several sketchy accounts.

3. This week at Balmoral, we have all been trying to help William and Harry come to terms with the _____ loss that they and the rest of us have suffered.

4. Raised by residents of the park, goats graze freely on wild vegetation during the _____ months of rain, then are rounded up when the dry season arrives.

5. How, then, could this race _____ of spirituality clothe in myths the profound horror of its life?

6. She nearly fell down by _____ over my stretched leg.

7. Instead of lava, ash, and sulfur dioxide, these volcanoes _____ mud and methane.

8. Republicans want to drastically _____ what the federal government spends this year. Democrats and the White House do not.

9. And the struggles of men have _____ the many problems—not just economic, but social and cultural—facing the country today.

10. Local media are covering every aspect of the scare with a _____ appetite.

11. To most of us, this might sound like no big deal, _____ to Apple coming out with a faster smartphone than Microsoft.

12. The _____ monument bestrode the harbour.

13. You should select according to your needs and avoid investment _____.

14. The man is very _____; he keeps open house for his friends and fellow-workers.

15. But the meat must be cooked, which will kill any _____ pathogens before you eat it.

IV. Try to paraphrase the following sentences, paying special attention to the underlined parts.

1. The lava was certainly deadly, but scientists believe that the far-reaching effects of the Siberian traps <u>lie in their ability</u> to alter the Earth's climate.

   _____

2. The deadly belch of the Laki traps lasted for 8 months, but 250 million years ago, <u>the massive slashes in the Earth's crust</u> let out their noxious gases for hundreds of thousands of years.

   _____

3. The Siberian traps are <u>the likely culprit</u> for the extreme global climate change behind the mass extinction.

   _____

4. Over thousands of years, <u>greenhouse gases</u> belched out by the traps accumu-lated <u>in deadly quantities</u>.

   _____

5. These putrid oceans released vast amounts of hydrogen sulphide into the atmosphere, marking the final death toll for the few remaining species on land already <u>battling drought and famine.</u>

   _____

   _____

V. Discuss with your partner about each of the three statements and write an essay in no less than 260 words about your understanding of one of them.

1. Our planet has a troubled and turbulent past: five catastrophic natural events have caused mass extinctions of life on Earth.

   _____

2. Our existence is more fragile than we imagine.

   _____

3. Huge flood basalts, asteroid impacts, gamma ray bursts...they do happen. And they will happen again.

   _____

   _____

VI. List four websites where we can learn more about Naomi Miles and natural disasters and provide a brief introduction to each of them.

1. _____
   _____
   _____ .

2. _____
   _____
   _____ .

3. _____
   _____
   _____ .

4. _____
   _____
   _____ .

Text B

Spyware on Your Cell Phone?

by Jessica Ramirez

Sometime in early 2007, Richard Mislan, an assistant professor of cyberforensics at Purdue University, started getting phone calls and e-mails from people around the world—all looking for help with the same problem. "They thought someone was listening in on their cell-phone calls," he says. "They wanted to know what they could do to confirm it was happening."

Mislan, who has examined thousands of phones at the Purdue Cyber Forensics Lab, politely disregarded some callers as a little paranoid. Others, he thought, had reason to be concerned. A decade ago the idea that anyone with little technical skill could turn a cell phone into a snooping device was basically unrealistic. But as the smart-phone market proliferates—it grew 86 percent in the United States alone last year—so do all the ethical kinks that come with it. Among them is a growing sector of perfectly legal smart-phone spyware apps that are peddled as tools for catching a cheating spouse or monitoring the kids when they're away

disregard /ˌdɪsrɪˈgɑːd/ *vt.* give little or no attention to

paranoid /ˈpærənɔɪd/ *n.* a person afflicted with paranoia 偏执狂

snoop /snuːp/ *v.* to find out private things about sb, especially by looking secretly around a place

proliferate /prəˈlɪfəreɪt/ *v.* grow rapidly

kink /kɪŋk/ *n.* an eccentric idea

peddle /ˈpedəl/ *v.* sell or offer for sale from place to place

from home. But what they can effectively do, for as little as $15 or as much as several hundred, is track a person with a precision once relegated to federal authorities. "Not only can you look at a person's e-mail or listen to their calls, in some cases you can also just turn on the microphone [on a smart phone] and listen to what the person is doing any time you want," says Chris Wysopal, cofounder and <u>CTO</u> of Veracode, a software-security company.

tether /ˈteðə/ *v.* tie sth so that it cannot move very far
vendor /ˈvendə/ *n.* a company that sells a particular product

Turning what is essentially cell-phone-bugging software into a business model is not a bad idea, technically speaking. The smart-phone market—largely dominated by the Symbian, Research in Motion, and iPhone operating systems—has 47 million users in the United States and is expected to exceed 1 billion worldwide by 2014, according to Parks Associates, a market-research firm. In most cases, people's lives are <u>tethered</u> to these handsets. It's how we e-mail, text, search, and, on occasion, even call someone. And the dependence just continues to grow. Last year consumers paid for and downloaded more than 670 million apps that can turn a phone into everything from a book reader to a compass. Smart-phone users effectively carry a real-time snapshot of what happens in their daily lives. This is what makes the smart phone the perfect way to track someone.

Among the top commercial spyware <u>vendors</u> who have ventured into this space are FlexiSPY, MobiStealth, and Mobile Spy. While the services vary, what they do is essentially the same. According to all three spyware Web sites, a person must have legal access to a smart phone to install a piece of spyware. For example, if you're spying on a family member, that means the phone is family property. If you're an employer monitoring your employee, the phone should be company-owned. To install the spyware, you have to have the phone in your possession for at least a few minutes to download the app. (There are apps that can be downloaded remotely, but that's less common and not legal.) In Mobile Spy's case, once the software is installed, you can log into your Mobile Spy web account to view e-mails, text messages, pictures taken, videos shot, calendar entries, incoming and outgoing calls, and GPS coordinates. MobiStealth and FlexiSPY take it a step further and allow a person to remotely record any conversations that take place near the cell phone. "The most threatening [part] is that it's pretty impossible to tell if this is happening to you," says Mislan. That's because once the spyware app is on the phone it is virtually undetectable to the average user. There is no typical corresponding app icon, nor is it listed on any menu. At best, it may show up with a <u>generic</u> name like "iPhone app" or "BlackBerry app," so that it appears to be a regular part of the system.

There is nothing illegal about making these apps, and almost all makers have disclaimers on their Web sites warning people not to use their products illegally. "Our software is for very specific uses," says Craig Thompson, support coordinator of Retina-X Studios, the creator of Mobile Spy. "We do what we can to discourage inappropriate use." Still, there is no way to know if someone is using the app to monitor his or her child (legal) or stalk an ex (not so much). Illegal use of spyware has already been reported in states such as Washington, Oklahoma, and Texas. According to Wysopal of Veracode, in addition to state and local laws, the federal Computer Fraud and Abuse Act and the Wiretap Act technically offer some protection for consumers. But even if someone discovers spyware on their phone, prosecuting the <u>perpetrator</u> can be difficult. "The problem with this law is the crime has to rise to the level of a <u>felony</u> for the FBI to investigate, [and] that typically involves $5,000 or more in damages," Wysopal says. "I don't really know what the damages are for someone installing [mobile spyware] and reading your e-mails."

Jeff Troy, acting deputy assistant director for the FBI's Cyber Division, says the issue is a growing concern for his organization because of how fast the smart-phone market is evolving. "I do think there is need for additional cyber laws to address this," he says.

Until that happens, the best solution may well be preventive. According to BlackBerry maker Research in Motion, "BlackBerry smartphones include a firewall that can be set to prevent an app (like spyware) from making external connections; and passwords can also be required to authorize downloading an application to the device." Google's Android gives apps limited access to phone resources by default, but that can be changed manually, so the best bet is to lock the phone and/or SIM card whenever you're not using it. Google has also recently activated a "kill switch" on its phone to remotely disable apps "that violate the Android Market Developer Distribution Agreement or other legal agreements, laws, regulations or policies." Of the trio, Apple probably has the most user-friendly safety net, because all apps must be approved by its app store. To even get most spyware apps on an

generic /dʒɪˈnerɪk/ *adj.* any product that can be sold without a brand name

perpetrator /ˈpɜːpətreɪtə/ *n.* someone who perpetrates wrongdoing

felony /ˈfelənɪ/ *n.* a serious crime (such as murder or arson)

Apple iPhone, a person would have to jailbreak it,
which voids the warranty.

jailbreak /ˈdʒeɪlbreɪk/ *n.* an escape from jail

If the software is already on a phone, Mislan says there is little that consumers
can do on their own to confirm this. Even if you're positive you are being spied
on, doing something like replacing the SIM card is not always enough to wipe a
phone clean of the problem. In some cases, Mislan advises consumers to reach out
to companies like SMobile Systems that offer security solutions for cell phones—a
growing market in themselves.

Wysopal says that as with so much that's technology-related, something big
has to break before things change in the smart phone—spyware space. "You'll
have to see someone important, like a politician, have their phone compromised,"
he says. "If that happened, it would be a wake-up call."

(approximately 1160 words)

Reading Time: _____   Reading Rate: _____

Cultural Notes

1. **cyberforensics:** (or computer forensics) is the application of investigation
   and analysis techniques to gather and preserve evidence from a particular
   computing device in a way that is suitable for presentation in a court of
   law. The goal of computer forensics is to perform a structured
   investigation while maintaining a documented chain of evidence to find
   out exactly what happened on a computing device and who was
   responsible for it.
2. **CTO:** Chief Technology Officer

Comprehension Exercises

I. Answer the following questions based on the text.

1. What can we learn from Mislan's concern on some callers?
2. Why did many people call Richard Mislan for help?
3. What's the cause of Mislan's wrong?
4. How do spyware makers warn people not use their products illegally?
5. What threatens the user most once the spyware is installed on the smart
   phone?

6. What must a person do in order to install a piece of spyware on a smart phone according to the three spyware web sites?

II. Decide whether each of the following statements is true or false according to the text.

1. The use of spyware apps is against the law.
2. The use of spyware apps is forbidden by federal authorities.
3. The research by Parks Associates was mentioned show the great development potential of the smart-phone market.
4. It can be concluded from the passage that the author believes smart-phones are technically necessary for us.
5. Ten years ago, it was unbelievable that anyone with little technical skill could turn a cell phone into a spying device.

III. Select the most appropriate word or phrase and use its proper form to complete each of the following sentences.

perpetrator	paranoid	tether	vendor	snoop
proliferate	coordinate	kink	peddle	felony
disregard	effective	generic	reason	jailbreak
assistant	threaten	compromise		

1. He was so crazy about diverse experiments that he _____ his wife's feelings, which caused her in great distress.
2. In fact, some experts worry that if people become too _____ about online privacy, it could have deleterious effects.
3. Consumers should never worry some junior police officer is _____ their data.
4. Despite the difficulties, investors assume such deals will continue to _____ .
5. Perhaps it is only by a _____ in my nature, strong in me even in those days, that I felt in such an existence, the share of the great majority, something amiss.
6. It was an absurd and untrue story, but Brown and Bossie _____ it hard.
7. We should _____ our plan to our resources.
8. To do this, copyright owners have to agree or give permission for their material to be shared through a _____ license that gives permission in advance.
9. The lawsuit alleges that the _____ was inspired by his obsession with the controversial video game.

10. A new message appears on the screen saying your _____ is ready.

11. However, since he had to go to the city on some business, his _____ would buy on his behalf.

12. He _____ that since she had not answered his letter she must have left here.

13. If you can use a word correctly and _____, you comprehend it.

14. The judge told him to desist from _____ his wife.

15. Many people _____ their lives so that they have to be together.

IV. Try to paraphrase the following sentences, paying special attention to the underlined parts.

1. Mislan, who has examined thousands of phones at the Purdue Cyber Forensics Lab, politely <u>disregarded some callers as a little paranoid</u>.

2. But what they can effectively do, for as little as $15 or as much as several hundred, is <u>track a person with a precision</u> once relegated to federal authorities.

3. But even if someone discovers spyware on their phone, <u>prosecuting the perpetrator can be difficult</u>.

4. <u>Of the trio</u>, Apple probably has the most user-friendly safety net, because all apps must be approved by its app store.

V. Discuss with your partner about each of the three statements and write an essay in no less than 260 words about your understanding of one of them.

1. A decade ago the idea that anyone with little technical skill could turn a cell phone into a snooping device was basically unrealistic.

2. There is nothing illegal about making these apps, and almost all makers have disclaimers on their Web sites warning people not to use their products illegally.

3. "The problem with this law is the crime has to rise to the level of a felony for the FBI to investigate, [and] that typically involves $5,000 or more in damages," Wysopal says. "I don't really know what the damages are for someone installing [mobile spyware] and reading your e-mails."

_____
_____

VI. List four websites where we can learn more about Jessica Ramirez and cyberforensics and provide a brief introduction to each of them.

1. _____
_____
_____ .

2. _____
_____
_____ .

3. _____
_____
_____ .

4. _____
_____
_____ .

Twenty Minutes' Reading

You are required to read the following two sections within 20 minutes.

Section A

It is a curious paradox that we think of the physical sciences as "hard", the social sciences as "soft", and the biological sciences as somewhere in between. This is interpreted to mean that our knowledge of physical systems is more certain than our knowledge of biological systems, and these in turn are more certain than our knowledge of social systems. In terms of our capacity to sample the relevant universes, however, and the probability that our images of these universes are at least approximately correct, one suspects that a reverse order is more reasonable. We are able to sample earth's social systems with some degree of confidence that we have a reasonable sample of the total universe being investigated. Our knowledge of social systems, therefore, while it is in many ways extremely inaccurate, is not likely to be seriously overturned by new discoveries. Even the folk knowledge in social systems on which ordinary life is based in earning, spending, organizing, marrying, taking part in political activities, fighting and so on, is not very dissimilar from the more sophisticated images of the social system derived from the social sciences, even though it is built upon the very imperfect samples of personal experience.

In contrast, our image of the astronomical universe, of even of earth's geological history, can easily be subject to revolutionary changes as new data comes in and new theories are worked out. If we define the "security" our image of various parts of the total system as the probability of their suffering significant changes, then we would reverse the order of hardness and see the social sciences as the most secure, the physical sciences as the least secure, and again the biological sciences as somewhere in between. Our image of the astronomical universe is the least secure of all simply because we observe such a fantastically small sample of it and its record-keeping is trivial as compared with the rich records of the social systems, or even the limited records of biological systems. Records of the astronomical universe, despite the fact that we see distant things as they were long ago, are limited in the extreme.

Even in regard to such a close neighbour as the moon, which we have actually visited, theories about its origin and history are extremely different, contradictory, and hard to choose among. Our knowledge of physical evolution is incomplete and highly insecure.

1. The word "paradox" (Line 1, Para. 1) means "_____".
    A. implication
    B. contradiction
    C. interpretation
    D. confusion
2. According to the author, we should reverse our classification of the physical sciences as "hard" and the social sciences as "soft" because _____.
    A. a reverse ordering will help promote the development of the physical sciences
    B. our knowledge of physical systems is more reliable than that of social systems
    C. our understanding of the social systems is approximately correct
    D. we are better able to investigate social phenomena than physical phenomena
3. The author believes that our knowledge of social systems is more secure than that of physical systems because _____.
    A. it is not based on personal experience
    B. new discoveries are less likely to occur in social sciences

C. it is based on a fairly representative quantity of data

D. the records of social systems are more reliable

4. The chances of the physical sciences being subject to great changes are the biggest because _____ .

   A. contradictory theories keep emerging all the time

   B. new information is constantly coming in

   C. the direction of their development is difficult to predict

   D. our knowledge of the physical world is inaccurate

5. We know less about the astronomical universe than we do about any social system because _____ .

   A. theories of its origin and history are varied

   B. our knowledge of it is highly insecure

   C. only a very small sample of it has been observed

   D. few scientists are involved in the study of astronomy

Section B

Over the past decade, thousands of patents have been granted for what are called business methods. Amazon.com received one for its "one-click" online payment system. Merrill Lynch got legal protection for an asset allocation strategy. One inventor patented a technique for lifting a box.

Now the nation's top patent court appears completely ready to scale back on business-method patents, which have been controversial ever since they were first authorized 10 years ago. In a move that has intellectual-property lawyers abuzz the U.S. Court of Appeals for the Federal Circuit said it would use a particular case to conduct a broad review of business-method patents. In *re Bilski*, as the case is known , is "a very big deal", says Dennis D. Crouch of the University of Missouri School of law. It "has the potential to eliminate an entire class of patents."

Curbs on business-method claims would be a dramatic about-face, because it was the Federal Circuit itself that introduced such patents with its 1998 decision in the so-called state Street Bank case, approving a patent on a way of pooling mutual-fund assets. That ruling produced an explosion in business-method patent filings, initially by emerging internet companies trying to stake out exclusive rights to specific types of online transactions. Later, move established companies raced to add such patents to their files, if only as a defensive move against rivals that might beat them to the punch. In 2005, IBM noted in a court filing that it had been issued more than 300 business-method patents despite the fact that it questioned the legal basis for granting them. Similarly, some Wall Street investment films armed themselves with patents for financial products, even as they took positions in court cases opposing the practice.

The *Bilski* case involves a claimed patent on a method for hedging risk in the energy market. The Federal Circuit issued an unusual order stating that the case would be heard by all 12 of the court's judges, rather than a typical panel of three, and that one issue it wants to evaluate is whether it should "reconsider" its state street Bank ruling.

The Federal Circuit's action comes in the wake of a series of recent decisions by the supreme Court that has narrowed the scope of protections for patent holders. Last April, for example the justices signaled that too many patents were being upheld for "inventions" that are obvious. The judges on the Federal Circuit are "reacting to the anti-patent trend at the Supreme Court", says Harold C. Wegner, a patent attorney and professor at George Washington University Law School.

6. Business-method patents have recently aroused concern because of _____.
   A. their limited value to business
   B. their connection with asset allocation
   C. the possible restriction on their granting
   D. the controversy over authorization

7. Which of the following is true of the *Bilski* case?
   A. Its ruling complies with the court decisions.
   B. It involves a very big business transaction.
   C. It has been dismissed by the Federal Circuit.
   D. It may change the legal practices in the U.S.

8. The word "about-face" (Line 1, Para 3) most probably means_____.
   A. loss of good will   B. increase of hostility
   C. change of attitude   D. enhancement of dignity

9. We learn from the last two paragraphs that business-method patents_____.
   A. are immune to legal challenges
   B. are often unnecessarily issued
   C. lower the esteem for patent holders
   D. increase the incidence of risks

10. Which of the following would be the subject of the text?
   A. A looming threat to business-method patents.
   B. Protection for business-method patent holders.
   C. A legal case regarding business-method patents.
   D. A prevailing trend against business-method patents.

Unit Ten
The Familiar Essay (II)

Fame

By Melvin Howards

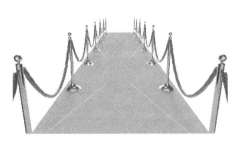

Fame is very much like an animal chasing its own tail who, when he captures it, does not know what else to do but to continue chasing it. Fame and the <u>exhilarating</u> celebrity that accompanies it, force the famous person to participate in his or her own destruction. Ironic isn't it?

Those who gain fame most often gain it as a result of possessing a single talent or skill: singing, dancing, painting, or writing, etc. The successful performer develops a style that is marketed aggressively and gains some popularity, and it is this popularity that usually convinces the performer to continue performing in the same style, since that is what the public seems to want and to enjoy. But in time, the performer becomes bored singing the same songs in the same way year after year, or the painter becomes bored painting similar scenes or portraits, or the actor is tired of playing the same character repeatedly. The demand of the public holds the artist hostage to his or her own success, fame. If the artist attempts to change his or her style of writing or dancing or singing, etc., the audience may turn away and look to confer fleeting fickle fame on another and then, in time, on another, and so on and so on.

Who cannot recognize a <u>Tennessee Williams</u> play or a novel by <u>John Updike</u> or <u>Ernest Hemingway</u> or a poem by <u>Robert Frost</u> or <u>W. H. Auden</u> or <u>T. S. Eliot</u>? The same is true of painters like <u>Monet</u>, <u>Renoir</u>, <u>Dali</u> or <u>Picasso</u> and it is true of movie makers like <u>Hitchcock</u>, <u>Fellini</u>, <u>Spielberg</u>, Chen Kai-ge or Zhang Yimou. Their distinctive styles marked a significant change in the traditional forms and granted them fame and fortune, but they were not free to develop other styles or forms

exhilarating /ɪgˈzɪləreɪtɪŋ/ *adj.* causing strong feelings of excitement and happiness

197

because their audience demanded of each of them what they originally presented. Hemingway cannot even now be confused with Henry James or anyone else, nor can Frost be confused with Yeats, etc. The unique forms each of them created, *created them*. No artist or performer can entirely escape the lure of fame and its promise of endless admiration and respect, but there is a heavy price one must pay for it.

Fame brings celebrity and high regard from adoring and loyal fans in each field of endeavor and it is heady stuff. A performer can easily come to believe that he or she is as good as his or her press. But most people, most artists do not gain fame and fortune. What about those performers who fail, or anyone who fails? Curiously enough, failure often serves as its own reward for many people! It brings sympathy from others who are delighted *not* to be you, and it allows family and friends to lower their expectations of you so that you need not compete with those who have more talent and who succeed. And they find excuses and explanations for your inability to succeed and become famous: you are too sensitive, you are not interested in money, you are not interested in the power that fame brings and you are not interested in the loss of privacy it demands, etc. —all excuses, but comforting to those who fail and those who pretend not to notice the failure.

History has amply proven that some failure for some people at certain times in their lives does indeed motivate them to strive even harder to succeed and to continue believing in themselves. Thomas Wolfe, the American novelist, had his first novel *Look Homeward, Angel* rejected 39 times before it was finally published and launched his career and created his fame. Beethoven overcame his tyrannical father and grudging acceptance as a musician to become the greatest, most famous musician in the world, and Pestalozzi, the famous Italian educator in the 19th century, failed at every job he ever had until he came upon the idea of teaching children and developing the fundamental theories to produce a new form of education. Thomas Edison was thrown out of school in fourth grade, at about age 10, because he seemed to the teacher to be quite dull and unruly. Many other cases may be found of people who failed and used the failure to motivate them to achieve, to succeed, and to become famous. But, unfortunately, for most people failure is the end of their struggle, not the beginning. There are few, if any, famous failures.

Well then, why does anyone want fame? Do you? Do you want to be known to many people and admired by them? Do you want money that usually comes with fame? Do you want the media to notice everything you do or say both in public and in private? Do you want them hounding you, questioning you and trying to undo you? In American politics it is very obvious that to be famous is to be the target of everyone who disagrees with you as well as of the media. Fame turns all the lights on and while it gives power and prestige, it takes the *you* out of you: you must be what the public thinks you are, not what you really are or could be. The politician, like the performer, must please his or her audiences and that often means saying things he does not mean or does not believe in fully. No wonder so few people trust politicians. But we have not answered the question at the beginning of this paragraph: why does anyone want fame? Several reasons come to mind: to demonstrate excellence in some field; to gain the admiration and love of many others; to be the one everyone talks about; to show family and friends you are more than they thought you were. Probably you can list some other reasons, but I think these are reasonably common.

Is it possible to be famous and to remain true to yourself, the real you? Perhaps, but one is hard pressed to come up with the names of those who have done their thing their way and succeeded in the fame game. Many political dissidents around the world, in particular, Aung San Suu Kyi of Burma, is a rare exception to the rule that says maintaining unpopular views or unpopular attitudes or approaches in any field will destroy you. The famous Irish writer Oscar Wilde, a very successful writer of stories, poems and plays, was known for his most unusual clothing and eccentric behavior, social and sexual. This behavior brought him to the attention of the mother of a young man Oscar was intimate with and she accused him. He was furious about this and sued the young man's mother which led to a trial and imprisonment for two years. He remained true to himself and paid a heavy price for it by being ostracized and defamed.

Time magazine of June 17, 1996 devoted a good deal of its issue to discussing people (25 in America) who are the most influential in the country in their opinion. They added a short essay on who are the most powerful people in America and no one on the first list appeared on the second list, and strangely enough, none of the people on either list was described as famous, although I think several surely are. Can we really distinguish influential people and powerful people from those who are famous? Maybe, but their list of influential people includes Jerry Seinfeld the comedian and TV star, Courtney Love the singer and drug addict whose fame has come largely through her husband

hound /haʊnd/ *vt.* to urge insistently; nag
dissident /dɪsɪdənt/ *n.* one who disagrees; a dissenter
ostraciz /ɒstrəsaɪz/ *vt.* to exclude from a group

Kurt Cobain, the guitarist who committed suicide, and the list includes Oprah Winfrey the talk show host and Calvin

wayfarer /ˈweɪfeərə/ *n.* one who travels, especially on foot

nonlinear /nɒnˈlɪnɪəl/ *adj.* not in a straight line

Klein the clothing designer. All of these people are famous, but I believe, not very influential in the sense that they change the way most of us think or act. In *Time* magazine's list we find a Supreme Court justice, Sandra Day O'Connor, who is no more influential or powerful than any of the other 8 justices. President Clinton is not considered influential but is considered powerful! You decide if you think famous and influential and powerful are closely related, or different.

I believe that fame and celebrity, influence and power, success and failure, reality and illusion are all somehow neatly woven into a seamless fabric we laughingly call reality. I say to those who desperately seek fame and fortune, celebrity: good luck. But what will you do when you have caught your tail, your success, your fame? Keep chasing it? If you do catch it, hang on for dear life because falling is not as painful as landing. See you soon famous and almost famous, <u>wayfarers</u> on this unbright, <u>nonlinear</u> planet!

(approximately 1450 words)

Reading Time: _____   Reading Rate: _____

Cultural Notes

1. **Tennessee Williams** (1911—1983): a major American playwright of the twentieth century who received many of the top theatrical awards for his work. He won the Pulitzer Prize for Drama for A *Streetcar Named Desire* in 1948 and for *Cat on a Hot Tin Roof* in 1955. In addition, *The Glass Menagerie* (1945) and *The Night of the Iguana* (1961) received New York Drama Critics' Circle Awards.

2. **John Updike** (1932—2009): an American novelist, short story writer and poet, internationally known for his novels *Rabbit, Run* (1960), *Rabbit Redux* (1971), *Rabbit Is Rich* (1981), and *Rabbit at Rest* (1990). They follow the life of Harry "Rabbit" Angstrom, a star athlete, from his youth through the social and sexual upheavals of the 1960s, to later periods of his life, and to final decline. Updike's oeuvre has been large, consisting of novels, collections of poems, short stories, and essays. He has also written a great deal of literary criticism.

3. **Ernest Hemingway** (1899—1961): an American novelist, short-story writer

and journalist. He received the Pulitzer Prize in 1953 for *The Old Man and the Sea,* and the Nobel Prize in Literature in 1954.

4. **Robert Frost** (1874—1963): an American poet. His works frequently employed themes from the early 1900s rural life in New England, using the setting to examine complex social and philosophical themes. A popular and often-quoted poet, Frost was honored frequently during his lifetime, receiving four Pulitzer Prizes.

5. **W. H. Auden** (1907—1973): an Anglo-American poet, regarded by many as one of the greatest writers of the 20th century. His work is noted for its stylistic and technical achievements, its engagement with moral and political issues, and its variety of tone, form, and content. The central themes of his poetry are love, politics and citizenship, religion and morals, and the relationship between unique human beings and the anonymous, impersonal world of nature.

6. **T.S. Eliot** (1888—1965): a poet, dramatist and literary critic. He received the Nobel Prize in Literature in 1948. His works include the poems *The Love Song of J. Alfred Prufrock, The Waste Land, The Hollow Men, Ash Wednesday,* and *Four Quartets;* the plays *Murder in the Cathedral* and *The Cocktail Party*; and the essay "Tradition and the Individual Talent."

7. **Claude Monet** (1840—1926): also known as Oscar-Claude Monet or Claude Oscar Monet, a founder of French impressionist painting, and the most consistent and prolific practitioner of the movement's philosophy of expressing one's perceptions before nature, especially as applied to plein-air landscape painting. The term Impressionism is derived from the title of his painting *Impression, Sunrise.*

8. **Pierre-Auguste Renoir** (1841—1919): a French artist who was a leading painter in the development of the Impressionist style. As a celebrator of beauty, and especially feminine sensuality, it has been said that "Renoir is the final representative of a tradition which runs directly from Rubens to Watteau". If something was not beautiful, Renoir would not paint it. This was the core of his artistic philosophy.

9. **Salvador Dali** (1904—1989): a Spanish surrealist painter born in Figueres, Catalonia, Spain. Dali was a skilled draftsman, best known for the striking and bizarre images in his surrealist work. His painterly skills are often attributed to the influence of Renaissance masters. His best known work, *The Persistence of Memory*, was completed in 1931. Salvador Dali's artistic repertoire also included film, sculpture, and photography. He collaborated with Walt Disney on the Academy Award-nominated short cartoon *Destino,*

which was released posthumously in 2003. He also collaborated with Alfred Hitchcock on Hitchcock's film *Spellbound*.

10. **Pablo Picasso** (1881—1973): a Spanish painter, draughtsman and sculptor. As one of the most recognized figures in twentieth-century art, he is best known for co-founding the Cubist movement and for the wide variety of styles embodied in his work. Among his most famous works are the proto-Cubist *Les Demoiselles d'Avignon* (1907) and his depiction of the German bombing of Guernica during the Spanish Civil War, *Guernica* (1937).

11. **Sir Alfred Joseph Hitchcock** (1899—1980): an iconic and highly influential British filmmaker and producer, who pioneered many techniques in the suspense and thriller genres.

12. **Federico Fellini** (1920—1993): an Italian film director. Known for a distinct style which meshes fantasy and baroque images, he is considered as one of the most influential and widely revered film-makers of the 20th century.

13. **Steven Allan Spielberg** (1946—   ): an American film director, producer and screenwriter. Spielberg is a three-time Academy Award winner and is the highest grossing filmmaker of all time; his films having made nearly $8 billion internationally. *Forbes* magazine places Spielberg's net worth at $3 billion. In 2006, the magazine Premiere listed him as the most powerful and influential figure in the motion picture industry. *Time* listed him as one of the 100 Greatest People of the Century. And at the end of the twentieth century, *Life* named him the most influential person of his generation.

14. **Aung San Suu Kyi** (1945—   ): a nonviolent pro-democracy activist in Myanmar. In 1990 she won the Sakharov Prize for Freedom of Thought and in 1991 she won the Nobel Peace Prize.

Comprehension Exercises

I. Answer the following questions based on the text.

1. What does the writer mean by comparing fame to an animal chasing its own tail?

2. What is the heavy price that artists or performers must pay for being famous?

3. According to the writer, why do so few people trust politicians?

4. What is the difference between being famous and being influential?

5. What is suggested, rather than plainly stated, in the essay?

II. Decide whether each of the following statements is true or false according to the text.

1. Most persons gain their fame because of a single talent or skill.
2. Fame, to some extent, is destroyed by the famous persons themselves.
3. Political dissidents are no exception to the rule that maintaining unpopular view or unpopular attitudes or approaches in any field will destroy you.
4. We can distinguish influential people and powerful people from the famous people.
5. For some people failure is the beginning of struggle, not the end.

III. Select the most appropriate word or phrase and use its proper form to complete each of the following sentences.

exhilarate	maintain	question	undo	weave
exception	ostracize	hound	linear	hostage
chase	original	confer	amply	sympathy
proven	fickle	devote		

1. I heard an interview with one of the bell ringers and he said it was an exhausting job but _____ when they can make the music they want; something called a full peal.
2. His security apparatus has beaten and arrested thousands, tried scores of dissidents in kangaroo courts, _____ others into exile, throttled the press and jammed the airwaves.
3. _____ world peace is our unshirkable internationalist duty.
4. It must also win the hearts of Gadhafi's friends in order to _____ him.
5. The children are _____ one another among the bushes.
6. Don't fire! He hijacked a girl as a _____ .
7. The police detained the suspected thief for further _____ .
8. No one will give me back the years spent in prison or _____ the tortures sustained.
9. These are _____ together through our languages, economic practices, social interactions and belief systems.
10. In a national survey last week, only 3% of respondents expressed any _____ for the cause.
11. Murray has _____ that his 253-yard performance in his first extended action was no fluke.
12. Alas, such is the _____ nature of the gold market on any given day recently.

13. _____ reports cited tainted rice protein concentrate and wheat gluten as the suspected compounds.

14. About 270, 000 are thought to have temporary residency, but even that does not _____ many benefits.

15. Only when we realize the importance of helping each other can we be _____ to building a harmonious society.

IV. Try to paraphrase the following sentences, paying special attention to the underlined parts.

1. Fame and the exhilarating celebrity that accompanies it, force the famous person to <u>participate in his or her own destruction</u>.

2. The demand of the public <u>holds the artist hostage</u> to his or her own success, fame.

3. Fame brings celebrity and high regard from adoring and loyal fans in each field of endeavor and <u>it is heady stuff</u>.

4. <u>Fame turns all the lights on</u> and while it gives power and prestige, <u>it takes the you out of you</u>: you must be what the public thinks you are, not what you really are or could be.

5. Perhaps, but one is hard pressed to come up with the names of those <u>who have done their thing their way</u> and succeeded in the fame game.

V. Discuss with your partner about each of the three statements and write an essay in no less than 260 words about your understanding of one of them.

1. Fame and the exhilarating celebrity that accompanies it, force the famous person to participate in his or her own destruction.

2. No artist or performer can entirely escape the lure of fame and its promise of endless admiration and respect, but there is a heavy price one must pay for it.

3. I believe that fame and celebrity, influence and power, success and failure, reality and illusion are all somehow neatly woven into a seamless fabric we laughingly call reality.

VI. List four websites where we can learn more about Robert Frost or T.S. Eliot and provide a brief introduction to each of them.

1.

2.

3.

4.

Text B

The Vice of Punctuality
By Robert Lynd

"Punctuality with the Englishman," says M. André Maurois, "is more than a habit. It is a vice." This is a severe judgment, but, from a strictly moral point of view, it is probably a true one. To the strict moralist—at least, to the Puritan—every form of self-indulgence is a vice, and undoubtedly punctuality is a form of self-indulgence. It is rooted in laziness and a desire to avoid trouble. The Englishman, being one of the laziest of men, was the first to discover the fact that, if he were habitually punctual, he

punctuality /pʌŋktʃuˈæləti/ *n.* not late; happening, doing something, etc, at the exact time: prompt

self-indulgence *n.* excessive indulgence of one's own appetites and desires

superfluous /suːˈpɜːfluəs/ *adj.* being beyond what is required or sufficient

would be spared a great deal of superfluous work and worry, and so he set about preaching the gospel of punctuality, which is merely a branch of the gospel of the higher selfishness. Needless to say, he lauded his vice as a virtue, and it is only the more logical moralists of the Continent who have seen through his pretences.

It is useless to deny that the unpunctual man excels the punctual both in energy and endurance. Even the unpunctual schoolboy is a model to his punctual coeval in these respects. How smoothly the day passes for the punctual fourteen-year-old! He glides through the day as easily as a tram along its lines! Sitting down in good time to breakfast, he has leisure to practise the art of gluttony almost before the sun is warm. Rising seasonably from the table, he sets off for school under no shadow of fear of an irate master's reproof. He saunters into school in the mood of Pippa, and is in his seat in class before the bell has rung and in time to receive his by-no-means-easy- to-placate master's glance of approval. And so he passes through the day, effortless, careless, and, I cannot help thinking, spiritually idle.

Compare with his the lot of the unpunctual boy, whose day is one long series of strenuous efforts. First, he has to make an effort to get out of bed, expending energy on what his punctual fellow has accomplished with lazy ease. At the breakfast-table, again, his brain is working hard, calculating exactly how many seconds he can afford in which to bolt his food before rushing off to an institution in which he is almost sure to be received, not with commendation, but with frowns. Only half-fed—for the unpunctual boy of necessity eats sparingly, like the saints and the ascetics —he tumbles out of the house, banging the door after him with the energy of a gymnast. See him running along the street, and you will note in him none of those marks of indolence which were all too conspicuous in the deportment of his punctual predecessor. His breath comes fast; his face is flushed; every step he takes is that of a boy doing his utmost, like a hero trying to score a try for the honour of his school. He is so bent on

gospel /ɡɒspəl/ n. also gospel truth; something that is completely true

laud /lɔːd/ vt. to give praise to; glorify

coeval /kəʊiːvəl/ adj. originating or existing during the same period; lasting through the same era

gluttony /ɡlʌtəni/ n. excess in eating or drinking

reproof /rɪpruːf/ n. a remark that expresses blame or disapproval

bolt /bəʊlt/ vt. to eat (food) hurriedly and with little chewing; gulp

ascetic /əsetɪk/ n. a person who renounces material comforts and leads a life of austere self-discipline, especially as an act of religious devotion

deportment /dɪpɔːtmənt/ n. a manner of personal conduct; behavior

doing his best and arriving at his school in good time that, when he mounts a tram, he finds that in his absorption in duty, he has not even had leisure to tie his shoelaces. At the school gates the empty playing-fields tell him that the

approbation /ˌæprəˈbeɪʃən/ *n.* an expression of warm approval; praise

tribulation /ˌtrɪbjʊˈleɪʃən/ *n.* great affliction, trial, or distress; suffering

penance /ˈpenəns/ *n.* an act of self-mortification or devotion performed voluntarily to show sorrow for a sin or other wrongdoing

bell has already rung and that he will have to face a reception in the schoolroom that only the bravest can face with equanimity. He braces himself for the ordeal; and the acute observer will perceive that the unpunctual schoolboy has to brace himself a score of times in the course of the day for once that this is required of the punctual. He lives in a fury of moral energy, indeed, that ought to have received, but did not receive, the approbation of Samuel Smiles. My own schoolmaster agreed with Samuel Smiles. He did not even look from his desk as he thought out words withering enough to discourage all moral effort on my part in the future. "Y," he said coldly, "if you cannot arrive in class in time, you will kindly stay away altogether." Such was the reward of virtue, of an output of energy of which no other boy in the class was capable or, at least, which no other boy in the class dreamed of emulating.

I doubt whether the punctual have the slightest conception of what the unpunctual go through—of their exhausting labours, of their endless tribulations. They seem to think that other people like being late for the sake of being late, whereas there is no one who suffer more from being late than the late-comer, there is very little fun for a middle-aged-man in bolting half an egg and running quarter of a mile to catch a morning train to town. No one, intent on his own comfort and eager to get through a day as lazily as possible, could think of doing such a thing. It is a form of penance that the unpunctual have to go through for not having been ease-loving enough in childhood to discover the art of living with a minimum of effort.

The unpunctual, again, are accused of selfishness. Theatre goers are continually complaining of the selfishness of those who arrive late in the stalls. The accusation is false. I know, for, being one of the most selfish of men, I always make a point of arriving at the theatre in time for purely selfish reasons. I have not the courage to endure the miseries of being late—to face the silent hatred of women whom there is no room to pass without crushing their knees or treading on their feet and the fury of fat men whom there is scarcely room to pass at all. To arrive in time at a theatre or a football match I regard as one of the luxuries of life. If I have to choose between disturbing other people and being disturbed myself, I prefer—for purely selfish reasons—being disturbed myself. For, since I am naturally unpunctual, I can make allowances for the late-comers and understand what they are suffering. Some of them, I tell myself, have been held up in traffic blocks. Others have

estuary /ˈestʃuəri/ n. the part of the wide lower course of a river where its current is met by the tides
famish /ˈfæmɪʃ/ vt. to cause to endure severe hunger
clamour for to demand noisily
egotist /ˈiːɡətɪst/ n. a selfish, self-centered person
caprice /kəˈpriːs/ n. an inclination to change one's mind impulsively

been kept fuming in the hall, while their wives and daughters were held prisoners upstairs by their mirrors. Others are the victims of slow clocks and watches. Every man who has ever been late knows that there are twenty good reasons for being late, whereas there is only one good reason for being punctual—self-love.

Our hatred of unpunctuality is, I think it can be shown, mainly a selfish hatred and, therefore, a vicious hatred. It is not from virtue, for example, that we object to being kept late for dinner. I have heard a fussily punctual fellow, after he had been kept waiting twenty minutes for dinner, saying: "My God, I could kill that cook." It was scarcely a Christian sentiment. Yet even I, who am frequently late for meals, hate to be kept waiting for one. I remember spending a summer holiday in a cottage on an estuary in which breakfast was never on the table before eleven. In London, I have no objection to an eleven o'clock breakfast, but on a holiday I like to be up early and am ready for breakfast by ten. The woman who looked after us, however, lacked the art of doing things easily, and, morning after morning, we hung about, famished, clamouring for food like young birds in a nest. Self, self, self—we thought nothing of the woman and the desperate efforts she was making in the kitchen. We were equally self-centred when, arriving back for lunch at half past one, we were kept waiting for it till four. It was not that, after our late breakfast, we were starving, but that the woman by her unpunctuality was interfering with our timetable. The whole day seemed to be wasted in waiting for meals that did not come. There is a kind of false gnawing that afflicts the body—or is it the soul? —when cooks are unpunctual. I used to feel it in the cottage about a quarter past ten at night when dinner had not appeared.

The truth is, in a selfish world, we feel that other people should always be punctual. Imagine the effect of short-tempered egotists, as most of us are, if the morning papers were constantly delivered late, if the first post arrived according to the caprice of an unpunctual postman, if no milk arrived for breakfast and the only explanation were the moral grandeur of the milkman. Italy, it is commonly said, went through a revolution largely in order to ensure the punctuality of trains. The wise men of the past said: "Better later than never"; but who nowadays echoes the ancient philosophy when the fish is not delivered in time for lunch? In a mechanized world, we insist that life must imitate the smoothness of a machine, and that other people must live, not according to their temperament, but in obedience to a time-table. This, it must be admitted, is for a highly organized society a convenience, but it is also a pursuit of the line of least resistance. There is nothing noble about it: it is merely Epicureanism on a practical plane. In demanding punctuality from others, we primarily seek, not their good, but our own happiness and comfort. Is that vicious? The Puritans, and M. Maurois among them, would say, "Yes." I cannot quite agree with them. I like other people to be punctual. As for myself, however, unpunctuality happens to be one of the things that have given me such character as I possess.

(approximately 1610 words)

Reading Time: _____   Reading Rate:_____

Cultural Notes

1. **Robert Lynd** (1879—1949): an Irish writer, an urbane literary essayist and strong Irish nationalist.

2. **M. André Maurois:** French biographer, novelist and essayist, best known for biographies that maintain the narrative interest of novels.

3. **Puritan:** Protestants believe in Puritanism. Puritanism is a religious reform movement in the late 16th and 17th centuries that sought to "purify" the Church of England of remnants of the Roman Catholic "popery" that the Puritans claimed had been retained after the religious settlement reached early in the reign of Queen Elizabeth I. Puritans became noted in the 17th century for a spirit of moral and religious earnestness that informed their whole way of life, and they sought through church reform to make their lifestyle the pattern for the whole nation. Their efforts to transform the nation contributed both to civil war in England and to the founding of colonies in America as working models of the Puritan way of life.

4. **Epicureanism:** This term has two distinct, though cognate, meanings. In its popular sense, the word stands for a refined and calculating selfishness, seeking not power or fame, but the pleasures of sense, particularly of the palate, and those in company rather than solitude. In the other sense, Epicureanism signifies a philosophical system, which includes a theory of conduct, of nature, and of mind.

Comprehension Exercises

I. Answer the following questions based on the text.

1. What does the unpunctual usually suffer from?
2. Why does the author make a point of being punctual in theatre-going?
3. Why punctuality is so valued in modern society according to the author?
4. Why does the author regard punctuality as a vice rather a virtue?
5. How does the author argue about his point?

II. Decide whether each of the following statements is true or false according to the text.

1. Englishmen are punctual because they are lazy.
2. The author agreed with M. André Maurois that punctuality is a vice.
3. The unpunctual boy makes more strenuous efforts than the punctual.
4. The punctual have the slightest conception of what the unpunctual go through, such as their exhausting labours or their endless tribulations according the author.
5. As for the author, unpunctuality happens to be one of the things that have given him character as he possesses.

III. Select the most appropriate word or phrase and use its proper form to complete each of the following sentences.

punctual	indulge	approbate	clamour for	tribulation
superfluous	proof	bolt	discourage	laud
dream	see through	reward	caprice	accord
famish	coeval	compare		

1. Train _____ fell during the first bout of bad weather this winter, according to Network Rail figures.
2. After decades of _____ and accumulating debt, our accounts cannot be settled in a few years.
3. The light box now seems _____, with its uniform brightness and the fiddlyness of setting it up.
4. Indeed, critics and fans world-wide ceaselessly _____ his tonal purity and perfect diction in several languages.
5. We also trust that readers can _____ the commercial and ideological motives of our competitor-critics.

6. The family were asking for _____ , but to prove someone's sexual preference is very difficult.

7. It's just hit me like a _____ from the blue what the grand plan is.

8. In modem society, the parking conflict is more and more acute, so underground parking whose integrated benefit is outstanding has been _____ gradually.

9. I suppose a dearth of food can _____ you and make you anxious to believe any promise of a better life, regardless of your mental faculty.

10. That case and others like it led to a growing _____ a change in the law.

11. When they measure themselves by themselves and _____ themselves with themselves, they are not wise.

12. Teachers should _____ their students from smoking and drinking.

13. They reinforced good behavior with some kind of _____ to direct a child's pattern of behavior.

14. We now have a big house of which we could not have _____ years ago.

15. _____ to traditions, the selectmen are required by law to perambulate the bounds every five years.

IV. Try to paraphrase the following sentences, paying special attention to the underlined parts.

1. "Punctuality with the Englishman," says M. André Maurois, "is more than a habit. It is a vice."

2. Compare with his the lot of the unpunctual boy, whose day is one long series of strenuous efforts.

3. Such was the reward of virtue, of an output of energy of which no other boy in the class was capable or, at least, which no other boy in the class dreamed of emulating.

4. It is a form of penance that the unpunctual have to go through for not having been ease-loving enough in childhood to discover the art of living with a minimum of effort.

5. There is a kind of <u>false gnawing</u> that afflicts the body—or is it the soul?

_____

_____

V. Discuss with your partner about each of the three statements and write an essay in no less than 260 words about your understanding of one of them.

1. To the strict moralist—at least, to the Puritan—every form of self-indulgence is a vice, and undoubtedly punctuality is a form of self-indulgence.

_____

_____

2. I doubt whether the punctual have the slightest conception of what the un-punctual go through—of their exhausting labours, of their endless tribula-tions.

_____

_____

3. Every man who has ever been late knows that there are twenty good reasons for being late, whereas there is only one good reason for being punctual—self-love.

_____

_____

VI. List four websites where we can learn more about Robert Lynd or punctuality and provide a brief introduction to each of them.

1. _____

_____

_____ .

2. _____

_____

_____ .

3. _____

_____

_____ .

4. _____

_____

_____ .

Twenty Minutes' Reading

You are required to read the following two sections within 20 minutes.

Section A

In our culture, the sources of what we call a sense of "mastery" —feeling important and worth-while—and the sources of what we call a sense "pleasure"—finding life enjoyable—are not always identical. Women often are told "You can't have it all." Sometimes what the speaker really is saying is: "You chose a career, so you can't expect to have closer relationships or a happy family life." or "You have a wonderful husband and children—What's all this about wanting a career?" But women need to understand and develop both aspects of well-being, if they are to feel good about themselves.

Our study shows that, for women, well-being has two dimensions. One is mastery, which includes self-esteem, a sense of control over your life, and low levels of anxiety and depression. Mastery is closely related to the "doing" side of life, to work and activity. Pleasure is the other dimensions, and it is composed of happiness, satisfaction and optimism. It is tied more closely to the "feeling" side of life. The two are independent of each other. A woman could be high in mastery and low in pleasure, and vice versa. For example, a woman who has a good job, but whose mother has just died, might be feeling very good about herself and in control of her work life, but the pleasure side could be damaged for a time.

The concepts of mastery and pleasure can help us identify the sources of well-being for women, and remedy past mistakes. In the past, women were encouraged to look only at the feeling side of life as the source of all well-being. But we know that both mastery and pleasure are critical. And mastery seems to be achieved largely through work. In our study, all the groups of employed women rated significantly higher in mastery than did women who were not employed.

A woman's well-being is enhanced when she takes on multiple roles. At least by middle adulthood, the women who were involved in a combination of roles— marriages, motherhood, and employment were the highest in well-being, despite warnings about stress and strain.

1. It can be inferred from the first paragraph that _____.
    A. for women, a sense of "mastery" is more important than a sense of "pleasure"
    B. for women, a sense of "pleasure" is more important than a sense of "mastery"
    C. women can't have a sense of "mastery" and a sense of "pleasure" at the same

time

D. a sense of "mastery" and a sense of "pleasure" are both indispensable to women

2. The author's attitude towards women having a career is _____.

A. critical

B. positive

C. neutral

D. realistic

3. One can conclude from the passage that if a woman takes on several social roles, _____.

A. it will be easier for her to overcome stress and strain

B. she will be more successful in her career

C. her chances of getting promoted will be greater

D. her life will be richer and more meaningful

4. Which of the following can be identified as a source of "pleasure" for women?

A. Family life.

B. Regular employment.

C. Multiple roles in society.

D. Freedom from anxiety.

5. The most appropriate title for the passage would be _____.

A. The Well-being of Career Women

B. Sources of Mastery and Pleasure

C. Two Aspects of Women's Well-Being

D. Freedom of Women in Society

Section B

Beauty has always been regarded as something praiseworthy. Almost everyone thinks attractive people are happier and healthier, have better marriages and have more respectable occupations. Personal consultants give them better advice for finding jobs. Even judges are softer on attractive defendants. But in the executive circle, beauty can become a liability.

While attractiveness is a positive factor for a man on his way up the executive ladder, it is harmful to a woman.

Handsome male executives were perceived as having more integrity than plainer men; effort and ability were thought to account for their success.

Attractive female executives were considered to have less integrity than unattractive ones; their success was attributed not to ability but to factors such as luck.

All unattractive women executives were thought to have more integrity and to be more capable than the attractive female executives. Interestingly, though, the rise of the unattractive overnight successes was attributed more to personal relationships and less to ability than was that of attractive overnight successes.

Why are attractive women not thought to be able? An attractive woman is perceived to be more feminine and an attractive man more masculine than the less attractive ones. Thus, an attractive woman has an advantage in traditionally female jobs, but an attractive woman in a traditionally masculine position appears to lack the "masculine" qualities required.

This is true even in politics. "When the only clue is how he or she looks, people treat men and women differently," says Ann Bowman, who recently published a study on the effects of attractiveness on political candidates. She asked 125 undergraduates to rank two groups of photographs, one of men and one of women, in order of attractiveness. The students were told the photographs were of candidates for political offices. They were asked to rank them again, in the order they would vote for them.

The results showed that attractive males utterly defeated unattractive men, but the women who had been ranked most attractive invariably received the fewest votes.

6. The word "liability" (Line 5, Para. 1) most probably means "_____".
   A. misfortune B. instability C. disadvantage D. burden
7. In traditionally female jobs, attractiveness _____.
   A. reinforces the feminine qualities required
   B. makes women look more honest and capable
   C. is of primary importance to women
   D. often enables women to succeed quickly
8. Bowman's experiment reveals that when it comes to politics, attractiveness ____.
   A. turns out to be an obstacle
   B. affects men and women alike
   C. has as little effect on men as on women
   D. is more of an obstacle than a benefit to women
9. It can be inferred from the passage that people's views on beauty are often ____.
   A. practical B. prejudiced C. old-fashioned D. radical
10. The author writes this passage to _____.
   A. discuss the negative aspects of being attractive
   B. give advice to job-seekers who are attractive
   C. demand equal rights for women
   D. emphasize the importance of appearance

Unit Eleven Short Story

Text A

The Shocks of Doom
By O. Henry

There is an aristocracy of the public parks and even of the vagabonds who use them for their private apartments. Vallance felt rather than knew this, but when he stepped down out of his world into chaos his feet brought him directly to Madison Square.

Raw and astringent as a schoolgirl—of the old order—young May breathed austerely among the budding trees. Vallance buttoned his coat, lighted his last cigarette and took a seat upon a bench. For three minutes he mildly regretted the last hundred of his last thousand that it had cost him when the bicycle cop put an end to his last automobile ride. Then he felt in every pocket and found not a single penny. He had given up his apartment that morning. His furniture had gone toward certain debts. His clothes, save what were upon him, had descended to his man-servant for back wages. As he sat there was not in the whole city for him a bed or a broiled lobster or a street-car fare or a carnation for buttonhole unless he should obtain them by sponging on his friends or by false pretences. Therefore he had chosen the park.

And all this was because an uncle had disinherited him, and cut down his allowance from liberality to nothing. And all that was because his nephew had disobeyed him concerning a certain girl, who comes not into this story—therefore, all readers who brush their hair toward its roots may be warned to read no further. There was another nephew, of a different branch, who had once been the prospective heir and favorite. Being without grace or hope, he had long ago

vagabond /ˈvæɡəbɒnd/ *n.* someone who has no home and travels from place to place; a tramp
astringent /əˈstrɪndʒənt/ *adj.* sharp and penetrating; severe
austerely /ɔːˈstɪəli/ *adv.* in a severe or stern or grave fashion
carnation /kɑːˈneɪʃən/ *n.* a flower that smells sweet. Men often wear a carnation on their jacket on formal occasions 康乃馨
sponge /ˈspʌndʒ/ *vi.* (*informal*) to live by relying on the generosity of others
disinherit /ˈdɪsɪnˈherɪt/ *vt.* prevent deliberately (as by making a will) from inheriting
liberality /ˌlibəˈræliti/ *n.* the quality of being generous

disappeared in the mire. Now dragnets were out for him; he was to be rehabilitated and restored. And so Vallance fell grandly as Lucifer to the lowest pit, joining the tattered ghosts in the little park.

Sitting there, he leaned far back on the hard bench and laughed a jet of cigarette smoke up to the lowest tree branches. The sudden severing of all his life's ties had brought him a free, thrilling, almost joyous elation. He felt precisely the sensation of the aeronaut when he cuts loose his parachute and lets his balloon drift away.

mire /'maɪə/ *n.* deep mud; a bad or difficult situation that you cannot seem to escape from

dragnet /'dræɡnet/ *n.* a system in which the police look for criminals or other wanted persons, using very thorough method

rehabilitate /ˌriːhə'bɪlɪteɪt/ *vt.* to help (a person) to re-adapt to society after illness or imprisonment or other events

tattered /'tætəd/ *adj.* wearing ragged or torn clothing

sever /'sevə/ *vt.* to cut through something complete

elation /ɪ'leɪʃən/ *n.* a feeling of great happiness and excitement

aeronaut /'ɛərənɔːt/ *n.* a pilot or navigator of a lighter-than-air craft, such as a balloon

lounger /'laʊndʒə(r)/ *n.* someone who does not work and wastes time

cohort /'kəʊhɔːt/ *n.* a group or band of people

musty /'mʌsti/ *adj.* stale or moldy in odor or taste

bummer /'bʌmə/ *n.* (*slang*) one that depresses, frustrates, or disappoints

pretzel /'pretsəl/ *n.* glazed and salted cracker typically in the shape of a loose knot or a stick

The hour was nearly ten. Not many loungers were on the benches. The park-dweller, though a stubborn fighter against autumnal coolness, is slow to attack the advance line of spring's chilly cohorts.

Then arose one from a seat near the leaping fountain, and came and sat himself at Vallance's side. He was either young or old; cheap lodging-houses had flavored him mustily; razors and combs had passed him by; in him drink had been bottled and sealed in the devil's bond. He begged a match, which is the form of introduction among park benchers, and then began to talk.

"You're not one of the regulars," he said to Vallance. "I know tailored clothes when I see 'em. You just stopped for a moment on your way through the park. Don't mind my talking to you for a while? I've got to be with somebody. I'm afraid—I'm afraid. I've told two or three of those bummers over there about it. They think I'm crazy. Say—let me tell you—all I've had to eat to-day was a couple of pretzels and an apple. To-morrow I'll stand in line to inherit three millions; and that restaurant you see over there with the autos around it will be too for me to eat in. Don't believe it, do you?

"Without the slightest trouble," said Vallance, with a laugh. "I lunched there yesterday. Tonight I couldn't buy a five-cent cup of coffee."

"You don't look like one of us. Well, I guess those things happen. I used to be a high-flyer myself years ago. What knocked you out of the game?"

"I—oh, I lost my job," said Vallance.

"It's undiluted Hades, this city," went on the other. "One day you're eating from china, the next you are eating in China—a chop-suey joint. I've had more than my share of hard luck. For five years I've been little better than a panhandler. I was raised up to live expensively and do nothing. Say—I don't mind telling you—I've got to talk to somebody, you see, because I'm afraid—I'm afraid. My name's Ide. You wouldn't think that old Paulding, one of the millionaires on Riverside Drive, was my uncle, would you? Well, he is. I lived in his house once, and had all the money I wanted. Say, haven't you got the price of a couple of drinks about you—er—what's your name—"

"Dawson," said Vallance. "No; I'm sorry to say that I'm all in, financially."

"I've been living for a week in a coal cellar on Division Street," went on Ide, "with a crook they called 'Blinky' Morris. I didn't have anywhere else to go. While I was out to-day a chap with some papers in his pocket was there, asking for me. I didn't know but what he was a fly cop, so I didn't go around again till after dark. There was a letter there he had left for me. Say—Dawson, it was from a big downtown lawyer, Mead. I've seen his sign on Ann Street. Paulding wants me to play the prodigal nephew—wants me to come back and be his heir again and blow in his money. I'm to call at the lawyer's office at ten to-morrow and step into my old shoes again—heir to three million, Dawson, and $10,000 a year pocket money. And—I'm afraid—I'm afraid."

The vagrant leaped to his feet and raised both trembling arms above his head. He caught his breath and moaned hysterically.

Vallance seized his arm and forced him back to the bench.

"Be quiet!" he commanded, with something like disgust in his tones. "One would think you had lost a fortune, instead of being about to

high-flyer *n.* a person who is extremely ambitious, or of great ability in a career

undiluted /ˌʌndaɪˈluːtɪd/ *adj.* not mixed with any other feeling or quality

panhandler /ˈpænhændlə/ *n.* a beggar

crook /krʊk/ *n.* (*informal*) a dishonest person or a criminal

cop /kɒp/ a fly cop: a plainclothes policeman

prodigal /ˈprɒdɪɡəl/ *adj.* giving or given in abundance; recklessly wasteful or extravagant

vagrant /ˈveɪɡrənt/ *n.* someone who has no home or work, especially someone who begs

hysterically /hɪˈsterɪkəlɪ/ *adv.* in a manner of being unable to control one's behavior or emotion

acquire one. Of what are you afraid?"

Ide <u>cowered</u> and shivered on the bench. He clung to Vallance's sleeve, and even in the dim glow of the Broadway lights the latest disinherited one could see drops on the other's brow <u>wrung</u> out by some strange terror.

cower /ˈkaʊə/ *vi.* to bend low and move back because of fear
wrung /rʌŋ/ *vt.* to extract (liquid) by twisting or compressing. Often used with "out"
soothingly /ˈsuːðɪŋli/ *adv.* trying to make someone feel calmer and less anxious, upset, or angry

"Why, I'm afraid something will happen to me before morning. I don't know what—something to keep me from coming into that money. I'm afraid a tree will fall on me—I'm afraid a cab will run over me, or a stone drop on me from a housetop, or something. I never was afraid before. I've sat in this park a hundred nights as calm as a graven image without knowing where my breakfast was to come from. But now it's different. I love money, Dawson— I'm happy as a god when it's trickling through my fingers, and people are bowing to me, with the music and the flowers and fine clothes all around. As long as I knew I was out of the game I didn't mind. I was even happy sitting here ragged and hungry, listening to the fountain jump and watching the carriages go up the avenue. But it's in reach of my hand again now—almost—and I can't stand it to wait twelve hours, Dawson—I can't stand it. There are fifty things that could happen to me—I could go blind—I might be attacked with heart disease—the world might come to an end before I could—"
Ide sprang to his feet again, with a shriek. People stirred on the benches and began to look. Vallance took his arm.

"Come and walk," he said, <u>soothingly</u>. "And try to calm yourself. There is no need to become excited or alarmed. Nothing is going to happen to you. One night is like another."

"That's right," said Ide. "Stay with me, Dawson—that's a good fellow. Walk around with me awhile. I never went to pieces like this before, and I've had a good many hard knocks. Do you think you could hustle something in the way of a little lunch, old man? I'm afraid my nerve's too far gone to try any panhandling"

Vallance led his companion up almost deserted Fifth Avenue, and then westward along the Thirties toward Broadway. "Wait here a few minutes," he said, leaving Ide in a quiet and shadowed spot. He entered a familiar hotel, and strolled toward the bar quite in his old assured way.

"There's a poor devil outside, Jimmy," he said to the bartender, "who says he's hungry and looks it. You know what they do when you give them money. Fix up a sandwich or two for him; and I'll see that he doesn't throw it away."

"Certainly, Mr. Vallance," said the bartender. "They ain't all fakes. Don't like to see anybody go hungry."

Ide folded a liberal supply of the free lunch into a napkin. Vallance went with it and joined his companion. Ide pounced upon the food ravenously. "I haven't had any free lunch as good as this in a year," he said. "Aren't you going to eat any, Dawson?

"I'm not hungry—thanks," said Vallance.

"We'll go back to the Square," said Ide. "The cops won't bother us there. I'll roll up the rest of this ham and stuff for our breakfast. I won't eat any more; I'm afraid I'll get sick. Suppose I'd die of cramps or something to-night, and never get to touch that money again! It's eleven hours yet till time to see that lawyer. You won't leave me, will you, Dawson? I'm afraid something might happen. You haven't any place to go, have you?"

"No," said Vallance, "nowhere to-night. I'll have a bench with you."

"You take it cool," said Ide, "if you've told it to me straight. I should think a man put on the bum from a good job just in one day would be tearing his hair."

"I believe I've already remarked," said Vallance, laughing, "that I would have thought that a man who was expecting to come into a fortune on the next day would be feeling pretty easy and quiet."

"It's funny business," philosophized Ide, "about the way people take things, anyhow. Here's your bench, Dawson, right next to mine. The light don't shine in your eyes here. Say, Dawson, I'll get the old man to give you a letter to somebody about a job when I get back home. You've helped me a lot to-night. I don't believe I could have gone through the night if I hadn't struck you."

pounce /paʊns/ vi. to spring or swoop with intent to seize someone or something

ravenously /ˈrævənəsli/ adv. extremely hungrily

cramp /kræmp/ n. a severe pain in part of human body, e.g. stomach, when a muscle becomes too tight

bum /bʌm/ n. someone, especially a man, who has no home or job, and who asks people for money

philosophize /fɪˈlɒsəfaɪz/ vi. to discuss or speculate in a philosophical manner

"Thank you, " said Vallance. "Do you lie down or sit up on these when you sleep? "

For hours Vallance gazed almost without winking at the stars through the branches of the trees and listened to the sharp slapping of horses' hoofs on the sea of asphalt to the south. His mind was active, but his feelings were dormant. Every emotion seemed to have been eradicated. Ide felt no regrets, no fears, no pain or discomfort. Even when he thought of the girl, it was as of an inhabitant of one of those remote stars at which be gazed. He remembered the absurd antics of his companion and laughed softly, yet without a feeling of mirth. Soon the daily army of milk wagons made of the city a roaring drum to which they marched. Vallance fell asleep on his comfortless bench.

asphalt /'æsfælt/ *n.* pitch; a black sticky substance that becomes hard when it dries, used for making the surface of roads

dormant /'dɔ:mənt/ *adj.* lying asleep or as if asleep; inactive

eradicate /ɪ'rædɪkeɪt/ *vt.* to completely get rid of; to tear up by the roots

antics /'æntɪks/ *n.* behavior that seems strange, funny, silly, or annoying

mirth /mɜ:θ/ *n.* happiness and laughter

battered /'bætəd/ *adj.* old and in bad condition

sardonically /sɑ:'dɒnɪkli/ *adv.* scornfully or cynically mocking

At ten o'clock the next day the two stood at the door of Lawyer Mead's office in Ann Street.

Ide's nerves fluttered worse than ever when the hour approached; and Vallance could not decide to leave him a possible prey to the dangers he dreaded.

When they entered the office, Lawyer Mead looked at them wonderingly. He and Vallance were old friends. After his greeting, he turned to Ide, who stood with white face and trembling limbs before the expected crisis.

"I sent a second letter to your address last night, Mr. Ide," he said. "I learned this morning that you were not there to receive it. It will inform you that Mr. Paulding has reconsidered his offer to take you back into favor. He has decided not to do so, and desires you to understand that no change will be made in the relations existing between you and him."

Ide's trembling suddenly ceased. The color came back to his face, and he straightened his back. His jaw went forward half an inch, and a gleam came into his eye. He pushed back his battered hat with one hand, and extended the other, with leveled fingers, toward the lawyer. He took a long breath and then laughed sardonically.

"Tell old Paulding he may go to the devil," he said loudly and clearly, and turned and walked out of the office with a firm and lively step.

genially /dʒɪˈnɪəli/ *adv.* in a pleasant or friendly manner
reconcile /ˈrekənsaɪl/ *vt.* to bring (oneself) to accept

Lawyer Mead turned on his heel to Vallance and smiled.

"I am glad you came in," he said, genially. "Your uncle wants you to return home at once. He is reconciled to the situation that led to his hasty action, and desires to say that all will be as—"

"Hey, Adams!" cried Lawyer Mead, breaking his sentence, and calling to his clerk. "Bring a glass of water—Mr. Vallance has fainted."

(approximately 2230 words)

Reading Time: _____   Reading Rate: _____

Cultural Notes

1. **O. Henry:** the pen name of the American writer William Sydney Porter (1862—1910). Porter's 400 short stories are known for their wit, wordplay, characterization and the clever use of twist endings. O. Henry's stories are especially famous for their surprise endings, to the point that such an ending is often referred to as an "O. Henry ending." Most of O. Henry's stories are set in his own time, the early years of the 20th century. Many take place in New York City, and deal for the most part with ordinary people: clerks, policemen, waitresses, etc.

2. **Lucifer:** a name frequently given to Satan in Judeo-Christian belief because of a particular interpretation of a passage in the Book of Isaiah. More specifically, it is supposed to have been Satan's name before being cast out of heaven.

3. **Hades:** in Christian theology, the term *hades* refers to the abode of the dead, where the dead await Judgement Day either at peace or in torment.

4. **chop-suey:** a typical American-Chinese dish with different interesting stories about its origin. (Please surf the Internet for those stories.) With the Chinese meaning—mixed pieces (杂碎), the dish consists of meats (often chicken, beef, shrimp or pork), cooked quickly with vegetables such as bean sprouts, cabbage, and celery and bound in a starch-thickened sauce. It is typically served with rice but can become the Chinese-American form of chow mein

with the addition of deep-fried noodles.

Comprehension Exercises

I. Answer the following questions based on the text.

1. What impresses you most in this short story?
2. How did Mr. Vallance, previously a man of easy circumstances, become a park-dweller?
3. What were Ide's reactions when he learned that he would not receive the money? What did that show?
4. Why did Vallance faint at the end of the story?
5. Is the ending of the story surprising?

II. Decide whether each of the following statements is true or false according to the text.

1. Vallance knew there is an aristocracy of the public parks and even of the vagabonds who use them for their private apartments.
2. Vallance became penniless because his uncle disinherited him and cut down his allowance from liberality to nothing.
3. Ide became neurotic because he got a letter from a big downtown lawyer Mead.
4. We can infer from the story that things are always beyond people's expectation.
5. Mr. Vallance became fainted because he thought his uncle asked him back to inherit.

III. Select the most appropriate word or phrase and use its proper form to complete each of the following sentences.

astringent	liberality	rehabilitate	disinherit	genial
reconcile	philosophize	prodigal	hysterical	dormant
sever	cohort	pounce	sardonic	undiluted
cower	soothing	crook		

1. The elder Ho threatened to _____ Pansy if she ever married her close friend Gilbert Yeung, son of Emperor Group tycoon Albert Yeung Sau Shing.
2. His attentive behavior to herself and his sisters convinced her that their welfare was dear to him, and, for a long time, she firmly relied on the _____ of his intentions.
3. Scottish Conservative justice spokesman John Lamont said more had to be

done to _____ prisoners.

4. Trilling and his _____ were tempted by the glittering mirage of a worker's paradise.

5. The technique, developed at Strathclyde University in Glasgow, examines ethanol concentration in _____ samples and the residue of dried whisky.

6. Eight years have passed since Fellowship's last release, and during that time, Brian Blade has been more prodigious than _____.

7. Then the two of them go running _____ across the foyer and into the bathroom.

8. "No one has ever been able to make the American people _____ and not live the American life," Fleischer said.

9. The land had no electrical connection, so he bought oil lamps, which glowed _____ as he went about his evening chores, his routine of dinner and bedtime.

10. We hid ourselves behind the bushes, ready to _____ on the intruder.

11. They spend their time _____ about the mysteries of life.

12. The long _____ volcano of Mount St. Helens erupted in 1980.

13. At his best he could write funny, write sad, write _____ and write serious.

14. Bob was always _____ and welcoming.

15. It's difficult to _____ the demands of my job and the desire to be a good father.

IV. Try to paraphrase the following sentences, paying special attention to the underlined parts.

1. Now dragnets were out for him; he was to be rehabilitated and restored.

_____

_____

2. The sudden severing of all his life's ties had brought him a free, thrilling, almost joyous elation. He felt precisely the sensation of the aeronaut when he cuts loose his parachute and lets his balloon drift away.

_____

_____

3. The park-dweller, though a stubborn fighter against autumnal coolness, is slow to attack the advance line of spring's chilly cohorts.

_____

_____

4. He clung to Vallance's sleeve, and even in the dim glow of the Broadway lights the latest disinherited one could see drops on the other's brow wrung

out by some strange terror.

5. Soon <u>the daily army of milk wagons made of the city a roaring drum</u> to which they marched.

V. Discuss with your partner about each of the three statements and write an essay in no less than 260 words about your understanding of one of them.

1. And all this was because an uncle had disinherited him, and cut down his allowance from liberality to nothing. And all that was because his nephew had disobeyed him concerning a certain girl, who comes not into this story.

2. One day you're eating from china, the next you are eating in China—a chop-suey joint.

3. "I believe I've already remarked," said Vallance, laughing, "that I would have thought that a man who was expecting to come into a fortune on the next day would be feeling pretty easy and quiet."

VI. List four websites where we can learn more about O. Henry or his short stories and provide a brief introduction to each of them.

1.

2.

3.

4. _____

_____

_____.

Text B

Luck

By Mark Twain

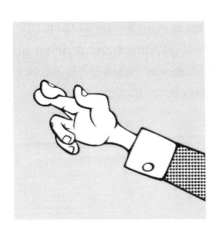

[Note—This is not a fancy sketch. I got it from a clergyman who was an instructor at Woolwich forty years ago, and who vouched for its truth.—M.T.]

It was at a banquet in London in honor of one of the two or three conspicuously illustrious English military names of this generation. For reasons which will presently appear, I will withhold his real name and titles and call him Lieutenant-General Lord Arthur Scoresby, Y.C., K. C.B., etc., etc., etc. What a fascination there is in a renowned name! There sat the man, in actual flesh, whom I had heard of so many thousands of times since that day, thirty years before, when his name shot suddenly to the zenith from a Crimean battlefield, to remain forever celebrated. It was food and drink to me to look, and look, and look at that demi-god; scanning, searching, noting: the quietness, the reserve, the noble gravity of his countenance; the simple honesty that expressed itself all over him; the sweet unconsciousness of his greatness, unconsciousness of the hundreds of admiring eyes fastened upon him, unconsciousness of the deep, loving, sincere worship welling out of the breasts of those people and flowing toward him.

The clergyman at my left was an old acquaintance of mine—clergyman now, but had spent the first half of his life in the camp and field and as an instructor in the military school at Woolwich. Just at the moment I have been talking about a veiled and singular light glimmered in his eyes and he leaned down and muttered confidently to me, indicating the hero of the banquet with a gesture:

illustrious /ɪˈlʌstrɪəs/ *adj.* well known and very distinguished
zenith /ˈzenɪθ/ *n.* the point of culmination; the peak
countenance /ˈkaʊntɪnəns/ *n.* appearance, especially the expression of the face
mutter /ˈmʌtə/ *vi.* to speak in a low voice
confidently /ˈkɒnfɪdəntli/ *adv.* obsolete trustfully

" Privately—he's an absolute fool."

This verdict was a great surprise to me. If its subject had been Napoleon, or Socrates, or Solomon, my astonishment could not have been greater. Two things I was well aware of: that the Reverend was a man of strict veracity and that his judgment of men was good. Therefore I knew, beyond doubt or question, that the

veracity /vəˈræsɪti/ *n.* adherence to the truth; truthfulness
preliminary /prɪˈlɪmɪnə ri/ *adj.* happening before something that is more important, often in order to prepare for it
quick /kwɪk/ be touched to the quick: to feel extremely upset
guileless /ˈɡaɪlləs/ *adj.* behaving in an honest way, without trying to hide anything or deceive people
galley-slave *n.* a slave or convict forced to ply an oar of a galley (a kind of ancient warship)
colors /ˈkʌləz/ *n.* complete success
cram /kræm/ *n.* preparation for an examination by learning a lot of information quickly
get plucked fail an exam
stupefy /ˈstjuːpɪfaɪ/ *adj.* amazing, astonishing

world was mistaken about this hero: he *was* a fool. So I meant to find out, at a convenient moment, how the Reverend, all solitary and alone, had discovered the secret.

Some days later the opportunity came, and this is what the Reverend told me:

About forty years ago I was an instructor in the military academy at Woolwich. I was present in one of the sections when young Scoresby underwent his preliminary examination. I was touched to the quick with pity, for the rest of the class answered up brightly and handsomely, while he—why, dear me, he didn't know *anything*, so to speak. He was evidently good, and sweet, and lovable, and guileless ; and so it was exceedingly painful to see him stand there, as serene as a graven image, and deliver himself of answers which were veritably miraculous for stupidity and ignorance. All the compassion in me was aroused in his behalf. I said to myself, when he comes to be examined again he will be flung over, of course; so it will be simply a harmless act of charity to ease his fall as much as I can. I took him aside and found that he knew a little of Caesar's history; and as he didn't know anything else, I went to work and drilled him like a galley-slave on a certain line of stock questions concerning Cesar which I knew would be used. If you'll believe me, he went through with flying colors on examination day! He went through on that purely superficial "cram ," and got compliments too, while others, who knew a thousand times more than he, got plucked . By some strangely lucky accident—accident not likely to happen twice in a century—he was asked no question outside of the narrow limits of his drill.

It was stupefying . Well, all through his course I stood by him, with something of the sentiment which a mother feels for a crippled child; and he always saved himself—just by miracle, apparently.

Now, of course, the thing that would expose him and kill him at last was mathematics. I resolved to make his death as easy as I could; so I drilled him and crammed him, and crammed him and drilled him, just on the line of questions which the examiners would be most likely to use, and then launched him on his fate. Well, sir, try to conceive of the result: to my consternation , he took the first prize! And with it he got a perfect ovation in the way of compliments.

consternation /kɒnstəˈneɪʃ ə n/ *n.* a feeling of worry, shock, or fear
ovation /əʊˈveɪʃən/ *n.* enthusiastic, prolonged applause
preposterous /priˈpɒstərəs/ *adj.* completely unreasonable or silly; absurd
prodigious /prəˈdɪdʒəs/ *adj.* enormous
gazette /gəˈzet/ *vt.* to announce or publish in an official journal or in a newspaper
sublimity /səˈblɪməti/ *n.* nobility in thought or feeling or style
cornetcy /ˈkɔːnɪtsɪ/ *n.* [military rank] a commissioned officer rank in cavalry troops, once the bearer of the Troop's flag or cornet (a musical instrument like a small trumpet)
repose /rɪˈpəʊz/ *n.* the act of resting or the state of being at rest
cornetcy /ˈkɔːnɪtsɪ/ *n.* the rank of a cornet

Sleep? There was no more sleep for me for a week. My conscience tortured me day and night. What I had done I had done purely through charity, and only to ease the poor youth's fall. I never had dreamed of any such preposterous results as the thing that had happened. I felt as guilty and miserable as Frankenstein. Here was a woodenhead whom I had put in the way of glittering promotions and prodigious responsibilities, and but one thing could happen: he and his responsibilities would all go to ruin together at the first opportunity.

The Crimean War had just broken out. Of course there had to be a war, I said to myself. We couldn't have peace and give this donkey a chance to die before he is found out. I waited for the earthquake. It came. And it made me reel when it did come. He was actually gazetted to a captaincy in a marching regiment! Better men grow old and gray in the service before they climb to a sublimity like that. And who could ever have foreseen that they would go and put such a load of responsibility on such green and inadequate shoulders? I could just barely have stood it if they had made him a cornet ; but a captain—think of it! I thought my hair would turn white.

Consider what I did—I who so loved repose and inaction. I said to myself, I am responsible to the country for this, and I must go along with him and protect the country against him as far as I can. So I took my poor little capital that I had saved up through years of work and grinding economy, and went with a sigh and bought a cornetcy in his regiment, and away we went to the field.

And there—oh, dear, it was awful. Blunders? —Why, he never did anything *but* blunder. But, you see, nobody was in the fellow's secret. Everybody had him focused wrong, and necessarily misinterpreted his performance every time. Consequently they took his idiotic blunders for inspirations of genius. They did, honestly! His mildest blunders were enough to make a man in his right mind cry; and they did make me cry—and rage

rave /reɪv/ *vi.* to roar or to speak wildly, irrationally, or incoherently
luster /'lʌstə/ *n.* glory, radiance, distinction, or splendor, as of achievement, reputation, or beauty
browse /braʊz/ *vt.* to inspect something in a leisurely and casual way
pell-mell *adv.* quickly and in an uncontrolled way
rout /raʊt/ *n.* a complete defeat in a battle, competition, or election

and rave, too, privately. And the thing that kept me always in a sweat of apprehension was the fact that every fresh blunder he made increased the luster of his reputation! I kept saying to myself, he'll get so high that when discovery does finally come, it will be like the sun falling out of the sky.

He went right along up, from grade to grade, over the dead bodies of his superiors, until at last, in the hottest moment of the battle of... down went our colonel, and my heart jumped into my mouth for Scoresby was next in rank! Now for it, said I; we'll all land in Sheol in ten minutes, sure.

The battle was awfully hot; the allies were steadily giving way all over the field. Our regiment occupied a position that was vital; a blunder now must be destruction. At this crucial moment, what does this immortal fool do but detach the regiment from its place and order a charge over a neighboring hill where there wasn't a suggestion of an enemy! "There you go!" I said to myself; "This *is* the end at last."

And away we did go, and were over the shoulder of the hill before the insane movement could be discovered and stopped. And what did we find? An entire and unsuspected Russian army in reserve! And what happened? We were eaten up? That is necessarily what would have happened in ninety-nine cases out of a hundred. But no, those Russians argued that no single regiment would come browsing around there at such a time. It must be the entire English army, and that the sly Russian game was detected and blocked; so they turned tail, and away they went, pell-mell , over the hill and down into the field, in wild confusion, and we after them; they themselves broke the solid Russian center in the field, and tore through, and in no time there was the most tremendous rout you ever saw, and the defeat of the allies was turned into a sweeping and splendid victory! Marshal Canrobert looked on, dizzy with astonishment, admiration, and delight; and sent right off for Scoresby, and hugged him, and decorated him on the field in presence of all the armies!

And what was Scoresby's blunder that time? Merely the mistaking his right hand for his left—that was all. An order had come to him to fall back and support our right; and, instead, he fell *forward* and went over the hill to the left. But the name he won that day as a marvelous military genius filled the world with his glory, and that glory will never fade while history books last.

phenomenal /fɪ'nɒmɪnəl/ *adj.* extraordinary; outstanding

He is just as good and sweet and lovable and unpretending as a man can be, but he doesn't know enough to come in when it rains. Now that is absolutely true. He is the supremest ass in the universe; and until half an hour ago nobody knew it but himself and me. He has been pursued, day by day and year by year, by a most phenomenal and astonishing luckiness. He has been a shining soldier in all our wars for a generation; he has littered his whole military life with blunders, and yet has never committed one that didn't make him a knight or a baronet or a lord or something. Look at his breast; why, he is just clothed in domestic and foreign decorations. Well, sir, every one of them is the record of some shouting stupidity or other; and, taken together, they are proof that the very best thing in all this world that can befall a man is to be born lucky. I say again, as I said at the banquet, Scoresby's an absolute fool.

(approximately 1740 words)

Reading Time: _____   Reading Rate: _____

Cultural Notes

1. **Samuel Langhorne Clemens** (1835—1910): better known by the pen name **Mark Twain**, an American humorist, satirist, lecturer and writer. Mark Twain is most noted for his novels *Adventures of Huckleberry Finn*, which has since been called the Great American Novel, and *The Adventures of Tom Sawyer*. He is also known for his quotations. Mark Twain enjoyed immense public popularity, and his keen wit and incisive satire earned him praise from both critics and peers. American author William Faulkner called Mark Twain "the father of American literature."

2. **Y. C.:** Yeomanry Cavalry

   K.C.B.: Knight Commander of the Bath—British military award conferred on someone in recognition of his outstanding service.

3. **Caesar** (Gaius Julius Caesar) (100 BC—44 BC): a Roman military and political leader. He played a critical role in the transformation of the Roman Republic into the Roman Empire.

4. **Frankenstein:** *the protagonist in the novel Frankenstein* written by the British author Mary Shelley. Shelley wrote the novel when she was 18 years old. The title of the novel refers to a scientist, Victor Frankenstein, who learns how to create life and creates a being in the likeness of man, but larger than average and more powerful. In modern popular culture, people have tended to refer to the creature as "Frankenstein" (especially in films since 1931), despite this being the name of the scientist. *Frankenstein* is a novel infused with some elements of the Gothic novel and the Romantic movement. The story has had an influence across literature and popular culture and spawned a complete genre of horror stories and films.

5. **The Crimean War** (1853—1856): The war was fought between Imperial Russia on one side and an alliance of France, the United Kingdom, the Kingdom of Sardinia, and the Ottoman Empire on the other. Most of the conflict took place on the Crimean Peninsula, with additional actions occurring in western Turkey, and the Baltic Sea region. The Crimean War is sometimes considered to be the first "modern" conflict and "introduced technical changes which affected the future course of warfare."

6. **Sheol:** the "abode of the dead", the "underworld", "the common grave of humankind" or "pit". In the Hebrew Bible, it is a place where both the bad and the good, slave and king, pious and wicked must go at the point of death. *Sheol* is the common destination of both the righteous and the unrighteous dead.

7. **Marshal Canrobert** (1809—1895): François Certain Canrobert, a marshal of France.

8. **baronet:** or the rare female equivalent, **baronetess**, is the holder of a hereditary title awarded by the British Crown known as a *baronetcy*. The current practice of awarding baronetcies was originally introduced in England and Ireland by James I of England in 1611 in order to raise funds.

Comprehension Exercises

I. Answer the following questions based on the text.

1. At the beginning of the banquet in London, what was the attitude of the narrator towards Scoresby?

2. Then, what was the dramatic change in the narrator's attitude? Why was there such a huge change?

3. How did Scoresby gain a glorious victory in a Crimean battlefield? What was the preliminary cause of the victory?

4. What impress you most in this humorous short story?

5. What is the message conveyed in this story?

II. Decide whether each of the following statements is true or false according to the text.

1. The Reverend was a man of strict veracity and his judgment of men was good.

2. Only the Reverend and Scoresby himself knew he was the supremest ass in the universe.

3. Scoresby did one blunder after another in the Crimean War.

4. Scoresby's success derived his good luck.

5. The clergyman instructed Scoresby in the military school at Woolwich about forty years ago.

III. Select the most appropriate word or phrase and use its proper form to complete each of the following sentences.

illustrious	preposterous	prodigious	veracity	preliminary
guileless	phenomenal	revere	stupefy	zenith
convenient	confident	verdict	rout	entire
color	rave	browse		

1. In Cricklewood Greats, Capaldi has created an _____ and eccentric history for Cricklewood Film Studios.

2. I can _____ promise that this year is going to be very different.

3. We have total confidence in the _____ of our research.

4. _____ results show the Republican Party with 11 percent of the vote.

5. Joanne was so _____ that Claire had no option but to believe her.

6. It seems that the honey had been left in the soldiers' path not in an act of flight from the advancing forces but as a poisonous bait to _____ them.

7. No matter how _____ the rule, it stays and stays, regardless of whether it works to accomplish its end.

8. China's imports have ballooned this year, thanks to its _____ stimulus spending and a rise in commodity prices.

9. She cried and _____ for weeks, and people did not know what to do.

11. And when our citizens are losing trust by the hour in institutions they once _____, only you can restore calm.

12. Two of the judges disagreed with the _____.

13. I live just by the market, and it's very _____ to go shopping.

14. If you like, you can even change the color of your eyes with _____ contact

lenses.

15. Everyone tends to forget what happened after the _____ of the British: In 1842 they invaded again, defeating every Afghan army sent out against them.

IV. Try to paraphrase the following sentences, paying special attention to the underlined parts.

1. It was at a banquet in London in honor of one of the two or three conspicuously illustrious English military names of this generation.

   _____

2. Two things I was well aware of: that the Reverend was a man of strict veracity and that his judgment of men was good.

   _____

3. All the compassion in me was aroused in his behalf.

   _____

4. Here was a woodenhead whom I had put in the way of glittering promotions and prodigious responsibilities, and but one thing could happen: he and his responsibilities would all go to ruin together at the first opportunity.

   _____

5. And the thing that kept me always in a sweat of apprehension was the fact that every fresh blunder he made increased the luster of his reputation!

   _____

V. Discuss with your partner about each of the three statements and write an essay in no less than 260 words about your understanding of one of them.

1. But, you see, nobody was in the fellow's secret. Everybody had him focused wrong, and necessarily misinterpreted his performance every time. Consequently they took his idiotic blunders for inspirations of genius.

   _____

2. I kept saying to myself, he'll get so high that when discovery does finally come, it will be like the sun falling out of the sky.

   _____

3. ...and, taken together, they are proof that the very best thing in all this world that can befall a man is to be born lucky.

_____

_____

VI. List four websites where we can learn more about Mark Twain or his short stories and provide a brief introduction to each of them.

1. _____

   _____

   _____.

2. _____

   _____

   _____.

3. _____

   _____

   _____.

4. _____

   _____

   _____.

Twenty Minutes' Reading

You are required to read the following two sections within 20 minutes.

Section A

The biographer has to dance between two shaky positions with respect to the subject. Too close a relation, and the writer may be objectivity. Not close enough, and the writer may lack the sympathy necessary to any effort to portray a mind, a soul—the quality of life. Who should write the biography of a family, for example? Because of their closeness to the subject, family members may have special information, but by the same token, they may not have the distance that would allow them to be fair. Similarly, a king's servant might not be the best one to write a biography of that king. But a foreigner might not have the knowledge and sympathy necessary to write the king's biography—not for a readership from within the kingdom, at any rate.

There is no ideal position for such a task. The biographer has to work with the position he or she has in the world, adjusting that position as necessary to deal with the subject. Every position has strengths and weaknesses: to thrive, a writer must try to become aware of these, evaluate them in terms of the subject, and select a position accordingly.

When their subjects are heroes or famous figures, biographies often reveal a democratic motive: they attempt to show that their subjects are only human, no better than anyone else. Other biographies are meant to change us, to invite us to become better than we are. The biographies of Jesus found in the Bible are in this class.

Biographers may claim that their account is the "authentic" one. In advancing this claim, they are helped if the biography is "authorized" by the subject, this presumably allows the biographer special access to private information. "Unauthorized" biographies also have their appeal, however, since they can suggest an independence of mind in the biographer. In book promotions, the "unauthorized" characterization usually suggests the prospect of juicy gossip that the subject had hoped to suppress. A subject might have several biographies, even several "authentic" ones. We sense intuitively that no one is in a position to tell the story of a life, perhaps not even the subject, and this has been proved by the history of biography.

1. According to the author, an ideal biographer would be one who _____.
   A. knows the subject very well and yet maintains a proper distance from him
   B. is close to the subject and knows the techniques of biography writing
   C. is independent and treats the subject with fairness and objectivity
   D. possesses special private information and is sympathetic toward the subject
2. The author cites the biographies of Jesus in the Bible in order to show that _____.
   A. the best biographies are meant to transform their readers
   B. biographies are authentic accounts of their subjects' lives
   C. the best biographies are the of heroes and famous figures
   D. biographies can serve different purpose
3. Which of the following statements is true, according to the passage?
   A. An authentic biography seldom appeals to its readers.
   B. An authentic biography is one authorized by the subject.
   C. No one can write a perfect biography.
   D. Authorized biographies have a wider readership.
4. An unauthorized biography is likely to attract more readers because _____.
   A. it portrays the subject both faithfully and vividly
   B. it contains interesting information about the subject's private life

C. it reveals a lot of accurate details unknown to outsiders

D. it usually gives a sympathetic description of the subject's character

5. In this passage, the author focuses on _____.

A. the difficulty of a biographer in finding the proper perspective to do his job

B. the secret of a biographer to win more readers

C. the techniques required of a biographer to write a good biography

D. the characteristics of different kinds of biographies

Section B

I was standing in my kitchen wondering what to have for lunch when my friend Taj called.

"Sit down," she said.

I thought she was going to tell me she had just gotten the haircut from hell. I laughed and said, "It can't be that bad."

But it was. Before the phone call, I had 30 years of retirement saving in a "safe" fund with a brilliant financial guru. When I put down the phone, my savings were gone. I felt as if I had died and, for some unknown reason, was still breathing.

Since Bernie Madoff's arrest on charges of running a $65 million Ponzi scheme, I've read many articles about how we investors should have known what was going on. I wish I could say I had reservations about Madoff before "the Call", but I did not.

On New Year's Eve, three weeks after we lost our savings, six of us Madoff people gathered at Taj's house for dinner. As we were sitting around the table, someone asked, "If you could have your money back right now, but it would mean giving up what you have learned by losing it, would you take the money or would you take what losing the money has given you?"

My husband was still in financial shock. He said, "I just want the money back." I wasn't certain where I stood. I knew that losing our money had cracked me wide open. I'd been walking around like what the Buddhists call a hungry ghost: always focused on the bite that was yet to come, not the one in my mouth. No matter how much I ate or had or experienced, it didn't satisfy me, because I wasn't really taking it in, wasn't absorbing it. Now I was forced to pay attention. Still, I couldn't honestly say that if someone had offered me the money back, I would turn it down.

But the other four all said that what they were seeing about themselves was incalculable, and they didn't think it would have become apparent without the ground of financial stability being ripped out from underneath them.

My friend Michael said, "I'd started to get complacent. It's as if the muscles of my heart started to atrophy(萎缩). Now they're awake, alive—and I don't want to go back."

These weren't just empty words. Michael and his wife needed to take in boarders to meet their expenses. Taj was so broke that she was moving into someone's garage apartment in three weeks. Three friends had declared bankruptcy and weren't sure where or how they were going to live.

6. What did the author learn from Taj's call?
   A. She had got an awful haircut.
   B. They had lost their retirement savings.
   C. Taj had just retired from work.
   D. They were going to meet for lunch.
7. How did the author feel in the following weeks?
   A. Angry.
   B. Disappointed.
   C. Indifferent.
   D. Desperate.
8. According to the passage, to which was she "forced to pay attention"?
   A. Her friends.
   B. Her husband.
   C. Her lost savings.
   D. Her experience.
9. Which of the following statements is CORRECT about her friends?
   A. Her friends valued their experience more.
   B. Her friends felt the same as she did.
   C. Her friends were in a better financial situation.
   D. Her friends were more optimistic than she.
10. What is the message of the passage?
   A. Desire for money is human nature.
   B. One has to be decisive during crises.
   C. Understanding gained is more important than money lost.
   D. It is natural to see varied responses to financial crises.

Unit Twelve
Environment Protection

The Price of Oil

By Peter Maass

More than 35 years ago, an offshore drilling rig spilled approximately three million gallons of oil into the waters near Santa Barbara. A massive slick covered hundreds of square miles and killed thousands of birds, seals and dolphins; the white beaches of California turned black with crude oil. Night after night, the TV networks showed oil-covered birds flopping in their death throes on fouled beaches. Popular outrage was heightened by the attitude of Fred Hartley, president of Union Oil, which operated the offending rig. In Senate testimony, he chided environmentalists and journalists for over-reacting to the loss of bird life.

The Santa Barbara spill was a galvanizing event that raised support for the first Earth Day, hastened the creation of the Environmental Protection Agency and led to state and federal moratoriums on new drilling. Today, drilling for oil and gas is barred off 90 percent of America's coastlines; it is allowed, mainly, in the Gulf of Mexico, though not near tourism-dependent Florida. The offshore moratoriums, along with a ban on drilling in the Arctic National Wildlife Refuge, are regarded as triumphs of the environmental movement.

But these victories came at a cost. As politicians in the White House and Congress are pushing again for exploration in coastal waters and drilling in ANWR, it is worth reconsidering the changes won by the

drilling rig *n.* special equipment or gear used for a particular purpose

slick /slɪk/ *n.* a smooth or slippery surface or area

throe /θrəʊ/ *n.* a condition of agonizing struggle or trouble

foul /faʊl/ *vt.* to make dirty or foul; pollute

testimony /ˈtestɪməni/ *n.* [Law] evidence given by a witness, esp. in court under oath

galvanizing /ˈgælvəˈnaɪzɪŋ/ *adj.* affected by emotion as if by electricity; thrilling

moratorium /mɒrəˈtɔːrɪəm/ *n.* a suspension of an ongoing or planned activity

environmental movement, but not only for the supply-enhancing reasons cited by advocates of extracting oil wherever it may be found. The latest battle has not touched upon a depressing fact: every barrel of oil that is not extracted from America must be drilled from someone else's backyard, often with little regard for the consequences. Because our appetite for energy has grown over the decades, new drilling, along with the damage it tends to create, has not been halted; it has been outsourced.

outsource /ˈaʊtsɔːs/ *vt.* obtain goods or services from an outside supplier
mangrove /ˈmæŋɡrəʊv/ *n.* any of several tropical evergreen trees or shrubs of the genus Rhizophora, having stiltlike roots and stems and forming dense thickets along tidal shores [植] 红树
wage /weɪdʒ/ *vt.* carry on (wars, battles, or campaigns)
Ecuador /ˈekwədɔː/ *n.* a republic in northwestern South America 厄瓜多尔
miasma /mɪˈæzmə/ *n.* a noxious atmosphere or influence
negligible /ˈneɡlɪdʒəbəl/ *adj.* not significant or important enough to be worth considering; trifling

Take a look at Nigeria, which has the misfortune of possessing more than 35 billion barrels of oil, much of it around the Niger Delta. When I visited last year, traveling through stunted mangrove swamps near Port Harcourt, there was a near-absence of birds, and oil was everywhere—not only dripping from rusty platforms atop the delta waters, but in the water itself, in the air, which smelled of petroleum, and in the gas flares that are a scalding feature of the injured landscape. Because of a host of political and economic ills triggered by the drilling, the Niger Delta is alive not with marine life but with violence—bands of tribal warriors wage an off-and-on war against one another and army troops.

Ecuador is another victim. After oil was discovered in its Oriente region in 1967, Texaco and a state-owned oil company operated an extraction program that, a quarter century later, had reduced parts of the Amazon to a deforested miasma of pollution and poverty. Chevron, which purchased Texaco, now faces a billion-dollar lawsuit accusing it of poisoning the land. Ecuador had a negligible foreign debt before oil was found but now owes $16 billion and, the greatest insult of all, more than 70 percent of the population now lives in poverty.

The harms suffered by these countries (and many others) are symptoms of what is known as the resource curse. Though it seems counterintuitive—countries with a lot of oil are lucky and rich, right?—a succession of studies, the most notable of which was conducted by the economists Jeffrey Sachs and Andrew Warner, show that countries dependent on natural-resource exports experience lower growth rates than countries that have nonresource economies, and they suffer greater amounts of repression and conflict too. The reasons are complex—and there are exceptions to these dismal rules—but in general, a reliance on oil discourages investment in other industries, makes governments less responsive to the desires of citizens and fosters corruption by officials seeking and receiving funds that are not their <u>due</u>. An oil state is, almost by definition, a dysfunctional state.

If those problems are not of urgent interest to Americans, it's because we do not pay much attention to the troubles of foreigners unless they threaten us directly; this is the <u>crux</u> of things. Perhaps understandably, many environmental groups indulge our inherent <u>parochialism</u> by devoting the <u>bulk</u> of their funds and publicity to domestic issues. For example, most of the "strategic initiatives" of the Sierra Club, with an annual budget of about $80 million, involve domestic matters, like protecting our forests and increasing citizens' participation in environmental decision-making. The Natural Resources Defense Council, which spent $52 million last year, keeps a "<u>Biogem Watchlist</u>," but only 3 of the 10 locations on it are outside the United States and Canada. Both groups have <u>lobbying</u> campaigns on Capitol Hill that focus on environmental issues with global <u>ramifications</u>, but if you want to learn about oil's impact in the countries that supply us, you would do best to look elsewhere. One of the best watchdogs on resource issues is Global Witness, a small organization in London that publishes excellent reports even though its 2004 budget of $3.4 million would not cover the fund-raising costs of its big American brothers. Although the big organizations express solidarity with environmental efforts overseas—N.R.D.C.'s motto is "The Earth's Best Defense"—their spending priorities indicate a narrower interest.

Of course, any effort to address the global consequences of our oil dependence faces an enormous obstacle—the apparent <u>bipartisan</u> consensus in Washington to make whatever compromises are necessary to ensure that America receives the ever-increasing quantities of petroleum that it requires. Although it is fashionable to blame oil companies and right-wing Republicans for caring <u>not a whit</u> about the downsides of resource extraction, the truth is that few Democrats have spoken of halting or minimizing oil imports because regime X or Y despoils its environment or represses its people. When it comes to oil, <u>expediency</u> is the rule, and a marvelously adaptable one. Because voters in Florida and California, which are scenic and

due /dju:/ *n.* something owed or deserved

crux /krʌks/ *n.* the basic, central, or critical point or feature

parochialism /pə'rəʊkɪəlɪzəm/ *n.* narrowly restricted in scope or outlook; provincial

bulk /bʌlk/ *n.* the major portion or greater part

lobby /'lɒbi/ *vt.* to try to influence public officials on behalf of or against (proposed legislation, for example)

ramification /ræmɪfi'keɪʃən/ *n.* the consequences or complications resulting from an action

bipartisan /baɪpɑ:tɪ'zæn/ *adj.* of, consisting of, or supported by members of two parties, especially two major political parties

not a whit not at all

expediency /ɪk'spi:dɪənsi/ *n.* appropriateness or suitability

prosperous, have made it clear they don't want or need oil rigs in their waters, Republicans in those states are nearly as vociferous as Democrats in opposing any loosening of the drilling bans. On offshore drilling, Jeb Bush and Arnold Schwarzenegger stand shoulder to shoulder with Barbra Streisand, though the governors' ecological sentiments do not necessarily extend beyond their coastal horizons.

vociferous /vəˈsɪfərəs/ *adj.* loud and forceful
gymnastics /dʒɪmˈnæstɪks/ *n.* complex intellectual or artistic exercises
cognition /kɒgˈnɪʃ ə n/ *n.* the mental process of knowing, including aspects such as awareness, perception, reasoning, and judgment
dissonance /ˈdɪsənəns/ *n.* a harsh, disagreeable combination of sounds; discord
anesthesia /ænɪsˈθiːzjə/ *n.* total or partial loss of sensation, especially tactile sensibility, induced by disease, injury, acupuncture, or an anesthetic, such as chloroform or nitrous oxide

The gymnastics of people like Schwarzenegger—probably the most famous Hummer owner in the world—are emblematic of the cognitive dissonance that runs in our national bloodstream. We demand clean beaches and untouched wildernesses at home but live in an energy-intensive fashion that leads other countries to sacrifice their waters and forests. This disconnect is easily explained. You don't need to alter your lifestyle much to help protect baby seals or punish Kathie Lee for supporting sweatshops, but you might need to suffer inconveniences—like higher gas prices, energy-conservation efforts and new taxes for alternative-fuels research—if better energy policies were adopted. In the end, the only red line that Americans insist upon, in terms of unacceptable ways for gasoline to be supplied to our cars, is that it must not come from ANWR or the waters off California and Florida. The politicians and environmental groups are, in many ways, just following the wishes of voters and donors.

If the protection of our environment comes at the expense of others, might it be an expression of selfishness rather than virtue? The more we focus on defending our environment, the less we may focus on environments outside our borders; activism can become anesthesia. Domestic restrictions on drilling have had the unintended effect of insulating our tender consciences from the worst impacts of oil extraction. Out of sight, out of mind. For that reason, could it be that drilling rigs within sight of Key West or in a part of Alaska that is an Alamo of conservationism would be a useful thing? Perhaps a few more drilling platforms in our most precious lands and waters would make us understand that the true cost of oil is not posted at the gas pump.

(approximately 1360 words)

Reading Time: _____   Reading Rate: _____

Cultural Notes

1. The Santa Barbara spill: On January 28, 1969, a Union Oil Company oil drilling platform 6 mi (10 km) off the coast of Santa Barbara, California, suffered a blowout, leading to a tremendous ecological disaster. Before it could be stopped, 3 million gal (11.4 million l) of crude oil gushed into the Pacific Ocean, killing thousands of birds, fish, sea lions, and other marine life. For weeks after the spill, the nightly television news programs showed footage of the effects of the giant black slick, including oil-soaked birds on the shore dead or dying. Many people viewed the disaster as an event that gave the modern environmental movement—which began with the publication of Rachel Carson's book *Silent Spring* in 1962—a new impetus in the United States.

2. Earth Day: one of two observances, both held annually during spring in the northern hemisphere, and autumn in the southern hemisphere. These are intended to inspire awareness of and appreciation for the Earth's environment. The United Nations celebrates an Earth Day each year on the March equinox, a tradition which was founded by peace activist John McConnell in 1969. A second Earth Day, which was founded by US politician Gaylord Nelson as an environmental teach-in in the late 1960s, is celebrated in many countries each year on April 22.

3. The Arctic National Wildlife Refuge (ANWR): a National Wildlife Refuge in northeastern Alaska. It consists of 19,049,236 acres (79,318 km²) in the Alaska North Slope region. Just to the west of it lies the Prudhoe Bay, which is North America's largest oil field, accounting for 17% of US domestic oil production. The question of whether to allow drilling for oil in ANWR has been a political football for every sitting American president since Jimmy Carter. In the 1990s and 2000s, votes about the status of the refuge occurred repeatedly in the US House of Representatives and Senate, but as of 2007 efforts to allow drilling have always been ultimately thwarted by filibusters, amendments, or vetoes.

4. The Niger Delta: the delta of the Niger River in Nigeria, is a densely populated region sometimes called the Oil Rivers because it was once a major producer of palm oil. Coincidentally, Nigeria has become Africa's biggest producer of petroleum, including many oil wells in the Oil Rivers. Some 2 million barrels a day are extracted in the Niger Delta. Since 1975, the region has accounted for more than 75% of Nigeria's export earnings. Much of the natural gas extracted in oil wells in the Delta is immediately burned, or flared, into the air at a rate of approximately 70 million m^3 per day. This is equivalent to 41% of African natural gas consumption, and forms the single largest source of greenhouse gas emissions on the planet. The environmental devastation associated with the industry and the lack of distribution of oil wealth have been the source and/or key aggravating factors of numerous environmental movements and inter-ethnic conflicts in the region, including recent guerilla activity by the Movement for the Emancipation of the Niger Delta (MEND).

5. **Texaco:** the name of an famous American oil retail brand. Its flagship product is its fuel. It was an independent company until it merged into Chevron Corporation in 2001.

6. **Biogem Watchlist:** a list of exceptional, imperiled ecosystems issued annually by The Natural Resources Defense Council (NRDC). NRDC launched the BioGems Initiative in 2001 to mobilize Americans to defend these ecosystems.

7. **Jeb Bush** (John Ellis "Jeb" Bush) (1953—   ): an American politician, and the 43rd Governor of Florida. He is a prominent member of the Bush family, the younger brother of President George W. Bush. Bush signed legislation to protect the Everglades and opposed federal plans to drill for oil off the coast of Florida.

8. **Arnold Schwarzenegger** (1947—   ): an Austrian-American bodybuilder, Golden Globe-winning actor, businessman and politician, and the 38th Governor of the U.S. state of California. In 2006 Schwarzenegger signed a bill creating the nation's first cap on greenhouse gas emissions. The law set new regulations on the amount of emissions utilities, refineries and manufacturing plants are allowed to release into the atmosphere. Schwarzenegger also signed a second global warming bill that prohibits large utilities and corporations in California from making long-term contracts with suppliers who do not meet the state's greenhouse gas emission standards.

9. **Barbra Streisand** (1942—   ): an American singer, film and theatre actress who has also achieved some note as a composer, political activist, film producer and director. She has won Oscars for Best Actress and Best Original Song as well as multiple Emmy Awards, Grammy Awards, and Golden Globe Awards. She has long been an active supporter of the Democratic Party and many of its causes, such as working against global warming.

10. **Alamo:** A battle between the Mexico army and the Texans who sought independence from Mexico in 1836. Some 145 Texans in the area took refuge in the fortified grounds of an old mission known as the Alamo on about

February 23th. Over the following two weeks, the Mexican forces continually strengthened to over 2000 troops. After periodic bombardment, the siege ended on the morning of 6 March when the Mexicans storm the Alamo fortress. During the battle, all of the Texan defenders were killed. Several non-combatants were spared. In the author's opinion, it is the Texans' conservatism that had led to their tragedy.

Comprehension Exercises

I. Answer the following questions based on the text.

1. What are the triumphs of the environmental movement as regarded by the author?
2. What are the symptoms of the resource curse?
3. Is the author satisfied with what the environmental groups have done? Why or why not?
4. What in the author's opinion is the obstacle to the efforts directed at the global consequences of America's oil dependence?
5. What are the author's suggestions to solving the environmental problems caused by oil drilling?

II. Decide whether each of the following statements is true or false according to the text.

1. The author advocates building some drilling platforms in American.
2. The environmental protection groups pay less attention to the land other than America.
3. All the countries dependent on natural-resource exports lower growth rates than countries that have nonresource economies, which is known as the resource curse.
4. Drilling for oil and gas off America's coastlines is banned because of the Santa Barbara spill.
5. These victories won by the American environmental movement brought disasters to other countries dependent on natural-resource export.

III. Select the most appropriate word or phrase and use its proper form to complete each of the following sentences.

budget	sacrifice	outsource	not a whit	vociferous
wage	at a cost	reliance	negligible	dissonance
due	approximate	chide	crux	parochial
expediency	foul	general		

1. They _____ the water by throwing in garbage.
2. Then, in early 2003, the decision was made to _____ a second war, in Iraq.
3. His blood pressure dropped and there was only _____ damage to blood cells from the pump.
4. The procedure may lead to anxiety and depression _____ to changes in body image.
5. Bank of America is at the _____ of the mortgage crisis in this country.
6. Evolution cares _____ how long you or I live, only that we survive to reproduce.
7. There are demonstrations in the streets almost every day, most of them urgent, _____ but good-humoured.
8. "President Obama is putting political _____ ahead of sound military and security judgment," Mr. Perry said.
9. It could be the meta cognitive _____ between the lyrics and the facts of life.
10. At present there are no women among the _____ 40 cosmonauts in the Russian space program.
11. In addition, of course, he is alert to the opportunity thus offered to _____ and condemn the UK government.
12. That provides a measure of willingness to punish, even _____ to the punisher.
13. But _____ on these personal devices potentially exposes sensitive corporate or personal information to the world.
14. The government has _____ $ 2,000,000 for education spending.
15. This balanced approach asks everyone to give a little without requiring anyone to _____ too much.

IV. Try to paraphrase the following sentences, paying special attention to the underlined parts.

1. Because our appetite for energy has grown over the decades, new drilling, along with the damage it tends to create, has not been halted; <u>it has been outsourced</u>.

_____

_____

2. <u>Because of a host of political and economic ills triggered by the drilling</u>, the Niger Delta is alive not with marine life but with violence.

_____

_____

3. When it comes to oil, expediency is the rule, <u>and a marvelously adaptable one</u>.

_____

_____

4. Domestic restrictions on drilling have had the unintended effect of <u>insulating our tender consciences</u> from the worst impacts of oil extraction.

_____

_____

5. Perhaps a few more drilling platforms in our most precious lands and waters would make us understand that <u>the true cost of oil is not posted at the gas pump</u>.

_____

_____

V. Discuss with your partner about each of the three statements and write an essay in no less than 260 words about your understanding of one of them.

1. Ecuador had turned its foreign debt into a credit of $16 billion after oil was discovered in the country, 70 percent of the Ecuador population now lives in poverty.

_____

_____

2. The harms suffered by these countries (and many others) are symptoms of what is known as the resource curse.

_____

_____

3. You don't need to alter your lifestyle much to help protect baby seals or punish Kathie Lee for supporting sweatshops, but you might need to suffer inconveniences.

_____

_____

VI. List four websites where we can learn more about environmental protection or pollution and provide a brief introduction to each of them.

1. _____
   _____
   _____.

2. _____
   _____
   _____.

3. _____
   _____
   _____.

4. _____
   _____
   _____.

Text B

Deal or No Deal

By Sharon Begley

It was time to get creative. In 2006, a head of government had signed a law requiring that greenhouse gases be cut 20 percent below 1990 levels by 2020 and 80 percent by 2050. The cuts will be carried out through a cap-and-trade system, like the one passed by the House of Representatives and introduced in the Senate, due to start in 2012. In an effort to reduce the cost of those greenhouse cuts, the executive reached out to his counterparts in Brazil and Indonesia, which have more than half of the world's remaining tropical forests. Because reducing deforestation is the cheapest way to mitigate climate change in the short term, he wanted utilities and other greenhouse emitters to be able to pay state governments in Brazil and Indonesia to preserve their forests, which ranchers and loggers keep whacking, yielding the same net gain for the atmosphere as reducing their own emissions of carbon dioxide. The details—how to measure the CO_2 cuts, how much to pay for preserving forests—will be worked out in the next few months, in time to set the rules for

cap-and-trade *adj.* denoting a scheme which allows companies with high greenhouse gas emissions to buy an emission allowance from companies which have fewer emissions, in a bid to reduce the overall impact to the environment 总量管制与排放交易计划

mitigate /ˈmɪtɪgeɪt/ *vt.* to make it less unpleasant, serious, or painful

emitter /ɪˈmɪtə/ *n.* a person or thing that emits

rancher /ˈræntʃə/ *n.* someone who owns or manages a large farm, especially one used for raising cattle, horses, or sheep

whacking /ˈwækɪŋ/ *adj.* enormous

cap-and-trade.

The official is Gov. Arnold Schwarzenegger of California, and his bilateral agreements with counterparts from Amazonas, Papua, and six other states in Brazil and Indonesia with millions of hectares of tropical forests illustrate why the impending failure to reach a new global climate accord isn't the disaster it might have been. Think "subnational." Although the 192 countries set to meet in Copenhagen next month will not reach a legally binding treaty setting out targets for greenhouse-gas reductions starting in 2012 (sources close to the negotiators say they have given up hope for that), cities, states, and provinces are on track to cut greenhouse gases. They see it as a way to retool their economies, draw high-paying jobs, and establish the industries of tomorrow, leapfrogging the sclerotic global talks. California's partnerships, for instance, will be the first time tropical forests are corralled into an international agreement. Not even the 1997 Kyoto climate treaty, which requires wealthy countries to reduce their emissions of six greenhouse gases 5.2 percent from 1990 levels, does that. "We will definitely keep moving ahead," says Anthony Brunello, California's deputy secretary for climate and energy.

That's the promise not only from states and provinces but also from businesses, especially those placing big bets on renewable energy and technologies to boost energy efficiency. Which raises a question that makes climate activists uneasy: why, exactly, was the Copenhagen meeting painted as the do-or-die moment—"the most important meeting since the end of the second world war," one green group called it—for averting calamitous climate change?

Seeing the failure of Copenhagen as something short of Armageddon is not contrarianism for contrarianism's sake. Just to be clear, if the world had agreed on what quantity of greenhouse-gas emissions to cut by when—on "targets and timetables," in the prevailing argot—it would have launched us down a path that could keep global warming below 2 degrees Celsius, relative to pre-industrial levels, which many climate scientists see as a point of no return. The meltdown of global climate talks is therefore a setback to efforts to avert the worst consequences of global warming. For instance, scientists foresee a massive rise in sea levels that would inundate coastal megalopolises from Shanghai to New

impending /ɪmˈpendɪŋ/ *adj.* something is going to happen very soon
sclerotic /skləˈrɒtɪk/ *adj.* of or relating to the sclerosis
corral /kəˈrɑːl/ *vt.* to capture or confine a person or animal
calamitous /kəˈlæmɪtəs/ *adj.* very unfortunate or serious
contrarianism /kəntˈreərɪən/ *n.* what a contrarian believes or does
meltdown /ˈmeltdaʊn/ *n.* sudden and complete failure of a company, organization or system
avert /əˈvɜːt/ *v.* to prevent something unpleasant from happening
inundate /ˈɪnʌndeɪt/ *vt.* to be covered with water

York, more frequent droughts and floods, a loss of glaciers that provide fresh water to tens of millions of people in India and China, lethal heat waves, and climate shifts that are as dangerous to farming as loss of sea ice is to polar bears. Already, yields of wheat in northern India have fallen due to climate change—not a good thing in a country that is currently importing grain to feed itself.

But for months there have been ample warning signs that the Copenhagen meeting was headed for a cliff. The Senate wasn't going to pass climate legislation in time, so other countries, getting déjà vu all over again, had no reason to believe the U.S. would abide by any emissions cuts the U.S. pledged in Copenhagen. Remember, the U.S. signed but never ratified the Kyoto climate treaty; to the rest of the world, America's climate promises aren't credible even with Obama in office. "The rest of the world has been asking, 'Why should we go ahead with this when the richest emitter hasn't stepped up to the plate?'" says Annie Petsonk of the Environmental Defense Fund, a veteran of climate negotiations. In addition, developing countries are demanding that wealthy nations cough up about $100 billion a year to help them switch from fossil fuels like coal to energy sources that do not emit carbon dioxide, such as wind and solar. China and India (the largest and fifth-largest greenhouse-gas emitters) refuse to even consider abiding by any globally agreed reductions, arguing that their per capita emissions remain a tiny fraction of America's. (India emits one ton of greenhouse gases per capita, compared with 20 in the U.S.) But the Senate would never have ratified a pact that exempted major developing countries such as China and India from mandatory greenhouse-gas cuts. That exemption made the Kyoto treaty such a nonstarter that President Clinton never even sent it to the Senate for ratification. So it wasn't that negotiations broke down. They'd never been on track in the first place.

There is good reason, then, to push the reset button and get it right rather than get it fast. By "right," I mean something that both reflects the important new science on greenhouse gases and makes political sense. Two international climate meetings are scheduled for 2010, when the world can try again to negotiate a binding pact. In the interim, negotiators can learn from the innovative steps that companies and subnationals are taking to reduce their greenhouse emissions. "There is enormous interest and commitment to greenhouse reductions at the subnational level," says Petsonk.

lethal /'li:θl/ *adj.* capable of causing a lot of damage

déjà vu /ˌdeɪʒɑːˈvuː/ (*French*) the feeling that one has already experienced the things that are happening to him now

ratify /'rætɪfaɪ/ *vt.* to give formal approval to a treaty or written agreement, usually by signing it or voting for it

cough up to be forced to pay or spend money that one would prefer not to

mandatory /'mændətərɪ/ *adj.* something have to be done because of a rule or a law

nonstarter /nɒnˈstɑːtə/ *n.* no chance of success

"So the message to business is clear: carbon constraints are coming."

impinge /ɪmˈpɪndʒ/ vi. (formal) to have a noticeable effect on sth/sb
ethanol /ˈeθənɒl/ n. another name for alcohol
cellulose /ˈseljuləʊs/ n. a substance that exists in the cell walls of plants and is used to make paper, plastic, and various fabrics and fibres

That's why businesses from Coca-Cola to Dow Chemical to Siemens are plunging ahead with "sustainability" programs, though each has a different reason. For biofuel companies, averting climate change is only one selling point, and arguably not the strongest one. Breaking free of dependence on foreign oil and creating jobs that can't be exported (it's cheaper to produce biofuel near its source and near where it will be used) are arguably more important. "Copenhagen is important, but it's probably not all that important," says CEO William Roe of Coskata, Inc., a biofuel company in Illinois. "It won't impinge significantly on what we're doing to try to develop next-generation biofuels. Energy security and competitiveness with oil will drive this industry."

For other businesses selling green tech, the market for their wares remains strong thanks to regional and state laws, such as Europe's requirements for greenhouse-gas reductions under the Kyoto treaty, which runs through 2012, and the rules in 29 U.S. states that say some percentage of electricity must be generated by zero-carbon fuels. "Whatever the outcome of Copenhagen, Siemens [the Germany-based electronics giant] will follow the path of green growth," says CEO Peter Löscher. In the last fiscal year, Siemens' green sales topped $34 billion (€23 billion), making it the world's biggest green company. And Coca-Cola still plans to phase out hydrofluorocarbons, greenhouse gases used as refrigerants, and to cut its greenhouse-gas emissions from manufacturing in developed countries 5 percent from 2004 levels by 2015. Copenhagen "won't really change anything," says Coke environment czar Jeff Seabright. "We're assuming a price on carbon is coming, but even without that we think we can increase energy efficiency 20 percent and still get a return of 20 percent."

Still, business wants clarity so it can assess which investments make financial sense. Chemical giants such as DuPont and Dow are developing next-generation ethanol (made from cellulose and other waste biomass, not corn, and in Dow's case using algae to turn carbon dioxide into ethanol) and solar-power roof shingles, for instance, and will keep at it. But they want to know how big the market will be, which depends on whether or not carbon emissions will be taxed heavily and therefore how much customers will pay for energy efficiency and other ways to avoid that cost.

Utilities in particular need to know if carbon will be priced, through either a tax or cap-and-trade. Enel, for instance, is

hydro /ˈhaɪdrəʊ/ *n.* short for hydroelectric
geothermal /ˌdʒi(ː)əʊˈθəməl/ *adj.* concerning heat that is produced inside the earth

Europe's second-biggest utility by installed capacity, with hydro, geothermal, wind, solar, and biomass facilities in Europe as well as the Americas. It is also Europe's largest provider of power from geothermal energy. The company had hoped for an agreement in Copenhagen so business would know the rules going forward; the financial appeal of, say, a geothermal facility depends on whether power plants that spew carbon dioxide will have to pay for the privilege of polluting, says Giuseppe Deodati, Enel's head of carbon strategy. "We would like to see a stable and reliable regulatory framework, which would act to stabilize the price of carbon in the long run," he says. "But even if Copenhagen produces only a general political commitment to greenhouse reductions, many countries will move forward with regional schemes, including [those in] Europe, to address climate change." Enel's own renewables projects, including the innovative Archimedes solar facility in Sicily that will harness the sun's power with giant mirrors, "will move on independently of Copenhagen."

(approximately 1570 words)

Reading Time: _____   Reading Rate: _____

Cultural Notes

1. **Armageddon:** It often refers to a terrible battle or war that some people think will lead to the total destruction of the world or the human race. The word "Armageddon", from Ancient Greek Ἁρμαγεδών, appears only once in the Greek New Testament, in Revelation 16:16. The word may come from Hebrew *har məgiddô* (רה גמידו), meaning "Mountain of Megiddo". "Mount" Megiddo is not actually a mountain, but a tell (a hill created by many generations of people living and rebuilding on the same spot) on which ancient forts were built to guard the Via Maris, an ancient trade route linking Egypt with the northern empires of Syria, Anatolia and Mesopotamia. Megiddo was the location of various ancient battles, including one in the 15th century BC and one in 609 BC. Modern Megiddo is a town approximately 25 miles (40 km) west-southwest of the southern tip of the Sea of Galilee in the Kishon River area.

2. **the Kyoto treaty:** The Kyoto Protocol to the United Nations Framework Convention on Climate Change (UNFCCC) is an international treaty that sets binding obligations on industrialized countries to reduce emissions of greenhouse gases. The UNFCCC is an environmental treaty with the goal of preventing "dangerous" anthropogenic (i.e., human-induced) interference of the climate system.

Comprehension Exercises

I. Answer the following questions based on the text.

1. Why do Brazil and Indonesia come into the executive's view?
2. What will work as a supplement to the potential failure of a new global climate accord?
3. What seems original to California's agreements with its counterparts?
4. Why are the businesses such as Coca-Cola, Dow Chemical and Siemens, etc. plunging ahead with "sustainability" programs?
5. Why does the market for the wares of the green tech businesses remain strong?

II. Decide whether each of the following statements is true or false according to the text.

1. The word "mitigate" in Para. 1 means "moderate".
2. The Copenhagen climate talks set out targets for greenhouse-gas cuts but failed.
3. Many climate scientists argue that it is hard to make the global temperature lower than the pre-industrial level.
4. The author predicted that the coming Copenhagen climate talk is destined to fail based on his analysis.
5. Copenhagen climate talk will be the decisive factor for the businesses to plunge ahead with "sustainability" programs.

III. Select the most appropriate word or phrase and use its proper form to complete each of the following sentences.

leapfrog	setback	reach out to	lethal	abide by
ratify	step up to the plate	on track	spew	impinge
avert	inundate	impend	cough up	exempt
detail	meltdown	mandatory		

1. That is why we have to be fast. We have to _____ all areas, to all isolated pockets of people, which, obviously, is the main challenge.

2. You have the power to protect your people and keep your development efforts _____.

3. It is already obvious that all four American systems have _____ over the European versions.

4. The move represents a _____ for the Middle East peace process.

5. He avoids any eye contact, quickly _____ his gaze when anyone approaches.

6. Their neighborhood is being _____ by the rising waters of the Colorado River.

7. Amorality and intelligence is probably the most _____ combination to be found within one personality.

8. Will China be peaceful and friendly and _____ the rules of international law and conventions, or will it use its heft to get its way?

9. He _____ to head the company's US office.

10. South Carolina claimed the power to _____ its citizens from the obligation to obey federal law.

11. He _____ his experiences at the Olympic Games.

12. This very recklessness makes me feel that these costly operations may be only the prelude to far larger events which _____ on land.

13. Even at these speeds, the rogue worlds could be _____ into orbit again, under the right conditions.

14. If nothing else, the recent _____ in the housing market has forced everyone to rethink the fundamentals of what a house is and what it can be.

15. European politicians are unlikely to _____ more, so much discussion behind the scenes is about how to lever up the rescue facility.

IV. Try to paraphrase the following sentences, paying special attention to the underlined parts.

1. In 2006, a head of government had signed a law requiring that greenhouse gases be cut 20 percent below 1990 levels by 2020 and 80 percent by 2050.

_____

_____

2. Seeing the failure of Copenhagen as something short of Armageddon is not contrarianism for contrarianism's sake.

_____

_____

3. But for months there have been ample warning signs that the Copenhagen

meeting <u>was headed for a cliff</u>.

4. Why should we go ahead with this when the richest emitter hasn't <u>stepped up to the plate</u>?

5. Still, business wants clarity so it can <u>assess which investments make financial sense</u>.

V. Discuss with your partner about each of the three statements and write an essay in no less than 260 words about your understanding of one of them.

1. Because reducing deforestation is the cheapest way to mitigate climate change in the short term, he wanted utilities and other greenhouse emitters to be able to pay state governments in Brazil and Indonesia to preserve their forests...

2. Remember, the U.S. signed but never ratified the Kyoto climate treaty; to the rest of the world, America's climate promises aren't credible even with Obama in office.

3. There is good reason, then, to push the reset button and get it right rather than get it fast.

VI. List four websites where we can learn more about Sharon Begley or climate change and provide a brief introduction to each of them.

1.

2.

3. _____

   _____

   _____.

4. _____

   _____

   _____.

Twenty Minutes' Reading

You are required to read the following two sections within 20 minutes.

Section A

The destruction of our natural resources and contamination of our food supply continue occur, largely because of the extreme difficulty in affixing legal responsibility on those who continue to treat our environment with reckless abandon. Attempts to prevent pollution by legislation, economic incentives and friendly persuasion have been net by lawsuits, personal and industrial denial and long delays—not only in accepting responsibility, but more importantly, in doing something about it.

It seems that only when government decides it can afford tax incentives or production sacrifices is there any initiative for change. Where is industry's and our recognition that protecting mankind's great treasure is the single most important responsibility? If ever there will be time for environmental health professionals to come to the frontlines and provide leadership to solve environmental problems, that time is now.

We are being asked, and, in fact, the public is demanding that we take positive action. It is our responsibility as professionals in environmental health to make the difference. Yes, the ecologists, the environmental activists and the conservationists serve to communicate, stimulate thinking and promote behavioral change. However, it is those of us who are paid to make the decisions to develop, improve and enforce environmental standards, I submit, who must lead the charge.

We must recognize that environmental health issues do not stop at city limits, county lines, state or even federal boundaries. We can no longer afford to be tunnel-visioned in our approach. We must visualize issues from every perspective to make the objective decisions. We must express our views clearly to prevent media distortion and public confusion.

I believe we have a three-part mission for the present. First, we must continue to press for improvements in the quality of life that people can make for themselves. Second, we must investigate and understand the link between environment and health. Third, we must be able to communicate technical information in a form that citizens can understand. If we can accomplish these three goals in this decade, maybe we can finally stop environmental degradation, and not merely hold it back. We will then be able to spend pollution dollars truly on prevention rather than on bandages.

1. We can infer from the first two paragraphs that the industrialists disregard environmental protection chiefly because _____.
   A. they are unaware of the consequences of what they are doing
   B. they are reluctant to sacrifice their own economic interests
   C. time has not yet come for them to put due emphasis on it
   D. it is difficult for them to take effective measures
2. The main task now facing ecologists, environmental activists and conservationists is _____.
   A. to prevent pollution by legislation, economic incentives and persuasion
   B. to arouse public awareness of the importance of environmental protection
   C. to take radical measures to control environmental pollution
   D. to improve the quality of life by enforcing environmental standards
3. The word "tunnel-visioned (Line 3, Para. 4) most probably means "_____".
   A. narrow-minded
   B. blind to the facts
   C. short-sighted
   D. able to see only one aspect
4. Which of the following, according to the author, should play the leading role in the solution of environmental problems?
   A. Legislation and government intervention.
   B. The industry's understanding and support.
   C. The efforts of environmental health professionals.
   D. The cooperation of ecologists, environmental activists and conservationists.
5. Which of the following is true according to the last paragraph?
   A. Efforts should be exerted on pollution prevention instead of on remedial measures.
   B. More money should be spent in order to stop pollution.
   C. Ordinary citizens have no access to technical information on pollution.
   D. Environmental degradation will be stopped by the end of this decade.

Section B

In the United States, the need to protect plant and animal species has become a highly controversial and sharply political issue since the passage of the Endangered Species Act in 1973. The act, designed to protect species' living areas, and policies that preserve land and forests compete with economic interests. In the 1990s, for example, the woodcutters in the Western United States were challenged legally in their attempt to cut trees for timber in the Cascade Mountains. The challenge was mounted to protect the endangered spotted owl (猫头鹰), whose remaining population occupies these forests and requires the intact, ancient forest for survival. The problematic situation set the interests of environmentalists against those of corporations and of individuals who stood to lose jobs. After months of debate and legal battles, the fate of the woodcutters—and the owls—was still undecided in mid-1992.

Similar tensions exist between the developed and the developing nations. Many people in industrialized nations, for example, believe that developing nations in tropical regions should do more to protect their rain forests and other natural areas. But the developing countries may be impoverished (使穷困), with populations growing so rapidly that using the land is a means to temporarily avoid worsening poverty and starvation.

Many of the changes to Earth that concern scientists have the potential to rob the planet of its biological richness. The destruction of Earth's ozone layer (臭氧层), for example, could contribute to the general process of impoverishment by allowing ultra-violet rays to harm plants and animals. And global warming could wipe out species unable to quickly adapt to changing climates. Clearly, protecting will come only through coordinated international efforts to control human population, stabilize the composition of the atmosphere, and preserve intact Earth's complex web life.

6. Why does the author say that the protection of endangered species is a highly controversial issue?
   A. Because people can't agree as to what species to protect.
   B. Because it is difficult to find an effective way to protect such species.
   C. Because it affects the interests of certain groups of people.
   D. Because it is a major problem involving a series of legal procedures.

7. According to the passage, the preservation of rain forests _____.

   A. may hamper a developing country in its fight against poverty

   B. benefits developed countries rather than developing countries

   C. should take priority over the control of human population

   D. will help improve the living conditions in developing countries

8. According to the passage, cutting tress to grow more food _____.

   A. will widen the gap between the developed and the developing countries

   B. is but a short-term relief to the food problem

   C. can hardly alleviate the shortage of food

   D. proves to be an effective way out for impoverished nations

9. Among "humanity's current problems" (which was mentioned in the last sentence of the passage), the chief concern of the scientists is _____.

   A. the impoverishment of developing countries

   B. the explosion of the human population

   C. the reduction of biological diversity

   D. the effect of global warming

10. The author's purpose in writing this passage is _____.

   A. to describe the difficulties in solving humanity's current problems

   B. to present the different views on humanity's current problems

   C. to analyze the contradiction between countries in dealing with humanity's current problems

   D. to point out that humanity's current problems can only be solved through the cooperation of nations